BORN
ADVENTURER

T0322738

About the Author

Stephen Haddelsey is the author of many books on Antarctic exploration history, including *Ice Captain*, *Shackleton's Dream* and *Icy Graves*, as well as other topics. He lives in Nottinghamshire.

Praise for Born Adventurer

'Some larger-than-life characters enter legend; others enter literature – the model for at least three fictional explorers, Frank Bickerton stuffed his life with event, and not only took part in the Australasian Antarctic Expedition of 1911–14, but was a treasure-hunter, served in both world wars ... and worked in the British film industry in its heyday ... What's here represents enough for several ordinary lives.'

Geographical Magazine

'The story and the way it's told are brilliant.'

Cross & Cockade Journal

'The author has done a fine job of piecing together Bickerton's story and providing an insight into this engaging character ... the sort of man without whom the expeditions could not have succeeded.'

Polar Record

BORN ADVENTURER

The Life of Frank Bickerton
Antarctic Pioneer

Stephen Haddelsey

Foreword by
Sir Ranulph Fiennes

*For my wife, Caroline,
without whose unflagging support and encouragement
this project would have remained permanently ice-bound.*

There are men it would be utter ruin to place in positions of staid and tranquil respectability, and yet who make good names. They are born to be adventurers.

Charles Lever, *The Diary and Notes of Horace Templeton*

Front cover image: Taken during the Australasian Antarctic Expedition by Frank Hurley. (State Library of New South Wales)

First published 2005
This paperback edition first published 2023

The History Press
97 St George's Place, Cheltenham,
Gloucestershire, GL50 3QB
www.thehistorypress.co.uk

British Library Cataloguing in Publication Data.
A catalogue record for this book is available from the British Library.

ISBN 978 1 80399 279 2

Typesetting and origination by The History Press
Printed and bound in Great Britain by TJ Books Limited, Padstow, Cornwall.

Trees for LYfe

Contents

List of Illustrations & Maps

ILLUSTRATIONS

1. Joseph Jones Bickerton. (Courtesy of Mrs Karen Bussell and Mrs Penny Stansfield)
2. Eliza Frances Bickerton (née Fox). (Courtesy of Mrs Karen Bussell and Mrs Penny Stansfield)
3. Francis Howard Bickerton, at 4 years old. (Courtesy of Miss Rosanna Bickerton)
4. Cocos Island, 1911. (Courtesy of Mr Angus MacIndoe and Mrs Sophia Crawford)
5. The Vickers REP D-type monoplane at Adelaide, October 1911. (Courtesy of Miss Rosanna Bickerton)
6. Frank Bickerton on the AAE, 1912, photographed by Frank Hurley. (Courtesy of the Mawson Antarctic Collection, South Australian Museum, Adelaide)
7. Bickerton in the air-tractor at Cape Denison. (Courtesy of the Mawson Antarctic Collection, South Australian Museum, Adelaide)
8. Bickerton working on the air-tractor in the hangar. (Courtesy of the Mawson Antarctic Collection, South Australian Museum, Adelaide)
9. The blizzard, by Frank Hurley. (Courtesy of the Mawson Antarctic Collection, South Australian Museum, Adelaide)
10. Bickerton in the trenches, c. 1916. (Courtesy of Miss Rosanna Bickerton)

MAPS

Foreword

Come with me, and learn that life is a stone for the teeth to bite on.
Vita Sackville-West, *The Edwardians*

Any expedition to Antarctica – or, indeed, to any of the world's most extreme and inhospitable regions – is almost wholly dependent, both for its success and for its ultimate survival, upon teamwork. In an age obsessed with the cult of personality, it is perhaps easy to forget that Scott, Shackleton, Amundsen and Mawson were not titans working in isolation, but leaders of teams. They worked in an environment where temperatures can hover around -40°C and the wind can maintain an all-year average of 50mph; where, during the winter months, there is no food to be hunted or scavenged; where there are no combustibles to be gathered; and where freezing drift-snow can so disorientate a man that he cannot find a shelter that stands just a few yards away. In these conditions, the man who fuels the stove or minds the storeroom becomes as essential as even the most fêted explorer.

It is in recognition of the vital importance of teamwork that the practice of awarding the Polar Medal en masse to all expedition members has been established. Knighthoods and Royal Geographical Society Founders' Medals are, by and large, the preserve of expedition leaders, but the award of that small bronze or silver hexagon on its white ribbon acknowledges the essential contributions made by Antarctica's other, often unsung heroes.

In the case of Sir Douglas Mawson's Australasian Antarctic Expedition of 1911–14, only Mawson himself, Frank Wild and the master of the Steam Yacht *Aurora*, John King Davis, had ever been south of the Antarctic Circle. The rest of the crew was made up of enthusiastic novices, some of whom had never even seen snow before. Mawson believed that youth, willingness and a general aptitude were often at least as important as experience. But he also recognised the need for certain specialist skills and knowledge. This is why he recruited men like the Swiss ski champion, Xavier Mertz, and the 22-year-old Englishman, Frank Bickerton – the hero of this book. Every explorer in Antarctica must be an innovator, willing to try new things – new approaches, new ideas and new technologies – if he is to survive. Scott took a balloon and Shackleton a motor car. Mawson journeyed south with an aeroplane and with wireless telegraphy. As the expedition's mechanical engineer, Frank Bickerton was intimately associated with both of these pioneering experiments. He also led a three-man sledging expedition that discovered the first meteorite ever to be found in the Antarctic – the crucial first step in establishing the continent as one of the world's richest meteorite fields.

The 'Heroic Age' of Antarctic exploration came to an end amidst the mud and blood of the First World War and many of the men associated with it returned only to be lost on the battlefields of Flanders and Gallipoli or in the waters of the Atlantic Ocean. Bickerton served in the trenches and with the Royal Flying Corps on the Western Front. He survived and went on to a variety of other adventures in Europe, North America and Africa and all of these episodes are covered in Stephen

Haddelsey's narrative. But it is, perhaps, as one of the little-known heroes of Antarctica – closely associated with Mawson and Shackleton – that his story achieves its greatest significance. Interest in mankind's conquest of the Antarctic has not been so intense for the best part of 100 years, with a spate of new biographies and television serials helping to spur the fascination. In this case, entirely new material relating to both Mawson's AAE and Shackleton's Imperial Trans-Antarctic Expedition has also been unearthed – no mean feat in this much-researched field.

It seems to me wholly appropriate that the life of Frank Bickerton should be remembered and celebrated, but not simply for his ground-breaking work on aero-engines and wireless and for his chance discovery of a meteorite. We should acknowledge him as a representative of all those other obscure adventurers without whose courage and sacrifices the great Antarctic continent would be as much of a mystery to us now, in the twenty-first century, as it was to our ancestors in the eighteenth.

Sir Ranulph Fiennes Bt, OBE

Acknowledgements

The extraordinarily varied life of Frank Bickerton has struck a chord in the imagination of practically every individual I have contacted during the long process of researching and writing this book. They have included, as well as family and friends, museum curators, broadcasters, film buffs and Polar and military historians. Many have not only expressed an interest in my subject but have also demonstrated an astonishing willingness to help in shedding light on Bickerton's numerous adventures. Sometimes their assistance has taken the form of granting me access to family papers or sharing their memories; sometimes it has involved the making of transcriptions of documents in their possession. Without their generosity, this book could never have been written.

I should like to take this opportunity to express my gratitude to all those who have helped and, most particularly, to the following: Karen Bussell for offering to put up a total stranger, for the constant flow of food and drink during my stay and for allowing me unrestricted access to family photographs and papers. David Madigan for transcribing portions of his father's expedition diaries. Anne Phillips and Elisabeth Dowler for allowing me to read and quote from Aeneas Mackintosh's Cocos Island diary. Patrick Garland for permission to quote from his father's RFC diary and for sharing with me his father's memories of serving with Bickerton during the First World War. The late Nigel Nicolson, for his memories of Bickerton's visit to the home of his mother, Vita Sackville-West. Anne Fright for permission to quote from the writings of Frank Wild. Trygve Norman for alerting me to the existence of ITAE correspondence in Finse. Angus MacIndoe and Sophia Crawford not only for their memories of Cuthbert and Eileen Orde, but also for allowing the reproduction of Orde's paintings, drawings and photographs. The late Jean Messervey, Hilda Chaulk-Murray, Chris Woodworth-Lynas and Judith Robertson for casting light on Bickerton's period in Newfoundland. Robert Stephenson for sharing with me his extensive knowledge of all things Antarctic. Bob Beck, historian of the Pasatiempo Golf Club, for his invaluable help in putting me on to Bickerton's trail in California. Leif Mills for his help with tracing the friendship of Bickerton and Frank Wild. Bryan Langley and Simon McCallum for background information on the Welwyn Film Studios. Sheila Fairfield, Stephanie Jenkins and Chris Rendle for their help with the Bickertons' Oxford background. The Mawson family, most particularly Andrew McEwin, Emma McEwin and Gareth Thomas, for permission to quote from the papers of Sir Douglas Mawson. Allan Mornement, for allowing me access to the wonderful diaries of Belgrave Ninnis. Elle Leane for sharing with me her detailed research into the *Adelie Blizzard*. The late Sally McNally, Elizabeth Pearce, Mrs Didi Cavendish, William Cavendish, Andrew Morritt and the Earl of Shrewsbury for their recollections of Bickerton. John Bell Thomson for help with tracing Bickerton's Antarctic friendships. Ralph Barker for his help with Bickerton's RFC career. Mark Offord for his research at the National Archives. Andrew Stevenson for helping me to save and collate the many photographs of Bickerton. My brother, Martin, for his shrewd comments on the shape and content of this book and for strug-gling through so many drafts.

Of course, the assistance of many institutions and museums has been essential to the completion of this project. For access to documents residing in their care, and for permission to reproduce the same, I am most grateful to: Robert Headland, of the Scott Polar Research Institute; the Syndics of Cambridge University Library; the Mitchell Library; the Royal Geographical Society; the National Archives at Kew; Hull University Archives; the US National Parks Service; the BBC; the British Film Institute; the Museums and Archives Service of Hampshire County Council; the West Sussex Record Office; the Imperial War Museum; the State Library of South Australia; the University of Sydney; the University of Cambridge; the Alexander Turnbull Library; the RAF Museum, Hendon; Stephen Rabson of P&O; and the Canterbury Museum at Christchurch.

Most notably, I should like to acknowledge my debt to Mark Pharaoh, of the Mawson Antarctic Collection in Adelaide, not only for his enthusiastic support and encouragement but also for reading and correcting the chapters covering the Australasian Antarctic Expedition.

Finally, I should like to offer my most sincere thanks to Sir Ranulph Fiennes for his generosity in supporting this book and for providing the foreword; to my editor, Jaqueline Mitchell, for her enormously helpful suggestions and advice at the manu-script stage; and to Bickerton's daughter, Rosanna, whose help has been crucial to the creation of this testament to her father's remarkable achievements. This list is not, indeed cannot, be comprehensive and I hope that those who have not been named individually will not think that their help and support is any the less appreciated. Every effort has been made to contact copy-right holders and I should like to crave the indulgence of any literary executors or copyright holders where these efforts have been unavailing.

Stephen Haddelsey, Southwell, July 2005

Introduction

my cousin Frank Bickerton ... was an ex RAF officer and had been to the South Pole with Amundsen in 1911.

Claude Walmisley, *Spacious Days*

This brief passage in the privately printed memoirs of a distant relative was the first reference I had ever come across to the name of Frank Bickerton. Given the distance of our relationship – he was my first cousin, three times removed – my ignorance of his career was not, perhaps, particularly surprising. But, now, my curiosity was roused. Why? Because even a casual student of Polar history knows that, while Captain Scott took a Norwegian, Tryggve Gran, on his last, fateful expedition, Amundsen was not accompanied by an Englishman when he made his assault on the fabled South Pole. Had he been so, perhaps the British establishment would have been at fewer pains to denigrate and tarnish his achievement with accusations of duplicity and foul play. If, then, there could be no possibility of a previously unsung British hero sharing the Norwegian's glory, who was the mysterious Frank Bickerton and why had his name been linked with that of Amundsen?

It soon became clear that, like most flawed reports, Claude Walmisley's account – though incorrect in a number of its essentials – also contained a kernel of truth. In reality, the closest Bickerton ever came to Amundsen was when the latter donated some of his huskies to the men of the Australasian Antarctic Expedition (AAE), then marooned on the great white continent. Bickerton could make no claim to Amundsen's laurels, but he had accompanied another 'Heroic Age' expedition – led not by a Norwegian but by an Australian named Douglas Mawson. The AAE, however, was never a Pole-seeking expedition; Mawson doubted the value of geographic- polar conquest for its own sake and instead dedicated himself to an exhausting combination of exploration and scientific study of the region as a whole. In particular, he laid great emphasis on geological, meteorological and magnetic observations and insisted on the kind of scientific professionalism and dedication exemplified by Professor Erich von Drygalski on his *Gauss* expedition of 1901–03. The accomplishments of the AAE have been best summarised by Dr Philip Ayres in his comprehensive 1999 study of Mawson.[1] They included, as well as the exploration and survey of 2,600 miles of previously unknown territory, the publication of scientific reports so comprehensive that the multiple volumes they filled were still being compiled and edited nearly thirty years after the return of the expedition. Given these achievements – and the almost unimaginable conditions in which they were obtained – it is not too bold to claim that the expedition was, in many ways, one of the most successful to be undertaken during the whole of the 'Heroic Age'. Furthermore, it is possible to make the claim without denigrating the attainments of Scott, Shackleton or Amundsen.

Frank Bickerton's contribution to the success of the AAE can be measured in a number of ways. Most importantly, perhaps, as its mechanical engineer, he was responsible for two of the expedition's pioneering experiments: with propeller-driven traction and with wireless telegraphy. Although the first did not live up to expectations, as was the case with similar trials with mechanised transport made by Scott and Shackleton, it is perhaps too easy to dismiss the utility of the 'air-tractor' and to ignore the fact that its ultimate failure was in large part due to damage done to the machine even before it left the shores of Australia. The use of wireless telegraphy, on the other hand, after initial teething troubles, was altogether more successful. It not only allowed direct communication between an Antarctic station and home, thereby removing much of the doubt and uncertainty resulting from complete isolation, but also enabled the transmission of time signals to determine longitude: an achievement promising huge potential benefits to future sledging parties. Bickerton's role in establishing, maintaining and operating the wireless station was absolutely crucial to success – as is amply demonstrated in the diaries of the expedition members and Mawson's official account of the expedition, *The Home of the Blizzard*, published in two huge tomes in 1915. In the closing days of 1912, he also led the three-man Western Sledging Party which, as well as exploring some 160 miles of uncharted coastline, discovered on 5 December the first meteorite ever to be found in Antarctica. As mechanical 'odd-job man' he contributed to the daily viability of the Main Base, which had been located, unintentionally and unknowingly, in one of the most inhospitable corners of the world's most inhospitable continent. Bickerton's varied work on the expedition was, therefore, of the greatest importance; but he made another, often ignored but equally vital contribution to its well-being – a contribution made, perhaps, quite unconsciously. In writing of his own battle against the elements on the *Kon-Tiki* expedition, Thor Heyerdahl noted that 'No storm-clouds with low pressure and dirty weather held greater menace for us than the danger of psychological cloudburst among six men shut up together for months... . In such circumstances a good joke was often as valuable as a life belt.'[2] In the huts of the AAE, battered almost incessantly by winds that gusted at more than 200mph, the same principle held true and, again, diaries and letters reveal that Bickerton's humour, selflessness and resourcefulness provided no insignificant antidote to the blue devils that inhabit the Antarctic wastes.

The members of the AAE were fêted on their return to civilisation in February 1914. Mawson was knighted and awarded the Founders' Medal of the Royal Geographical Society (RGS), while all who had ventured into the Antarctic Circle received the King's Polar Medal or, in the cases of those who had taken part in previous expeditions, bars to their existing medals. But, with the outbreak of the First World War, popular interest in Antarctic exploration rapidly waned and, when it revived, in England the focus was upon the heroic failure of Scott and upon the miraculous survival of Shackleton's British Imperial Trans-Antarctic, or *Endurance*, Expedition (ITAE) of 1914–17. Britain's possessive love affair with the Antarctic, which even Amundsen's Polar success failed to scotch, remained determinedly nationalistic in focus and there was little room for the consideration of what was seen as a foreign, albeit a Commonwealth, expedition – a strange neglect given that, while the expedition proclaimed itself to be Australian in inspiration, in funding and, by implication, in personnel, there had been a significant British contribution. Although Australian by adoption, Mawson himself was born in Yorkshire and John King Davis – master of the expedition ship, the *Aurora* – most of her crew, and four of the twenty-five men originally selected for the land parties were all British.

The expedition may have lacked the romantic appeal of an assault on the South Pole, more important perhaps in the first decades of the twentieth century than now, but its story possesses every attribute of great adventure. In a tiny wooden-hulled vessel, Bickerton and his companions braved seas that threatened to overwhelm or crush them; they raised their flags above lands never before trodden by man; they struggled against seemingly insurmountable odds, including weather conditions harsher than those to be found anywhere else in the world; and they faced conflict, madness and death. In battling against these odds and in its achievement of ultimate victory, the AAE was every inch as heroic as the better-known expeditions of the period. Bickerton and his fellows, of whatever nationality, were every bit as tenacious, resilient and courageous as their more famous contemporaries.

The AAE's photographer and cinematographer was Frank Hurley, now famous for his images of Shackleton's *Endurance* in its death throes. Hurley's photographs show Bickerton as dark complexioned, even saturnine: with a waxed moustache and an intense stare, he could have been a model for Errol Flynn's screen persona – a man of action, an adventurer, even a buccaneer. By his early twenties, he was already a Fellow of the RGS and had demonstrated a precocious willingness to turn adolescent dreams of exploration and adventure into reality, to become a man in the mould of such characters as Rider Haggard's Alan Quartermain or W.E. Johns' Biggles. Bickerton would have laughed at such suggestions but the comparison with fictional heroes is not as far-fetched as it might appear. In the late twenties, frequenting the glittering boudoirs of fashionable London, he became acquainted with the novelists Stella Benson and Vita Sackville-West. While the former fell passionately – and, ultimately, disastrously – in love with him, the latter was so impressed that she took him as the model for the character of the sardonic explorer Leonard Anquetil in her best-selling novel *The Edwardians* (1930). Nor was this Bickerton's only appearance in fiction. In 1912, his sister, Dorothea Bussell, included him in her novel *The New Wood Nymph*, and, as recently as 1989, some of his experiences in the Royal Flying Corps were included in Patrick Garland's novel *The Wings of the Morning*.

Given the company he kept, Bickerton's appearance in fiction is hardly surprising, though any novelist including the full gamut of his adventures might justly fear the incredulity of the audience. His part in the ground-breaking work of the AAE was but one in a series of exploits, any of which might be enough for a 'normal' individual. As well as accompanying Mawson's expedition, he dug for pirate treasure on the legendary Cocos Island in the Pacific Ocean. Shackleton recruited him for the *Endurance* expedition and he included Hurley, Frank Wild and Aeneas Mackintosh, the ill-fated leader of Shackleton's Ross Sea Party, among his Antarctic friends. He served in both world wars – as an observer and then fighter pilot in one of the RFC's elite scout squadrons during the First World War and as an RAF wing commander with a penchant for joyriding over enemy territory during the Second World War – and he was wounded four times, twice seriously. Despite a 40 per cent disability he joined a colony of veterans farming in Newfoundland under the leadership of Victor Campbell, of Scott's fatal *Terra Nova* expedition; he helped to found one of California's most prestigious golf clubs, a magnet for Hollywood glitterati; he travelled the length of Africa by train, plane and automobile; and he worked as an editor and screenwriter for the British film industry during its heyday.

Those who met Bickerton tended to remember him. They were struck, in the first instance, by his piratical looks and adventurous spirit and then, if they grew to know him better, by his modesty and shrewdness. But there are also occasional glimpses of a darker side to his nature; of an unwillingness to suffer fools and of an inability to empathise with those more emotionally susceptible than himself, the result being a capacity to wound, unintentionally, perhaps, but nonetheless deeply. Celebrated diarists such as Stella Benson and Charles Ritchie recorded their impressions of him and their records form a fascinating, if sometimes oddly contradictory portrait. Their descriptions can be further 'fleshed out' by the diaries and letters of the men who saw him during some of his most daring adventures, in the Antarctic and over the battlefields of the Western Front. Many refer to Bickerton's reticence, but it is clear that in the right company – the right company often being that of

intelligent women – he could also be a raconteur of no mean
ability: 'Nothing pleased those within his intimate circle more
than to get him to tell a story. The material always came from
some adventure of his own. Yet he always told the story through
the mouth of another. It would usually start: "I once knew a
man who ..." and then would follow a perfect gem: a narrative
not merely exciting in terms of action or suspense, but shrewd
in psychological situation and reaction. And always it would be
told in short, almost staccato, sentences with the expression of
a poker player.'[3] His anonymous obituarist in *The Times* stated
that Bickerton 'could never be persuaded to write his memoirs' and he laughed at the idea of regular diarising. Sometimes,
however, he felt compelled to record his experiences, though
not without ironically comparing himself with a tourist who
'industriously takes photos with a VPK and makes notes on a
Utility Scribbling Tablet'.[4] Crucially, a number of his writings
survive, allowing the reader to immerse himself in the astonishingly vivid and immediate descriptions of his sledging journey
across 160 miles of uncharted Antarctic coastline, scribbled in
pencil while 70mph winds threatened to shred the tent in which
he sheltered; of his engagements with hostile aircraft during the
Battle of Ypres; and of his travels through Africa in the early
thirties. The existence of these diaries makes it possible not only
to tell Bickerton's story but, in many instances, to tell it in his
own words.

Unfortunately, since Bickerton's surviving diaries are not
comprehensive, in completing this book, I can't help feeling
that his tale is, as yet, only partly told. If nothing else, the many
months spent in researching and writing about his life have
taught me to expect the unexpected, not to be surprised when
another previously unsuspected adventure suddenly comes
to light. There are still a few small gaps in the chronology and
remarkable tales may lie concealed in those nooks and crannies.
His obituarist tantalisingly mentions that 'he did, in recent years
and most reluctantly allow notes to be taken at his dictation' but

those autobiographical notes have remained well hidden and one can only wonder about the hair-raising tales that the ageing buccaneer dictated to his amanuensis. For the time being, I can only hope that, in telling the story of this 'born adventurer', I might have been able to capture some portion of his intrepidity and, perhaps, to exercise something of his own shrewdness 'in psychological situation and reaction'.

Author's Note

All quotations taken from previously unpublished diaries and letters are, so far as possible, reproduced as per the original with punctuation and spelling corrected only where this is essential for reasons of clarity.

One

Of Ice and Treasure

*I shall satiate my ardent curiosity with the sight of a part of the world
never before visited, and may tread a land never before imprinted by the
foot of man.*

Mary Shelley, *Frankenstein*

Saturday 2 December 1911, and, at the port of Hobart, Tasmania,
all eyes are trained on the Queen's Pier where the 600-ton Steam
Yacht *Aurora* is tied up. She's a businesslike looking vessel: built
for strength rather than beauty, with her three slender masts,
and the single, tall funnel, rising like a dismembered drainpipe,
giving her otherwise-clean lines a slightly ungainly aspect. She
sits low in the water, and her decks are crowded precariously
with canisters and boxes, stacks of timber and a bewildering assortment of items, of every conceivable size and shape,
crammed into all manner of nooks and crannies. Perhaps the
most unwieldy is a huge, coffin-shaped crate which the crew
mysteriously refer to as the 'Grasshopper'.

Around the harbour there's a carnival atmosphere, different
from that which prevails at a more routine sailing; the mood
is one of almost elated anticipation with excited spectators far

outnumbering anxious weeping wives or mothers. The men are in straw boaters and, among the usual seeming chaos of the dockside with its crates and cables, rats and seagulls, grease and dirt, the women shield their best frocks and their nostrils from contamination. Multicoloured bunting is conspicuous in the rigging of neighbouring ships and many of the spectators, young and old, are enthusiastically waving flags. The *Aurora* flies the pennant of the Royal Thames Yacht Club from her main topmast and the Commonwealth red ensign from her mizzen. The decks of a liner, the SS *Westralia*, berthed at the King's Pier just opposite, have been made available to the onlookers, though any gratuities are unlikely to appear in the purser's ledger. In the harbour, a multitude of smaller craft bob about; a lucky thing since the wharves are so densely packed that some members of the assembly seem in imminent peril of being pushed into the water. Nor is it merely the idle spectators, owners, merchants and families of the crew who are gathered to cheer the *Aurora* on her way. Among the relaxed, laughing crowd can be spotted public men, standing upon their dignity, and sweating beneath top hats and dark frock-coats. The bright Australian summer sun glances from their gold watch-chains and decorative fobs, and the drooping ostrich feathers in their wives' hats lend a touch of exoticism to the scene. The Premier, Sir Elliott Lewis, is present, as is His Excellency Sir Harry Barron, the Governor, attended by his aide-de-camp, Major Cadell, and the usual train of flunkies and minor officials. They, of course, are not here out of idle curiosity, but to read out valedictory telegrams and to place the stamp of imperial approval on the very first of Australia's Antarctic expeditions, to be led by Dr Douglas Mawson of the University of Adelaide. Tall and thin, Mawson conceals his nerves, stretched taut by his, as yet, unaccustomed position of total command, and passes the time in politely, even jovially, responding to the comments and questions of his various supporters. All the time his restless eye is monitoring the feverish preparations for departure. Simultaneously, he turns a deaf ear to the grunts and curses of the crew as they bark their shins and snag their clothing on the clutter strewn about the decks – a clutter which, they are all too aware, gives a distinctly unship-shape appearance to the *Aurora*.

Tense and expectant though he is, Mawson is willing to abrogate responsibility for the shipboard preparations to the *Aurora*'s master, John King Davis. Looking, at first glance, more like a haberdasher's assistant than an intrepid Antarctic veteran, Davis it is who decides precisely what latitude may be allowed the men as they make ready to cast off. Nonetheless, the security of the lashings has a very real interest for Mawson, for in each of those unwieldy crates is housed equipment and supplies upon which success or failure in the Antarctic depends. And he cannot help but mentally calculate the tensile strength of the ropes and tackle as he responds smilingly to another convivial remark or outstretched hand. All of a sudden, the ship shifts at her moorings, causing the landlubbers to take a step to balance themselves, and giving rise to a general alarm that she is about to depart. Many of the shore visitors rush to disembark, fearful of an unscheduled voyage to Antarctica, and it is a few moments before order is restored by the officers' assurances that notice of departure will be given in due form. At a few minutes to four the warning 'All visitors on shore' is heard, and the lazy swirl of smoke from the *Aurora*'s funnel gives place to a steady, thick black plume, billowing in time with the increasingly determined throb of her engines. The order to let go is given and the green, oily water at her stern begins to boil with the rotation of the tough, four-bladed propeller. The crowd, grown somewhat restive with the imminence of departure, raises a cheer, though Mawson's pleasure is momentarily checked by the ill-informed shout of some anonymous wag: 'I hope you bring back the Pole!' On board, the decks become even more crowded, as those members of the expedition who are to accompany the *Aurora* to Macquarie Island line the rail and wave and cheer in reply. Among them might be seen the burly figure of Frank Bickerton, strongly and darkly featured, and with a moustache that might grace the upper lip of a cavalry officer or a film star of a later decade. Being an Englishman and a stranger to Australia, he is not the focus of anyone's particular attention. His upraised hand doesn't acknowledge any specific handkerchief-wielding matron or girl, but merely offers a general salute to the expedition's well-wishers.

But the voyage is not yet fully under way, nor have all fare-wells been spoken. The Hobart Marine Board's motor launch *Egeria*, carrying the Governor and his lady, goes as far as Long Point before turning back, while an assorted jumble of other craft follow for a while in the *Aurora*'s wake. Once the ship is in the channel, the cases of dynamite and rifle cartridges are taken tenderly on board, as the crew of HMS *Fantome* cheers from across the water. Finally, the Nubeena Quarantine Station is reached and the expedition's forty-eight Greenland huskies are shipped and tethered round the ship's bulwarks, howling and whining their reluctance throughout the procedure and no doubt recollecting the trauma of their recent passage from England. As the ship's head is turned southwards, the lashings are checked again and the expeditioners descend to the ward-room, the adrenalin churning in their blood, as the *Aurora*'s propeller churns the ocean. At 8.30 p.m. she slips past the signal station at Mount Nelson, and the Morse lamp is used to signal the message, 'Everything snug on board; ready for anything. Good-bye.'

Frank Bickerton was just 22 years of age when he set sail for the Antarctic. Rather incongruously, a life that was to become extraordinary for its adventurousness and intrepidity had begun in the safe and highly respectable surroundings of suburban Oxford. Born on 15 January 1889, he was the second child of well-to-do, middle-class parents – conservative and ambitious – and hardly the kind of people likely to encourage an only son in the haphazard and dangerous career of an explorer. His father,

Joseph Jones Bickerton, was the son of a tobacconist, but he had worked hard to improve the standing of his family and, despite his involvement in a minor electoral scandal in 1880, he had risen to become a councillor and town clerk. He had also reinforced his position as a pillar of Oxford society by linking himself to an impressive array of civic institutions: becoming clerk of the peace, clerk to the Charity Trustees and the Police Committee, and a proctor of the university chancellor's court. In this last capacity, his name had been linked with that of Oscar Wilde, Bickerton acting as plaintiff's proctor when Wilde was pursued for non-payment of a bill for Masonic regalia.[1] Before their marriage, his second wife, Eliza, had described her 44-year-old fiancé as 'an elderly looking party' with 'a good deal of bald head' and a 'cold and formal air'.[2] But the Councillor was also a man of action, within a limited sphere, serving as a captain in the Oxford City Yeomanry and contributing to the city's sporting life by winning a series of rowing trophies with the four-man *Endeavour* crew.

At the time of his accidental drowning in the waters off Torcross in Devon – his son would later state that he had been 'murdered by the sea, fetching a small child's wooden spade that had floated away'[3] – Joseph Bickerton's estate had been worth over £11,000.* In the two years that intervened between the town clerk's death and that of his wife in 1896, this estate had mysteriously dwindled by nearly half. Years later, Frank's sister, Dorothea, wrote a semi-autobiographical novel in which she offered a possible explanation for the loss. The heroine's mother, like Eliza, was from an affluent Devon family and younger than her husband; after his premature death 'she took up bridge and gambled heavily. She got into debt.... Then, after a few days' illness, she had died quite suddenly,'[4] just as pneumonia had carried off Eliza in only four days. Despite the loss of capital – whether through maternal extravagance or other causes – in

---

* Approximately £700,000 in today's terms.

financial terms, Frank's inheritance gave him security and even affluence. In other terms, he seems to have inherited his father's strength and energy with, at least, a tincture of his mother's recklessness. Deprived of both parents by the age of 7, he might also have been shorn of the discipline and example that would have focused his abilities.

Frank and Dorothea became the wards of their maternal uncle, Dr Edward Lawrence Fox, a resident of Plymouth, a bachelor and a man of stubborn, mildly eccentric and intellectual habits. From the leafy suburbs of a city steeped in scholarly rigour and industry, the young Bickerton now moved to a port that epitomised England's traditions of seafaring and adventure. It was from here that the *Mayflower*, Drake's *Golden Hind* and Darwin's *Beagle* had sailed. The very house in which Bickerton now lived, 9 Osborne Place, was a mere stone's throw from the Hoe, where Drake had played his Armada-defying game of bowls; and from his new home's upper windows the boy could see Boehm's colossal statue of the buccaneer-cum-admiral staring belligerently out to sea. More recently, the town had become the birthplace of one of Britain's most celebrated Antarctic explorers: Captain Robert Falcon Scott.

It was in these surroundings that Bickerton's independent and unconventional spirit began to burgeon. To his guardian's horror, one of its earliest manifestations was his schoolboy decision to decorate his middle-class forearms with tattoos, a serpent on his right and a bird and snake on his left being, as he later told his great-niece, 'the best he could afford at the time'.[5] All in all, perhaps the attitude of the young Bickerton is best encapsulated in a photograph taken of him when aged about 10. In it he impishly defies Victorian mores by sticking out his tongue at the camera, an early display of the rebelliousness that would characterise much of his subsequent career. Not that such independence was unprecedented: there were intrepid spirits to be found on both sides of his family. His mother's forebears included a number of diplomatists who had served a budding empire in the far-flung corners of the world and the Bickertons claimed kinship with two admirals, the younger of whom had served under Nelson in the Mediterranean. Perhaps romantic stories of their foreign postings and nautical adventures, told to entertain an orphan in a strange house, had sown the seed – given to the child a desire to abandon the paths more commonly beaten by those of his background and education.

Although his early schooling remains something of a mystery – he may have been tutored at home – in September 1901, Bickerton became a pupil at one of England's most prestigious public schools: Marlborough College. The usual onward destinations for aspiring young Marlburians included Oxford, Cambridge and Sandhurst but, after only three rather undistinguished years at the college, Bickerton defied any such expectations and instead opted to pursue a career in mechanical engineering. His first step on this path was to embark on a four-year course at London's City & Guilds (Technical) College. The exact date of his enrolment is uncertain but 1906 seems the most probable year as this would have allowed him to take full advantage of the College's first series of aeronautics lectures, delivered in 1910. Nonplussed by this unusual choice, his family might have been reassured by the thought that an engineering qualification at least offered the chance of a remunerative profession. After all, his father's youngest brother, Charles Howard Cotton Bickerton, had pursued a successful engineering career, albeit in the fetid climate of India. It would not be long before they were again forced to review their assumptions. After completing his studies at City & Guilds, Bickerton spent some time working at one of the large iron foundries in Bedford. It was here that he met the intrepid Aeneas Mackintosh, whose mother lived in Bedford and who was, at the time, courting a local girl named Gladys Campbell. Although Mackintosh was ten years Bickerton's senior, the two men formed a strong and enduring friendship. Already a veteran of Sir Ernest Shackleton's British Antarctic Expedition (BAE) of 1907–09, Mackintosh was a man

of proven daring, even recklessness, and it was under his tute-
lage that Bickerton's lust for adventure would at last spill over
into action.

On 1 March 1911, the two men sailed on the Royal Mail Steam
Packet *Oruba*, bound for Cocos Island, a jungle-covered rock so
steeped in the myths of pirate gold that Robert Louis Stevenson
had taken it as the model for his *Treasure Island*. The tiny island
lies 550 miles south-west of the Panama Canal and, according to
the legends, the single largest cache hidden there consists of the
treasures of the city of Lima. In 1821, faced with the approach
of the liberating army of Simon Bolivar, those city dignitar-
ies and ecclesiastics still loyal to Spain rather naively entrusted
their bullion to an English sea captain named Thompson, on
the understanding that he would hide the treasure on their
behalf. Faced with such a temptation – by 1911 the treasure was
being valued at £20 million – Thompson cut his cables and ran
his brig, the *Mary Dier*, out to sea. Evading the Peruvian gun-
boats, he made his way to Cocos Island and buried his ill-gotten
gains, adding them to the innumerable other hoards reputedly
buried by buccaneers such as Dampier and Bonito the Bloody.
Thompson and his crew were later captured by a Peruvian man
o'war and all but Thompson, who promised to disclose the
whereabouts of the treasure, were summarily executed. The
slippery captain then succeeded in eluding his captors and, after
various adventures, washed up on the shores of Newfoundland
a sick and dying man. For once, he failed to engineer a dramatic
escape, and died sometime around 1838 – but not before dis-
seminating, mostly through the offices of an erstwhile shipmate
called Keating, enough clues and maps to occupy generations of
would-be treasure seekers. It seems to have been one of these
maps that prompted Bickerton's voyage to Cocos Island.

In the years between Thompson's death and 1911, many
expeditions had set out with the intention of retrieving the
pirates' hidden treasure. This one, however, was different for
two reasons. Firstly, its sponsors were women, who insisted on

safeguarding their investment by accompanying their male business partners. Secondly, they intended to donate their eagerly anticipated discoveries to philanthropic causes, most particularly the establishment of a new London orphanage.

On their voyage southwards, Bickerton and Mackintosh passed the time discussing their enterprise with the former's RGS acquaintance, the ill-fated explorer of South America, Major Percy Harrison Fawcett. He was on his way to continue his work with the Bolivian Boundary Survey and, as well as telling them of Cocos Island's history, he further whetted their appetites with stories of another treasure, buried by the Jesuits in Bolivia. Separating from Fawcett at Colón, Bickerton and Mackintosh caught a train to Panama, where they were joined by the expedition's sponsors, Mrs Barrie Till and Miss Davis, and by the other members of the expedition. These included an American called Stubbins, Colonel Gonzales – the official representative of the Costa Rican government – and a man named Atherton – a resident of Panama whom Mackintosh considered 'the swiniest swine that ever swanked'.[6] After tedious days during which Mackintosh tried, and repeatedly failed, to hire a suitable vessel to carry them to Cocos, and Bickerton fished and went alligator hunting, the party eventually sailed on 8 April on board a cargo steamer, the SS *Stanley Dollar*, which was to drop them off at Cocos en route to San Francisco. They landed on the island three days later and took up residence in a three-room shack vacated by an earlier expedition. Standing near an inlet, the hut was shaded by palms, and a rich crop of oranges, limes and coconuts weighed down the nearby trees: it seemed as though they had discovered a tropical paradise.

The next few days were spent in rowing round the island in search of likely-looking caves and inlets and in clearing paths through the dense equatorial jungle, searching for the 'flat stone, with markings on it'[7] that the ladies had been told would infallibly lead them to the treasure. No one, apparently, troubled to enquire why anyone possessed of such precise knowledge had failed to retrieve the treasure for themselves. They found no stone, but discovered instead millions of small red ants, which swarmed over them and left them covered with painful bites. They took to blasting their way into rocky outcrops, using dynamite they found in another abandoned tin hut, and all the time squinting at scratches on the rocks, 'which we all try to shape into anchors, arrows or such-like shapes!'[8] After nearly three weeks on the island, tormented by insects of every description and often drenched by tropical storms, with no sign of success, tempers began to fray and all grew tired of 'this stupid and ridiculous "clue" to the hypothetical Treasure'.[9] For Bickerton and Mackintosh, the main, if not the only, pleasure of the expedition became the opportunities they had for exploring the island in each other's company:

> Today being a holiday, Sunday, we were allowed to have it by ourselves. So Bick and I have decided to make a journey up the river as far as we can. At 9 a.m. we started off taking with us some biscuits, tea, jam and sugar, also my compass and aneroid. We have found that the only way of getting anywhere here – if it can be managed – is to go by the river. So we adopted this method and went along, jumping from stone to stone with occasional misses! Which we paid for by getting wet up to the knees… . We took photos as we went along – all the way we passed through the thick tropical vegetation: giant ferns, shrubs that a botanist would revel in but to us it was a wild chaos of growth which it would require someone versed in botany to know the names of. Occasionally we had to scramble over large trees that had fallen and bridged themselves across the river.[10]

Climbing gradually, after some two hours of travelling they reached a cascade. Above it, they found a large, level plateau which they then proceeded to explore. Thinking the cascade an easy landmark to identify, however, Mackintosh failed to take careful compass bearings. Soon the two explorers were lost and disorientated, hacking their way through

> Royal Palms, ferns of every variety – orchids, long grass-like Iris Lily leaves which cut one like a razor if you should happen to scrape along it…. . We at this time found ourselves in rather a predicament in not being able to find our way … as we went on we could see no signs, but were getting more and more involved in the mess. Bick climbed the highest trees round, but could get no view of any definite object except a glimpse of the sea, but this did not help us as we did not know in which direction to make for it. After wandering about for at least four hours – hopelessly lost – Bick discovered a decent high tree. Up this he climbed – when at the top he made out the sea and headland to the Northward of us, and what we took to be the High Peak of the island to the SW.[11]

Proceeding in a northerly direction, they found their way to the cascade and then, via the river, back to the hut, after a ten-hour excursion. Both men agreed that 'in spite of being wet through and having lost our way' – for more than five hours – 'we considered we had spent a most enjoyable day.'

Working days continued in the same vein. They hacked through the equatorial forests in search of likely-looking slabs of rock; blasted holes (on 9 May, 'Bick swarmed up the rocks and placed the charge and fuse – 14 sticks of dynamite!'[12]); and rowed into coves which Mackintosh, a ship's officer, thought impassable to boats laden with treasure but which the ladies considered probable hiding places. All to no avail; relations declined still further, with constant rows and disagreements, and the return of the ship on 13 May came as a relief to them all.

On 10 April, at a time when Bickerton was hacking and blasting his way through the equatorial rainforest of Cocos Island, Douglas Mawson was laying before the Fellows of the Royal

Geographical Society in London his plans for a predominantly Australian expedition to Antarctica. As with most expedition leaders of the 'Heroic Age' of Antarctic exploration, funding was perhaps the single greatest obstacle he faced and, in addressing the Fellows, he was not only seeking their approval but also making a direct appeal to their generosity. His Antarctic credentials were such that he could expect to command the undivided attention of his auditors. In March 1909, aged just 26, he had returned from Shackleton's BAE, having completed a record-breaking 1,260-mile unsupported man-hauled sledging journey in his quest for the South Magnetic Pole. He had also made the first ascent of the volcanic Mount Erebus and drawn the most accurate map of South Victoria Land to that date.

The area of Antarctic coast that he now wished to explore stretched from Cape Adare, directly to the south of New Zealand and the westernmost point of Captain Scott's *Terra Nova* expedition, to the Gaussberg, south of the Indian Ocean and the easternmost line of Professor Erich von Drygalski's German expedition of 1901–03. Only one landing, lasting but a few minutes, had been made in his chosen area: by the French expedition led by Dumont D'Urville of the *Astrolabe* in January 1840. Naming the region after his wife, D'Urville called it Terre Adélie or, in its anglicised form, Adelie Land. The only other expeditions that had ventured into the same region were those led by the Englishmen John Biscoe (1830) and John Balleny (1838–39) and the United States Exploring Expedition, led by Charles Wilkes of the *Vincennes* between 1838 and 1842. To all intents and purposes, then, a stretch of virgin territory some 2,000 miles wide lay facing Australia across the great Southern Ocean. Mawson's objective was to explore it, chart it, and to undertake a detailed scientific analysis of its climatic and magnetic phenomena, its meteorology and its geology. In addition, the expedition's vessel would carry out detailed oceanographic work on its way to and from the site of the expedition's Main Base.

Mawson's lecture was a huge success – a success that is, in all ways but one: while he had fired the imaginations of many of his listeners, he only managed to persuade the RGS to subscribe £500 to the expedition's kitty. Though not in itself ungenerous, this contribution made only very small inroads into the £45,000 that he estimated the expedition would cost. In his fund-raising speeches and private applications an assortment of justifications rubbed shoulders: the possible existence of rich mineral deposits, the advancement of science, and the need for Australia to stake its claim in Antarctica before it was gazumped by a more aggressive and less scrupulous imperial power. In Sydney, Mawson's friend and supporter, Professor Edgeworth David, even went so far as to compare 'Dr Mawson's objective with the Yukon, and suggested that large discoveries of gold were possible'.[13] For all their passion, however, these appeals had an Achilles' heel: they lacked the glamour attaching to an attempt on the geographic South Pole. As a geologist, Mawson saw little of interest in such a conquest, preferring instead to dedicate his resources to the rigorous scientific study of the region. This meant that, in marketing his expedition, he must find other means by which to appeal to donors seeking a cause célèbre, particularly the wealthy Australians attending the coronation of King George V. One way to capture the attention of both public and sponsors was to include, and advertise, the use of innovative technology in his plans. It was these plans that would soon involve Bickerton in one of Antarctic exploration's most daring experiments to date.

In 1908, *The Sphere*[14] had challenged 'motorists, submariners, bear-drivers, and aeronauts' to better the record of 460 miles from the Pole and, although that objective remained firmly outside Mawson's field of interest, the challenge and its popular appeal would not have been lost on him. Shackleton, a self-publicist nonpareil, had long ago impressed upon him the importance of capturing the public imagination. He had also shown him that mechanised transport could be used for this purpose by taking on the BAE a 15hp Arroll-Johnston motor car, donated by William Beardmore, the Clydeside shipbuilder, after whom a glacier was dutifully named. More recently, in January 1911, Scott's *Terra Nova* had unloaded at McMurdo Sound three tracked motor sledges designed by the Wolseley Company of Birmingham. In both cases, publicity had been as much a consideration as utility.

Perhaps inspired by the Antarctic balloon flights made during Scott's National Antarctic (*Discovery*) Expedition on 4 February 1902 and during Drygalski's *Gauss* expedition two months later, Mawson decided that he would be the first to take an aeroplane to the Antarctic. Scott's balloon, quaintly named the *Eva*, had cost an extravagant £1,300 and, at the edge of the Great Ice Barrier, it had made two flights, reaching a maximum altitude of 800 feet. But the balloon had leaked and its further use was abandoned. Drygalski's ascent had been rather more successful, reaching 1,600 feet. There were, however, huge risks inherent in such experiments and these had been amply demonstrated in 1897 when, in an attempt to cross the North Pole in a balloon called the *Ornan*, the Swedish aeronaut Salomon Andrée and his two companions died of exposure. Their bodies wouldn't be discovered until 1930. But no expedition to the Antarctic was devoid of danger and Mawson, convinced that the benefits – not least in terms of publicity – would more than outweigh the risks, remained bent on achieving Antarctica's first powered flight. With this aim in mind, he purchased an REP monoplane from the Vickers Company for £955 4s 8d. An obvious use for an aeroplane in the Antarctic would be spotting leads, or channels, in the ice wide enough for the expedition ship to push through, but since Mawson's machine would have to be transported in a crate, there would be little chance of utilising it in that way. Besides, the problems of launching an aeroplane from a ship would not be seriously addressed until the exigencies of war led to systematic research under the auspices of the Royal Naval Air Service. Once assembled at the spot chosen for the expedition's Main Base, however, the monoplane could be used for reconnaissance and survey work.

Such an experiment – an astonishingly daring one given that Louis Blériot's pioneering cross-Channel flight had only taken place in July 1909 and that, in 1911, no one had ever taken off from ice or snow – required the recruitment of men with very particular skills and experience. The expedition staff of thirty was to be made up almost entirely of graduates from the universities of Adelaide, Sydney and Melbourne, but Mawson recognised that in Australia, a country that had not witnessed its first powered flight until Houdini's exploit at Digger's Rest in March 1910, aviators were likely to prove rather thin on the ground. In making up the shortfall, he demonstrated a willingness to listen to the advice of friends and colleagues in England. Kathleen Scott, wife of Captain Scott and herself an aviation enthusiast, assisted him not only in the choice of an aeroplane, but also in the selection of a pilot: Lieutenant Hugh Evelyn Watkins of the 3rd Battalion, the Essex Regiment. Although a competent mechanic himself, Watkins would need the assistance of another engineer to maintain the machine in Antarctic conditions. The man selected for this role was Bickerton, who volunteered for the expedition immediately upon his return from Cocos Island.

Although Bickerton had been unable to attend Mawson's address at the RGS in April, the two did meet through their mutual acquaintances among the Society's Fellows. Bickerton's application for a Fellowship, made in October 1910, had been the first real demonstration of his interest in exploration and, despite his inexperience, he had articulated his enthusiasm sufficiently well for his two sponsors, William Scoresby Routledge and Edward A. Reeves, to agree that he was 'likely to become a useful and valuable Fellow'. Australian by birth, Routledge was husband to Katherine Pease Routledge (the surveyor of Easter Island) and descendant of the redoubtable whaler and father of Arctic science, William Scoresby. He was also irascible and cantankerous: he lacked friends at the best of times and there is no evidence of an acquaintance with Mawson. Indeed, he may not even have been acquainted with Bickerton, as the Society's regulations required that only one of an applicant's two sponsors should know him personally.

Reeves was a very different character: a family man, a lifelong servant of the RGS and a committed spiritualist, he had also been of immeasurable service to Mawson in obtaining for the AAE a loan of specialist surveying equipment to a value of £439 4s. As well as looking after the Society's important collection of maps, he served as its Instructor in Surveying and the list of his pupils reads like a veritable *Who's Who* of British exploration. In the period leading up to Bickerton's election, Reeves' students had included, among others, Captain 'Titus' Oates, Major Fawcett, Ernest Shackleton and John King Davis, Mawson's friend and master of the *Aurora*. The approval of this highly respected and influential member of the RGS's establishment must have weighed heavily in Bickerton's favour. He also benefited from the support of another of Mawson's professional acquaintances and a fellow veteran of the BAE: Aeneas Mackintosh. To a man of Mawson's rigidly scientific bent, the Cocos Island expedition might have seemed nothing more than a fool's errand. On the other hand, Bickerton's willingness to undertake such an errand could be considered indicative of a spirit of adventure that, if suitably disciplined, would not be out of place on an expedition to discover his own ice-bound El Dorado. Another Englishman recruited at about this time was Lieutenant Belgrave Ninnis of the Royal Fusiliers, who was to take charge of the expedition's dogs. In his diary, Ninnis recorded that 'Mackintosh swore by Bickerton, and urged Mawson to take him.'[15] Mawson was convinced and offered the young Englishman his chance.

Within three weeks of his return from Cocos Island, Bickerton received a letter of appointment from Mawson, written as the Australian travelled from London to Marseilles, on the first leg of his long journey back to Adelaide. In the letter, for-warded by Captain Davis, Bickerton was instructed to 'rub up on your navigation with Reeves if opportunity presents itself'[16] and, over the next few weeks, he accepted Reeves' tuition in navigation and route surveying. Reeves believed that 'anyone with a fair knowledge of mathematics and ... able to give most of his time to the subject' could be taught to find his latitude and longitude 'and do quite useful surveying in about three months'.[17] Although Bickerton's engineering background made him at least reasonably competent in mathematics, the time available for him to devote to his studies fell far short of Reeves' expectations. On 13 July, he and Ninnis journeyed to Reigate to meet their tutor and practise their star observations on the hilltops and high common lands in the area. The two would-be Antarctic navigators became thoroughly lost and one can only assume that, as they tramped their way round leafy suburbia, the irony of their situation was not lost upon them. Despite these setbacks, however, and between bouts of 'sweating together at the Geographical', the two young men also found time for 'lunching together at Lyons, and in fact, hunting in couples'.[18]

Mawson had also advised Bickerton to 'learn all you can of the engine during the next few weeks'. It was good advice. The mechanical engineering syllabus that Bickerton had followed at City & Guilds was 'arranged to suit the requirements of ... Persons who desire to acquaint themselves with scientific prin-ciples underlying the particular branch of industry in which they are engaged'.[19] Despite this broad remit, however, Antarctic exploration had never been numbered among the industries considered by the college's founders. Furthermore, although he had attended City & Guilds' early aeronautics lectures, prior to volunteering for the AAE, Bickerton had enjoyed few opportu-nities to put his professors' teachings into practice. Nevertheless, Mawson considered his new recruit's recently acquired skills suf-ficient for the expedition's purposes. Bickerton's place among the small brotherhood of Antarctic explorers was assured and the cost of his passage to Australia, which Mawson expected him to meet from his own funds, was a small price to pay.

Instructed to accompany Watkins to Australia, on 11 August 1911 Bickerton boarded the P&O vessel the SS *China*. Mawson had booked their particular charge, the monoplane, onto the SS *Macedonia* and, despite Watkins' last-minute attempts to have the crate moved to the *China*, he and Bickerton were forced to sail without it. Fortunately, the machine travelled instead under the watchful eye of the expedition's fourth and final English recruit, Frank Wild, a veteran of both Scott's *Discovery* expedition and Shackleton's BAE. Although the AAE would eventually sail from Hobart, Mawson's employment at the University of Adelaide had made it more convenient for him to establish his expedition headquarters in that city. As the expedition members arrived in dribs and drabs, they were each thrown into an increasingly frenetic round of preparations. Bickerton and Watkins were no exception and, on 16 September, they stepped from the gangplank into a whirlwind of activity. As soon as Wild arrived with the aeroplane, they would be expected to devote their time to readying it for a series of exhibition flights intended to thrill the pounds, shillings and pence out of the pockets of the crowds of spectators. Until then, they must contribute to more general work.

The *Macedonia* docked on 30 September and Bickerton, Watkins and Wild were immediately employed in arranging for the huge crate to be carted to the Cheltenham Racecourse, about 8 miles from Adelaide. The two-seater REP D-type was brand-new and the Vickers company had been pleased to be associated with the first attempt at powered flight in the Antarctic; in seeking publicity for their involvement, they even claimed that it would be used in a 'final dash for the Pole'.[20] It had a five-cylinder fan-shaped engine, and a tubular-steel fuselage covered in doped fabric. With a total length of 36ft and a wingspan of 47ft, it could manage a cruising speed of 48 knots. Its large engine cowling and complicated exhaust manifold also made it distinctly ugly and the machine displayed little of the fragile grace of some other contemporary designs.

If, while examining the aeroplane, Bickerton felt any qualms about his lack of practical experience, they may well have been allayed when he learned that many of the other expedition members had even less knowledge of their allocated roles. Robert Bage, for instance, a lieutenant in the Royal Australian Engineers and the expedition's astronomer, claimed to know nothing of astronomy, and many others, despite their degrees, had little real practical experience in their specialist fields. In fact, there was nothing particularly exceptional in this apparently haphazard approach to recruitment. Mawson himself had been employed as the BAE's physicist, even though his field of expertise was geology. What mattered, he believed, besides a general aptitude, was youth and enthusiasm; and, more cynically, a lack of real experience might make the poor salary more tempting.

Hugh Watkins was one of the most experienced men on the team. Already an expert balloonist, he had taught himself to fly on a Howard-Wright biplane at Brooklands and qualified for his Royal Aero Club Aviator's Certificate (No. 25) on 15 November 1910. As well as being accustomed to carrying passengers, he was also a competent mechanic with considerable hands-on experience. The monoplane's first exhibition flight was scheduled for 5 October. The Governor of South Australia had volunteered to become Watkins' passenger on the inaugural flight and, thereafter, daring members of the public could venture into the skies upon payment of a not- inconsiderable £5; all proceeds would go to the AAE's still disturbingly empty kitty. Bickerton, Watkins and Wild spent three days preparing the machine and Watkins took it up for the first time on 4 October. The monoplane performed well but, on landing, a wing was slightly damaged and Bickerton spent much of the remainder of the day repairing it.

At six o'clock on the morning of 5 October, Watkins decided to try one last preliminary flight before the arrival of the

fare-paying public. This time, Frank Wild occupied the front
seat. The flight started well but things quickly went disastrously
wrong. In a letter to his friend Fred Pinfold, Wild described
what happened next: 'We got away beautifully and had got up
to about 100ft when the left wing was caught in an air eddy
and we came down like greased lightning, and struck the earth
at over seventy miles an hour, the aeroplane turning over and
pinning us both under it. It seemed a devil of a time before any
body came to help us, but really it was only about two minutes
when Bickerton and half a dozen more lifted the wreck up and
dragged us out.'[21]

Clearly, Wild was not aware that Watkins had begun to
experience difficulties almost as soon as they had taken off. To
Bickerton and the other spectators on the ground, it was obvious that the monoplane had side-slipped at 500ft and had rapidly
lost altitude. It seemed that Watkins had recovered the situation
because the aeroplane was seen to climb to around 150ft before it
struck the fatal eddies that Wild noted. When Bickerton reached
the wreckage there was a strong smell of petrol, the fragile wings
had crumpled with the impact, and the nose was bent and the
tail section was in pieces. In its 'Aeronautics' column *The Times*
regularly reported accidents like this: planes falling from the
skies, folding up in mid-air or colliding. All too often the pilots
and their passengers were killed outright; here, amazingly, both
men survived. Wild was badly bruised and shaken but he managed to walk to the jockeys' hospital unaided. Watkins' injuries,
though more serious, were not life-threatening, the worst of
them being a cracked sternum.

The aeroplane itself had suffered the most devastating
damage. Besides the obvious warping of its fuselage, Bickerton
soon discovered that one of the five cylinders had been broken.
With the necessary spare parts and time, it might have been put
back into 'flying order', but neither parts nor time were available. Mawson was furious. Any hope of recouping the costs of
the purchase by exhibition flights had been forfeited: no one

would pay £5 to see the broken machine trundle disconsolately along the ground. Not only had an opportunity for positive publicity been lost but, if news of the accident were not handled skilfully, it could backfire altogether and the expedition become the butt of journalistic humour. Lastly, any hope of a pioneering Antarctic flight, no matter how useful it might have proved, had now been permanently dashed. So far as Bickerton was concerned, a few short, fateful minutes had thrown his part in the expedition into doubt. He had been employed to maintain an aeroplane; now his special charge lay in ruins. Would the irate Mawson dismiss him, or would he be kept on as a mere appendant, devoid of any specified role?

There was just one ray of hope in the pervading gloom. It had never been certain that an Antarctic flight would be feasible, so there had always been the option of utilising the machine as a motor sledge for the hauling of heavy equipment. Now, Mawson decided that this should be their aim – if Bickerton had enough equipment and adequate skill to turn the mass of bent wreckage into a functioning 'air-tractor'. But attention must first be turned to the other preparations for the expedition. For the time being, all he could do was to strip the torn fabric from the twisted frame, make some rudimentary attempts to straighten it and smile at the name that some wag among the team gave to the machine: the 'Grasshopper'. The remaining conversion work would have to be completed in the Antarctic where, Bickerton believed, it could be 'repaired, assembled and fitted with sundry appliances to make it practicable for the usual climate of the country in which it was to work'.[22] In Mawson's eyes, Watkins' usefulness was now at an end and, since there was no possibility of his injuries being sufficiently healed for him to join the expedition, he returned to England.[23]

A few weeks later, Bickerton and his colleagues travelled from Adelaide to Melbourne where, at the house of Professor Orme Masson, they met some of the other expedition members for the first time. Masson was Professor of Chemistry at the University of Melbourne and President of the Australasian Association for the Advancement of Science; he had also been an active supporter of the AAE from its earliest days. The rest of the party included Mawson, George Ainsworth, Bage, Herbert Dyce Murphy, Cecil Madigan, Alec Kennedy, Percy Correll and Alfie Hodgeman. Ainsworth, a man supremely sure of himself and perhaps more than a little pompous, was to lead a small party to be landed on Macquarie Island, midway between Australia and the Antarctic coast. As well as conducting a detailed survey of the island, they would construct and operate a wireless station that would relay messages between Australia and the expedition's Main Base. Murphy, whom Mawson had selected to lead the westernmost of the three bases he planned to establish in Adelie Land, was urbane and highly educated, but also an experienced whaler in Arctic waters.

The next day they all joined the *Loongana*, in which they crossed the choppy Bass Strait to Tasmania and then followed the River Tamar to Launceston. To recover from the grogginess that they had all experienced on the crossing, Bickerton accompanied Madigan and Hodgeman on a walk up a hill that presented them with a fine view over the town, the river and the lush, if rather unkempt, countryside all around. During these early days, he and Madigan, a Rhodes Scholar at Oxford who was to serve as the expedition's meteorologist, struck up a friendship that would endure throughout the trials and tribulations of the coming months.

On 21 November, they travelled south to Hobart by train and were met by Eric Webb, the magnetician, and Wild, who had now recovered from the injuries sustained in the crash six weeks earlier. Not long afterwards, they went to inspect the *Aurora*, which had steamed into harbour on the 4th. Her passage from England had not been a smooth one. Between London and Cardiff, where the ship was scheduled to take on 500 tons of coal, the irascible Davis and his crew had fallen out over shipboard conditions. Threatened with a lawsuit for damages to personal kit, he had been obliged to dismiss them and appoint a scratch crew – hardly a satisfactory start to a voyage that would take his vessel into the most treacherous and difficult waters on the face of the globe.

The *Aurora* had been built in Dundee in 1876 and started her life as a whaler with the Dundee fleet. Except for those few expeditions, like Scott's *Discovery* expedition, that could afford to have a ship specially built, most chose old whalers as the closest they could come to a ready-made Antarctic exploration vessel. Typical of her kind, in many ways the *Aurora* was ideal. She was strong – her elastic wooden hull had been designed to withstand the cruel Arctic waters and her cutwater was protected by a sheath of iron; she combined steam power and sails, which would enable her to conserve her fuel for use among the pack ice; and she was comparatively cheap. As was usual with the Dundee whalers, the *Aurora* had spent a considerable portion of each year in the sealing grounds off Newfoundland. More unusually, she had also taken holidays from the routine, if highly dangerous, occupations of whaling and sealing. In 1884, she took part in the search for the seven survivors of Lieutenant A.W. Greely's 24-strong United States expedition to Lady Franklin Bay. Then, in 1894, she had been chartered for a treasure hunting expedition to, of all places, Cocos Island. Like all the other ships that braved the island's shark-infested waters, she returned without the hoped-for freight of pirate bullion.

In preparation for the voyage south, the ship had undergone a complete overhaul and refit at the South West India Docks on the Thames. Under Davis's watchful eye, she had been barquentine-rigged – square-rigged on the foremast and fore-and-aft rigged on her main and mizzen-masts – and her two-bladed propeller had been exchanged for a tougher, four-bladed model. Her hold had also been crammed with 3,000 cases of equipment and stores, but another 500 lay waiting in the quayside warehouse in Hobart. They included the 'aero-sledge' or 'air-tractor' as the erstwhile aeroplane was variously described and, once it was loaded, Bickerton noted rather ruefully that the 'enormous case on the *Aurora*'s boat skids' was 'viewed with displeasure by everybody on board'.[24] So much for the claim made by *The Times* that 'the monoplane has been chosen for the expedition principally on account of its portability.'[25] All the boxes had been colour-coded, the different coloured bands denoting the element of the expedition for which they were destined: the Macquarie Island party (no colour), the Main Base under Mawson's personal leadership (red), the central party under Wild's command (blue) and Murphy's far-western party (yellow). The warehouse became a hive of activity and even with the large doors thrown wide open to let in the sea breeze and the smells and sounds of the harbour, the men grew hot and dusty in the heat of the Australian summer.

A day later, another party of twelve arrived from Sydney on board the *Paloona*. They included the expedition's three surgeons – Doctors McLean, Jones and Whetter – and the wireless operator, Walter Hannam. After the aeroplane, the use of wireless was to be the expedition's second great innovation and no expense had been spared in the selection and purchase of the necessary equipment. Two complete sets of Telefunken apparatus were purchased from the Australasian Wireless Company, with motors and dynamos from Buzzacott of Sydney. In total there were to be four masts, two for Macquarie Island and two for the main Antarctic base, and these were built by Saxton and Binns, also of Sydney. Although each mast could be broken down into sections, their size and weight made them a considerable obstacle on the *Aurora*'s already cramped decks and it was precisely these problems that had dissuaded Scott from taking wireless equipment on the *Terra Nova*. To counterbalance the cost and inconvenience, if transmissions could be successfully sent and received, the expedition would set an important precedent and some of the doubt and uncertainty inherent in Antarctic exploration would be effectively removed. For the first time, an expedition would be able to announce both its success and, perhaps more importantly, its precise whereabouts. Mawson and his staff would become the first men to 'speak' to the wider world from a position hundreds of miles to the south of the Antarctic Circle. Then, as recipient of the messages on the mainland, Conrad Eitel, the AAE's secretary, would become the man to spread the news abroad. Bickerton would be expected to work closely with Hannam in the installation and maintenance of the wireless equipment.

Besides the arduous physical exertion required to stow everything safely on board the bulging *Aurora*, there was an assortment of other, less strenuous tasks. The men had to be measured for their all-in-one Jaeger woollen suits and Burberry jackets; then, of course, their spiritual welfare must be considered. On 26 November, the last Sunday before the *Aurora* sailed, the Bishop of Tasmania presided over a special service dedicated to the expedition. In his sermon, the Bishop paid tribute to the expedition's laudable scientific goals – the betterment of mankind through an increase in its knowledge – but he also acknowledged the spirit of adventure that ran through the enterprise and concluded with a prayer for both success and a safe return for all the young men. The next day, in a more-private ceremony, Bickerton invited Madigan to his room and the two men toasted the expedition in crème de menthe. The Premier of Tasmania, Sir Elliott Lewis, hosted a farewell party at the Museum on Friday 1 December, and all was set for departure.

Two

Tempest-Tossed

Now would I give a thousand furlongs of sea for an acre of barren ground.

William Shakespeare, *The Tempest*

As the *Aurora* headed southwards from Hobart, the glass was falling rapidly; the ship, her crew and the supernumeraries of the AAE were about to undergo their first trial. While the vessel rolled in the increasing swell, landsmen and crew sought to stabilise the shifting load, each acutely aware of the 6,000 gallons of inflammable kerosene, benzine and spirit in their all-too-fragile containers. At sunset on 4 December, two days out from Tasmania, the *Aurora* lurched as she was struck by southerly gales. Overburdened and sitting low in the water, she laboured in the roaring, granite-grey seas as the helmsman fought to keep her head to the wind and prevent her from being driven too far to the east. Percy Gray, the navigating officer, found that 'Nearly all the wretched land party are as sick as dogs'[1] and, given his seasickness during his recent voyage to Cocos Island, there is no reason to suppose that Bickerton was not among those 'puking in all directions'.[2] Davis divided the land parties into watches, placing Bickerton in Gray's middle watch, along with Wild, Hannam, Hodgeman and a geologist named Watson. They were told to stand ready to obey without hesitation the orders of the officers: the safety of the ship and of their colleagues might now depend upon their ability to tighten a lashing, brace a shifting crate, or haul upon a rope. And all the time they must try to avoid treading on the dogs, a pathetic mass of sodden, whimpering fur still cowering on a deck awash with their filth.

The next day, the storm grew in intensity as the prevailing westerly winds, the 'roaring forties', rushed down upon the *Aurora*. With no significant landmass to interrupt their course, the winds scoured the ocean with increasing violence, whipping the surface into spume and spray and generating enormous rolling waves. It seemed to Davis and his officers inevitable that some part, at least, of the invaluable and irreplaceable cargo must be lost overboard and, as Bickerton later noted, the air-tractor nearly became the first victim: 'During the gale encountered a few days out from Hobart, a sea came aboard and stove in one end of the case, causing the machine to protrude through the far end some 4ft, driving it through the inch planking and tin lining like a nail. The same sea passed on to demolish half the bridge.'[3] Toucher, the officer of the watch, only narrowly escaped with his life but, astonishingly, by the time the violence of the storm began to abate on the 8th, the damage was relatively limited. Besides the wrecking of the bridge and the injury to the air-tractor, a pump had been temporarily disabled, the drinking water was contaminated by seawater and, despite their special strengthening, some of the planks of the expedition's motor launch were staved in.

As the seas took on a gentler aspect, Bickerton assisted Gray and others in patching up the damage done during the storm; more comprehensive repairs would have to wait. In the calmer weather, the *Aurora*'s passengers found their sea legs and their spirits rose. In the more relaxed atmosphere, Gray in particular soon demonstrated an aptitude for practical jokes: 'I had a great

joke with Bickerton this afternoon. He asked me to throw him
an apple of which there is a case on the bridge. There is also a
case of eggs. I was on the bridge at the time and he was right aft
on the poop. Instead of an apple I threw him an egg, fairly hard.
He, thinking it was an apple, caught it over his head, and the
result was delightful! The spectators were greatly entertained!
Bickerton not quite so much!'[4] Bickerton vowed that he would
get even but with Gray on his guard and Macquarie Island fast
approaching, there was little enough time for him to engineer
his revenge. Landfall came at 4 a.m. on 11 December. The men
aboard the *Aurora* could congratulate themselves on having
passed the first test of the expedition; besides cuts, bruises and
seasickness, no member of the party was injured. They had run
the gauntlet and survived. Macquarie Island lay off the port side,
its grim outline marking a point some 850 miles south-south-
east of Hobart.

For the next year, the island would be home to five of
Mawson's men. Under Ainsworth's leadership, Leslie Blake,
Arthur Sawyer, Charles Sandell and Harold Hamilton were to
explore and chart the landscape, catalogue its fauna and flora,
and man the wireless station. The island also became the rendezvous for the seventeen members of the expedition who had
not been able to leave Hobart on board the *Aurora*. As the masses
of gear had been stowed away, it had become increasingly clear
that the ship could not possibly accommodate both equipment
and men. There had been some suggestion of reducing the size
of the landing parties, but Mawson avoided this extreme meas-
ure by hiring a support vessel, the *Toroa*, which rendezvoused
with the *Aurora* on the 13th and spent two days unloading the
Macquarie Island stores before returning to Tasmania.

While awaiting the arrival of the *Toroa*, Mawson and
Ainsworth surveyed the island and chose to position the expedition hut and the all-important wireless station on a promontory
to the north-east. Frank Wild and others prepared a 'flying fox',
or wire hoist, for the hauling of the heavy Telefunken wireless

equipment up the hillside, which rose steeply from the coast. Bickerton, meanwhile, worked with Gillies, the *Aurora*'s chief engineer, to put the motor launch back into working order. As soon as they made the launch seaworthy it joined the ship's whaleboat in a series of hazardous trips to and from the island, threading its way through the submerged rocks, carrying stores and men between ship and shore. Over the next few days, 10 tons of stores and equipment, plus fifty-five bleating, anxious sheep and all of the huskies were landed. Frank Hurley, the expedition's official photographer, captured the work and the wildlife on film. Shock-haired and inventive, he had been so anxious to join the staff that he had even volunteered to forego any remuneration for his services. Lugging his delicate equipment to any vantage point that offered the prospect of a good image, he filmed everything: parties of fifteen or twenty men struggling with the enormous wireless masts, looking, from a distance, like some monstrous centipede; elephant seals floundering in the surf among the rocks; and even the floating knots of writhing kelp. Somewhat less scientifically, he also recorded the men cavorting in the shadow of the monolithic wreck of the sealer *Gratitude*, clambering on to the blubbery backs of the seals and riding them down the beach and into the water. Around 3 p.m. on the 14th, approximately 2,500 miles due south, another photograph was being taken. It showed Amundsen and his four companions gazing at the Norwegian flag fluttering above their tent, at the geographic South Pole.

The work setting up the Macquarie Island base was not free of accidents – Wild was slightly injured while operating the fox, and Hannam nearly ruined components of the vital wireless equipment by leaving some of the crates open and exposed to the elements – but it proceeded rapidly. There were also certain regional delicacies to be enjoyed by the more adventurous: 'Near the rocky landing-place Wild, Hannam and Bickerton erected a tent... . In ideal surroundings, they were mainly concerned with the proximity of a certain gentoo penguin rookery which supplied their larder with choice steaks cut from the breast of this bird.'[5]

By 23 December everything had been prepared for the *Aurora*'s departure and, with the barometer falling and the sea rising, it was time to be off. As the *Aurora* steamed away from the island, George Ainsworth and his party could be seen waving and cheering, their good spirits apparently unaffected by their melancholy surroundings – 20 miles by 4 of tussock grass, swamp and black volcanic mountains. But they wouldn't be alone. Besides the seasonal population of sealers, there would be the constant flow of messages to and from the Antarctic. Sawyer and Sandell, the wireless operators, would be the first to hear of the heroic exploits and achievements of the Main Base party, and they would serve as the heralds of this news, conveying it, via Eitel, to the expectant outside world.

Over the next few days, the *Aurora* tore along before a brisk north-easterly breeze. She now carried a complement of fifty all told, divided into three watches, and the men were settling into a routine. Having worked with Gillies on the repairs to the motor launch and sharing a professional camaraderie, Bickerton was welcomed into the dark, clamorous engine room. In the months to come, he would remember these moments with particular affection: 'There are several little things though that we look forward to enjoying before civilisation is reached. For instance, coming down on the ship, or calm evenings on the pack. I often used to go down into the engine room and talk with the Chief and drink coffee and sometimes oil and run the jolly old engine. I am looking forward to this again awfully, what heaps we shall have to talk about.'[6]

But there was also the pleasure of the *Aurora* as a sailing ship. Despite the seasickness that he had suffered during the early days of his voyage to Cocos Island, in later years sailing would become one of Bickerton's passions. It was perhaps the experience of standing on the deck of the *Aurora* as she bowled south that planted the seed in his soul. The heaving of the decks on the swell, the crackling of the spread canvas and humming of the cordage; all must have been indescribably exhilarating to a man who had deliberately chosen to embark on such an adventure. While some, like 'Joe' Laseron, biologist-cum-taxidermist, might spend a disproportionate amount of their time leaning green-faced over the rails, Bickerton and others lent an increasingly capable hand with the day-to-day running of the ship. Even the grudging Davis admitted in his journal that the members of the landing parties assisted with 'bracing yards, making or furling sail, steering, hoisting boats in and out and other miscellaneous duties'. To his evident surprise, they also seemed to 'rather enjoy keeping watch'.[7]

The men, destined to spend the next year marooned together, were gradually getting to know one another. Some were clearly outstanding, like Frank Wild, who noted in his own journal the camaraderie developing between the men and expressed his regard for Bickerton on more than one occasion. Madigan's bond with the English engineer was also growing and, while still on Macquarie Island, he noted that 'I like Bickerton very much, he is a considerate and unselfish chap with a fine sense of humour.'[8] Then there was the rather acerbic New Zealand magnetician, Eric Webb, whose scepticism about the qualifications of some of his companions, even of Mawson's, grew day by day. Popular with everyone was Dr 'Dad' McLean, the chief medical officer: always happy to lend a hand, to have a go at just about anything and ever ready to round off the day with a song. Fat, cheery, rather coarse Hannam, whose role of wireless operator would necessitate close working with Bickerton, had already made himself popular by volunteering his not-inconsiderable talents in the galley. His welcome variations on the usual poor fare more than made up for his gaffe with the crate-opening on Macquarie Island, at least with most of the team. Morton Moyes, the fastidious meteorologist of the Western Base, shunned his company, while Madigan thought him 'commonplace and rude but very keen and competent'.[9] Most of the others were much less experienced men – some, like Percy Correll, little more than fresh-faced boys, bursting with enthusiasm for this, the first of their adventures. And over all of them loomed the austere, aloof Dr Mawson, who locked himself away with Davis, discussing, in the intervals between bouts of seasickness, charts and plans, crew and coal levels.

So far as the charts were concerned, they could be used only as a rough guide. Very few vessels had traversed the waters into which the *Aurora* was sailing and the notorious effects of Polar refraction or 'looming', a phenomenon similar to desert mirage, could well mean that land firmly sworn to by previous navigators might prove illusory. In the days to come, the *Aurora* would sail over Balleny's Sabrina Land, Wilkes's Cape Carr and D'Urville's Côte Clarie, proving that all three sightings were probably of large ice-masses rather than of land. On the 29th the watch cried 'Ice on the starboard bow!' and the decks resounded with the rush of feet. Many members of the AAE had never before left the shores of Australia, and they hung over the rail, awestruck as the ship swept past a small iceberg, her wake lapping against its silvery sides. This berg was merely the herald of a larger armada; one, a floating island, measured three-quarters of a mile long by half a mile wide. As they passed by, the waves thundered through the fissures and caves in its sides, making Alec Kennedy, the Western Base magnetician, think of '100 locomotives blowing off steam'.[10]

At 7 p.m. that evening, pack ice was spotted for the first time. This day marked the beginning of the long, tedious and dangerous game of cat-and-mouse, as Davis sought to find a path through the ice in order to land the shore parties. Skill and preparation were – and still are – vital to the navigator in Antarctic waters, but the part played by sheer luck cannot be overestimated. In January 1902, Scott's *Discovery* had broken through the ring of pack ice in only four days; it had taken others as many weeks. Every opportunity to push southwards must be grasped, every jagged path through the ice explored; but, all the time, they faced the risk that the ice would invite them in, only to close like a giant trap behind them, its teeth sawing with malicious tenacity at the hull.

The *Aurora* followed the outline of the pack as it trended gradually southwards, all the time skirting bergs which, for all their serene beauty, were capable of disembowelling the ship and sending her to an icy grave. The cutter *Sabrina*, consort to Balleny's *Eliza Scott*, had foundered in these waters in 1839 with the loss of all her crew. Fortunately, since Davis had already served under Shackleton as chief officer and then master of the *Nimrod* during the expedition of 1907–09, no one could doubt that he knew his business. All the time, around them, the ocean boomed in the hollows of bergs, sometimes close by, sometimes far distant; to Davis's ears, it sounded 'like distant thunder'. The lookouts strained their eyes in search of the longed-for 'water sky', a darkness that indicated clear water below, or a mottling that revealed an ice-strewn but navigable passage. At present, the sky showed only an uninterrupted whiteness, the reflection of the sun's rays on the ice, a phenomenon tiring to both the mind and the eyes and known as 'ice-blink'.

The pack grew ever more dense, the sought-after water sky as elusive as ever, and time and again it became necessary to turn the ship's bows westwards to clearer water. Every day that passed without progress to the south was a day lost and brought the end of the season closer. There was also the matter of fuel. Feeling their way along the edge of the pack and forcing the *Aurora's* bow into any narrow passage meant that serious inroads had been made into the 386 tons of coal shipped at Hobart. Once they located a suitable site for the Main Base, it would then be necessary to steam hundreds of miles to land Wild's central and Murphy's western parties, and still retain sufficient coal to escape the freezing pack. In 1902, Drygalski's exploration vessel, the *Gauss*, had become ice-locked as early as February, and the narratives of Arctic and Antarctic exploration are littered with similar accounts. Between 1829 and 1833, on board the *Victory*, Sir John Ross had been beset for four winters in Arctic waters. Sir John Franklin's ships *Erebus* and *Terror* had been similarly trapped in the winter of 1846 and their crews had perished in a futile attempt to sledge to safety. And, as lately as 1903 to 1904, Scott's *Discovery* had been hemmed in at McMurdo Sound at the south-west corner of the Ross Sea. For the *Aurora* to become imprisoned in the same manner would spell disaster for the scientific purposes of the expedition and could have dire consequences for the explorers themselves.

For the next few days, progress remained predominantly westward in orientation. Whenever a passage opened to the south it soon became a dead end, forcing the *Aurora* to swing round and head back to the open sea to continue her search. New Year's Day 1912 was ushered in in nearly full daylight, and the shore parties gathered on deck as the last eight bells of 1911 was sounded. Some marked the occasion by letting fly with their guns, while other, less bellicose celebrants banged mess tins together. Finally, there were group photographs on the bridge, although the poor light made Hurley pessimistic of the results.

On 2 January, Davis decided to refill the water tanks which had been only partly replenished at Macquarie Island. He gave the order to 'ice ship' and the *Aurora* was positioned against a large slab of the floe. Wild led Bickerton, Madigan, Kennedy, Hurley and Archie Hoadley on to the surface of the ice while, on board, a block and tackle was rigged in preparation. The men dropped on to the floe from the bowsprit and tethered the ship with an ice-anchor. Using picks and ice-saws to break the ice, they filled a large tank and then waited as it was swung upwards on to the deck. From the bridge, Davis looked on as the men hauled on the creaking ropes, and the tank rose with a jerky motion, oscillating like an enormous pendulum. He watched as it was refilled and made another precarious ascent, and then ordered Wild and his men back on board; with the heavy north-easterly swell there was a risk of the swinging tank colliding with and seriously damaging the rudder. Besides the danger to the ship, the operation did not run smoothly and, for a time, Bickerton and his colleagues found them- selves stranded on the ice, the sailors hauling on the anchor cable having allowed it to slip through their hands, so that the anchor disappeared into the sea. Fortunately, enough water had been brought aboard for immediate needs; should it become necessary, another attempt would be made when the swell had subsided. The same day, some of the sheep were slaughtered and their carcasses festooned the rigging like macabre bunting, dripping blood on the unwary.

On 3 January, the pack began to trend northwards, and the tension mounted. To have sailed so far west, only to be forced on to a course diametrically opposed to the one they desired to take must have seemed intolerable. But the next morning, at 5 a.m., land-ice was spotted on the port bow. This could be the long-sought-after southern continent, or it might be an ice-covered island or just an iceberg of colossal proportions. No matter at this moment because, as they rounded a corner at 7 a.m., an open track of southward trending sea opened before them. Clinging to the edge of the barrier, the *Aurora* plunged on, southwards at last. The only member of the expedition whose new-found optimism was alloyed with disappointment was Murphy. The difficulties encountered in discovering a route to the south had eaten so far into the ship's coal reserves that landing the planned three parties now seemed quite impossible. The Western Base would have to be abandoned and Murphy's men and equipment would be distributed between Mawson's and Wild's parties. As he and Mawson discussed the reallocation of the men, Wild requested that Bickerton should be allowed to join his team, but Mawson refused. The air-tractor and its engineer would be included in the Main Base party. Wild had also been discussing with his companions his plan to make an attempt on the South Pole, should Scott and Amundsen fail. Ninnis and Gray had already been recruited and, on 24 January, Gray noted, 'Wild is still dead keen on this Southern journey of his, there has been one more candidate enrolled, vis Bickerton, so that makes four out of the six.'[11]

As the wind began to rise, the ship sheltered in the lee of what they now knew to be an ice-island. For twenty-four hours, a gale blew ferociously, showering the ship with snow and confining the landsmen to their cabins and wardroom. When it eased, the *Aurora* headed south-south-east, diverging from the ice barrier which trended east-south-east. By the early evening of the 6th, the ship lay beneath another towering cliff of ice that stretched across her path, its face pitted with caves and grottoes carved by the action of the sea. They launched one of the boats, and Hurley photographed the *Aurora* in front of the largest cavern, whose vaulted ceiling arched 100ft and more above the ocean.

By 11 p.m. the ship had made her way into a wide bay, the unmistakable outline of ice-covered land forming its western boundary. At last, the members of the Australasian Antarctic Expedition caught their first glimpse of the great Antarctic continent, and the discovery of the coastline meant that a landing must shortly follow. Steaming round the bay, the ship entered another to the west, where she rode at anchor for a few hours. The next day, a heavy fall of snow had transformed her rigging into a magic white tracery and the decks were slippery underfoot. Soon she was under way again, threading her way between the numerous islets and bergs that strewed the bay, each with its population of screeching Adélie penguins, diving into the sea or launching themselves like black rockets back on to land. Soundings were taken every few minutes to minimise the ever-present danger of grounding. So far, no suitable landing place had been distinguished. Small stretches of rock could be seen at the base of some of the ice cliffs, but it was essential that the site of their base should provide access to the tops of the cliffs so that inland exploration could be undertaken. On the 8th, they steamed into what would come to be called Commonwealth Bay, and it was here, Mawson decided, that the Main Base would be established. In the afternoon, while he and Davis conferred in the chart-room, Wild came down to report the sighting of a rocky exposure that might be suitable for a base. Closer examination was called for.

By three o'clock, a landing party of eight had been selected, headed, of course, by Mawson himself. The others were Wild, Madigan, Kennedy, Webb, Bage, Hurley (to record the moment for posterity) and Bickerton. The weather was balmy, calm and crisp, as they turned the whaleboat's head towards the rocky promontory pointed out by Wild. The landscape was given a slightly bizarre aspect by the snowcapping of the islets: where the snow overhung the water, it had been gradually eaten away by the action of the waves, giving the islets the appearance of peculiar sea-toadstools or monstrous 'iced-cakes',[12] as Mawson called them. Looking for a suitable place to land, they made for a small inlet, taking soundings as they went. The inlet opened out into a beautiful, landlocked harbour, and soon the boat was drawn up alongside an ice-quay. The next moment, the snow on shore crackled beneath their boots – the first men to set foot on a tract of coastline some 2,000 miles long.

Cape Denison, as it would come to be called in honour of one of the expedition's benefactors, is about half a mile deep and something between a mile and a mile and a half in length. Immediately to the south, the ice trends gradually down towards the bay, while on either side of the slopes, precipitous ice cliffs rise to heights of up to 150ft. The bleakness of the site was alleviated by the bright sunshine and the beauty of the crescent-shaped bay stretching all about them. Mawson made his decision, and Wild concurred: this was the spot for the Main Base. Although much further west than had been anticipated, in all other respects, the site seemed ideal. It had a small area free from ice, a perfect boat harbour, a relatively gentle slope giving free access to the plateau above and cliffs that might be expected to shelter their habitation from the worst of the weather. While the leaders consulted, Bickerton and the others roamed about the site of their new home and, to relieve their high spirits, embarked on a brisk snowball fight. Hurley, meanwhile, set up his camera and began the process of recording.

By 7.30 p.m. the pioneers were back on board the *Aurora*. Time was of the essence, as it still remained to steam westwards and find a suitable location for Wild's base. The shallowness of the waters in the immediate vicinity of the shore made it impossible for stores to be unloaded directly on to the ice from the ship, so, instead, a ferry service would have to be run, taking men and equipment from the ship to the landing point. The motor launch had become Bickerton's responsibility and it was he who steered it across the bay with the whaleboat, loaded with perishable foodstuffs, in tow. Meanwhile the *Aurora* steamed to the west of the islets, seeking a more sheltered anchorage. By the time the launch reached the harbour, the weather had turned, the warm sunshine giving place to darkening skies and rapidly dropping temperatures. The wind, too, blew with increasing force and showered the men with tiny ice particles from the plateau above. All on board had dressed in their light summer clothes, little thinking that the warm, mellow weather could give way so rapidly to greyness and plummeting temperatures. The cold chilled them to the bone, and Archie Hoadley's unprotected hands soon showed the first signs of frostbite. The boats were rapidly unloaded, and the order given for a return to the ship, before the sea became too choppy. Emptied of their cargo, the two boats sat high in the water, bouncing over a rising sea that threatened to capsize them at any moment. When they reached the ship, ropes were thrown down so they might be taken in tow. Davis was anxious to get under way, and hoisting the boats back on board would take too long. He intended to find a safer anchorage and then bring them in. In the meantime, as the boats were taking in water, a handful of men remained in each to bail them out. In the launch, Bickerton turned off the engine and assisted Whetter and Johnnie Hunter with the bailing.

It was a bumpy ride, as the boats contended with the heavy seas and the ship's wake. The thermometer stood at 24°F

(-4.5°C) and the men grew numb with the cold. At last, 500yd from the ice cliffs, the *Aurora*'s anchors were let go, and caught in the seabed. Preparations were being made to bring the men aboard when, without warning, the painter snapped and a 45mph gale whirled the launch away from the ship's side, the distance widening with every second. If the launch were upset, the three men on board might be dead before they could be fished out of the freezing ocean. Their only chance was to restart the engine and fight their way back to the ship under their own steam. But the engine, soaked with salt water, would not fire. Those on board the *Aurora* could see Hunter's elbow bobbing up and down as he worked the pump, and Dr Whetter fumbling in the stern as he attempted to rig a jury-rudder, the proper rudder having been shipped when she was taken in tow. Bickerton, meanwhile, was hunched over the motor, desperately trying to coax it into life. By now, half a mile separated the vessels, and the launch was being drawn dangerously close to one of the smaller islets, against which the sea pounded with ever-increasing violence. If she struck the rock she must inevitably founder. A stone's throw from the wave-lashed, black rock, the engine fired at last. A cry of jubilation rose from the ship as the launch was seen to suddenly transform itself from a lump of driftwood, subject to the whim of the ocean, to a thing with life and a purpose of its own. They cheered again as it swept towards the ship's stern, the jury-rudder rendering its course a little uncertain. The occupants of the two boats clambered up the ship's sides, their friends clutching at their belts to haul them in. The whaleboat's crew first and then Bickerton and his companions were brought aboard, looking, Gray thought, 'more like snow men than anything where the spray had hit them'.[13] 'It was', McLean noted, 'a chilling reception from Adelie Land.'[14]

Despite her anchorage in the lee of the ice cliffs, for two days the blizzard thrashed the ship and it was not until the evening of the 10th that they regained the shore of Cape Denison, with unloading beginning in earnest the day after. On the night of the 11th, Bickerton joined the first party to sleep ashore, sharing a tent with George Dovers, the Western Base's cartographer, and Madigan. He remained on shore for the next two days, assisting with the unpacking; then, on the 13th, the blizzard returned, marooning them until the early hours of the 15th. Fortunately, as Ninnis noted, as well as their tents and reindeer sleeping bags, the party had 'enough food there to last 'em for about twenty years'.[15] Amusement at the expense of the local wildlife again became the order of the day, though this time it was the penguins' turn to suffer: 'Bickerton and Wild seized a few from a rookery full of furry chicks, and glissaded them down a slope. It was great fun to watch them try and stop, and then, when they succeeded, try and mount the slope again with their great webbed feet and pointed tails.'[16]

As soon as the wind died down, the motor launch was again in demand, hauling the two whaleboats and a raft, each piled high with stores, and Hurley took the opportunity to photograph Bickerton at the tiller, a battered and shapeless trilby on his head. Once landed, the crates were loaded on to sledges and hauled about 100yd inland, to protect them from any incursion of salt water. At last, on 18 January, the air-tractor's turn arrived, but the disembarkation of the elongated crate was not a gentle one. As Bickerton tersely noted, 'the damaged condition of the machine was not improved by a somewhat rude unpacking and landing – which was necessarily hasty.'[17] Once at the quay, they used the derrick, manufactured by Wild from wireless royal masts, to lift it on to the ice.

The rest of the unloading proceeded without any major upsets. With each journey, they brought five or six tons of supplies ashore: sledges, tents, food, fuel, hut timbers, wireless masts, rifles, laboratory equipment and the frantic dogs. Every successful trip rendered the Main Base more able to sustain itself through an Antarctic winter, made Mawson's dream of a ground-breaking Australian expedition more attainable. The only major obstacle to a rapid and efficient unloading was the weather, which constantly harried them with fierce, bitingly cold winds and forced them to return to the comparative safety of the ship. Every hour lost now increased the difficulty and danger of setting down Wild's party and brought ever closer the risk of the ship becoming locked in the ice. But nothing could be done when the blizzard whipped down from the plateau above, churning the mile or so of sea between the *Aurora* and the shore into an impassable maelstrom. Mawson believed that a landing had never been so hampered by adverse weather conditions. Nonetheless, by 19 January the work was complete; their accommodation and all the supplies required for a year on the Antarctic continent lay piled, somewhat indiscriminately, on shore. It only remained for the motor launch to be reshipped and for the members of the two land parties and the ship's officers to say farewell.

They congregated in the wardroom and broached a bottle of Madeira, but not just any Madeira. The bottle was itself an Antarctic veteran, having accompanied the *Challenger* oceanographic expedition of 1872. It had already travelled some 70,000 miles of the world's oceans even before it had been taken on board the *Aurora*. Mawson made a speech appropriate to the moment and they drank toasts in the crisp, yellow wine: to the imminent landing of Wild's central or, as it had now become, western party, to mutual success and to the explorers of the past who had set the example they now followed. Then, when all were gathered on deck again, Davis gave the order to weigh anchor.

As the dripping, weed-strewn anchors thudded against the sides, the eighteen members of the Main Base party clambered down to the whaleboat that bobbed on the ocean below. They pushed off and then began to strain at their oars, while those on deck raised three cheers to send them on their way. Already, the sailors were darting about the decks, obeying the orders of the officers, whose principal concern now was to sail westwards with all possible speed. Wild and his seven companions remained at the rail, shouting good wishes while the whaleboat lingered within earshot, and then waved their last farewells. Bickerton later admitted that it was at this rather belated point in his membership of the AAE 'that I realised properly what it meant. There were 18 of us at that moment in a whaleboat rowing to the shore half a mile away.... . The ship which brought us had gone, and anything we wanted from now on, we should have to do without for a year or so. We were committed to an adventure and it seemed to me very risky, but I had seen plenty of food, fuel and clothing landed, and the 17 faces round me looked eager and companionable.'[18] Fortunately, while uncertainty and trepidation were numbered among his feelings, excitement and enthusiasm were also present in abundance and 'looking around there occurred to me all manner of questions to ask this curious looking land where no one had ever been before.'[19]

Three

Terre Adélie

With bleak and with congealing winds,
The Earth in shining chains he binds;
And still as he doth further pass,
Quarries his way with liquid glass.

Charles Cotton, *Winter Quatrains XXVII*

The patch of black rock at Cape Denison was now adorned by
four tents and a miscellaneous jumble of crates, boxes, sledges
and the surviving twenty-nine Greenland huskies. To the men
climbing out of the whaleboat, the taste of vintage Madeira fresh
in their mouths, it must have presented a desolate scene. The sea
lapped on the one hand, on the other the barren ice slopes rose
up to the plateau. Either side, precipitous cliffs stretched as far as
the eye could see, their faces scoured down to blue glacial ice by
the recent gales. Confronted with the daunting prospect of carving some kind of existence from these repulsive surroundings,
the men might be forgiven for giving the *Aurora* a last, lingering
glance, as she rounded the western tip of Commonwealth Bay.

The most urgent task must be the erection of the main hut,
about 40yd from the shore and in the lee of a small outcrop of

rock. Bickerton remembered that over the next few weeks, 'We worked and slept hard at this time and found little time to talk and learn more of each other.'[1] But there were also opportunities to marvel at the weirdness of their new surroundings: 'one day when it was blowing too much for work four of us played bridge, shouting our bids in the flapping tent. A roar like thunder and very close and growing louder made us rush out. I imagined some blocks of ice as big as houses rolling down on us from the hill to the south. I was frightened, but there was nothing to see until we climbed a rocky hill and saw the glacier a mile or two away had dropped some bergs, each one flat topped and big enough for a parade ground.'[2]

Work continued throughout the rest of January and the extreme cold continued to be an obstacle. In particular, it rendered the rock-drills brittle and made it necessary for the men to carry sticks of dynamite in their pockets to keep them at a sufficient temperature for detonation. They laboured for sixteen hours a day, anxious to achieve as much as possible before the expected blizzards swept down upon them. At night they slept in their tents – Bickerton shared with Madigan and Ninnis – or in a temporary building made from benzine cases and sections of the crate that had housed the air-tractor. Bickerton might be reluctant to leave the machine exposed to the elements, but the men's need was greatest. While the weather held it shouldn't suffer to any great degree, no matter how forlorn and neglected it might appear: more like a drooping, wingless dragonfly than a grasshopper. Once they had finished the living accommodation they could build a hangar and, with luck, still get the machine under cover before the worst of the weather.

Blasting holes in the rock for the foundations, they tried to secure the heavy upright timbers with concrete, but the cold prevented it from setting and they had to rely on wedges and stones which they forced into the niches. The construction of the huts was made substantially easier by the fact that they were made from kits of carefully numbered parts, rather than raw timbers that had to be cut to size. The main hut was 24ft square and largely pyramidal in shape, the four roof slopes descending down well below the tops of the walls to form storerooms and a veranda that were then enclosed by outer walls. As well as providing a home for biological specimens and foodstuffs, these areas helped to insulate the interior. To ensure that no unexpected problems were encountered with the design, each of the huts had been fully constructed in Australia, before being dismantled and packed, ready for the outward voyage. Hodgeman, who had been employed as a draughtsman in the Government Works Department in Adelaide, was the architect.

Whatever Murphy's disappointment at the decision not to land a separate party under his command there was one real benefit to the main party: the addition of an extra hut to their accommodation. The largest hut would continue to provide living space where the men would sleep, cook, eat and undertake many of their indoor tasks. The second hut, however, would now be available as a workshop, accommodating lathes, vices and workbenches as well as the wireless equipment and dynamo. More space must mean more comfort and less disruption.

When Bickerton and his companions abandoned their tools on 24 January the site still looked chaotic, with boxes wrenched open and packing straw strewn about like tumbleweed, but the walls stood bolted into position and the planks of the floor had been laid. The following day they would start roofing the hut. As always, the underlying concern was the weather. All had, by now, become familiar with the symptoms of a change: the colour of the sky and the shape and movement of the clouds. They awoke the next day to find that the wind had increased and they must be cautious to avoid frostbite. Although the term 'wind-chill factor' wouldn't be coined for another thirty years (by the American scientist Paul Siple), painful personal experience was making Mawson's men all too familiar with the phenomenon. Even the lightest breeze increased the risk significantly: a wind of only 10mph could plunge an ambient temperature of

-20°F (-29°C) down to the equivalent of -47°F (-44°C). A wind speed of 25mph, however, could reduce the same temperature to -87°F (-66°C).[3] In Adelie Land, between January 1912 and January 1913, the average wind speed was 50mph.

By 30 January, the hut was all but complete and the men were able to sleep within its walls, exchanging sleeping bags for blankets. A few days later, Bickerton sat on the windward roof, pinning down the rubberoid sheeting that would protect the wood from the elements and help to seal the joints. The 'roof of the hut was put on in a gale,' he later admitted, 'and as the work was difficult there were air leaks in it for ever after.'[4] Below him, in the comparative shelter of the nearly finished hut, Xavier Mertz was also hammering, fastening slats to the interior of the roof. Mertz was one of the specialists recruited by Mawson while he was in Europe. With a doctorate in law from the University of Berne, he combined academic talent with a love of physically demanding challenges. By the age of 28, he had climbed Mont Blanc, and he had won the Swiss ski-jumping championship of 1908. It was these latter achievements that impressed Mawson. Mertz's understanding of the effects on the body of exertion at high altitudes and in low temperatures would be beneficial, while he also brought an expertise on skis which none of the other recruits could boast. Once they started the sledging expeditions, the dogs would need a pathfinder to follow and, on his skis, Mertz would be the ideal candidate. On the voyage from London, Davis had taken a dislike to the Swiss, thinking him an idler, but he was popular with the rest of the party and his lack of familiarity with the English language was more productive of humour than a real bar to understanding. Sitting on the roof, Bickerton encountered the Swiss's physical prowess firsthand as, with what Laseron termed 'his usual emphasis',[5] Mertz drove a long nail straight through the roofing timbers and into his colleague's vulnerable posterior. Such incidents, resulting from misunderstanding or clumsiness, soon became known as 'championships' and, for a while, Mertz's unintentional hit was a favourite with all. Later in the year, when the soreness had receded, Bickerton would joke about buying Christmas presents 'appropriate to the recipient', including among his projected gifts a 'hammer for X'.[6]

It was now time to concentrate on the subsidiary buildings: the workshop, which measured 16ft square, two huts for the magnetic work to be undertaken by Webb and the screens for Madigan's meteorological observations. To Bickerton's chagrin, Mawson deemed the housing of the aerosledge to be the least essential of the building works and the machine was left to repose 'half in and half out of a snow drift for some weeks'.[7] For the time being, he must be satisfied with stuffing up the exhaust pipes to protect the engine, so far as possible, from the incursion of drift snow. Since he was in charge of maintenance of the wireless transmitter and associated equipment, it seemed appropriate that he should share with Hannam the responsibility for building the hut intended to house it. First, the petrol motor and generator required solid foundations capable of withstanding the inevitable vibration. Once these were in place, they laid the floor around them; the walls and roof followed and then Hannam began the process of unpacking and installing the transmitter.

There were some welcome breaks in the building work. While some of the men busied themselves with the arrangement of stores, or the sealing of cracks in the walls by the judicious application of tarred paper, hunting parties were arranged to ensure a sufficient stock of meat throughout the winter months. During the brief Antarctic summer, thousands of penguins and seals came ashore to breed and rear their young, but for the rest of the year, the continent would be completely devoid of life and the men must survive on the stores they had brought with them and whatever they had managed to kill. The bay still teemed with seals but penguins were becoming increasingly scarce and even the youngest would soon be ready to take to the water; by the end of March the shores of Adelie Land would be deserted. Over the next few weeks, some hundreds of penguins were slaughtered, the bodies soon becoming completely frozen and thereby protected from decay. Bickerton quickly established himself as one of the best shots in the party and his services would later be called upon to support the collecting activities of Laseron and Johnnie Hunter, whose main responsibility was to gather, catalogue and conserve zoological specimens.

They still intended to start serious sledging journeys as soon as the huts were finished and before the Antarctic autumn gave place to winter, when conditions would become too extreme for work at any distance from the base. Towards the end of February, Mawson decided that an attempt should be made to place a series of flags marking out the best route down the ice slopes. If the safest descent were indicated, much time might be saved by returning sledging parties. It was no exaggeration to say that lives might well be preserved, as weary, snow-blind sledgers would otherwise have to orient themselves using the shape of the bay beneath them and the angles of *sastrugi* – crests of snow and ice whipped into the semblance of waves by the blizzard. He chose Bage and Madigan to accompany him, and asked Bickerton, Hurley and Mertz to assist in the earlier stages of the journey, helping to haul the heavily laden sledge up the ice slopes before the real route-surveying began. The rest of the men must continue with the construction work.

The support party wasn't expected to spend even a night on the plateau, but this would be Bickerton's opportunity to get away from the routine of building work and to start what might seriously be called exploring. Of course, the expedition had already discovered Commonwealth Bay and Cape Denison itself, but those successes were entirely due to the efforts of Davis and his crew. Now, the turn of the land party had arrived. Naturally enough, Mawson oversaw the preparations: selecting the equipment and packing the sledge, ensuring that the essentials were stowed securely, including tent, food, cooker, fuel, sleeping bags and navigational and scientific equipment. They began on the evening of 29 February, all six men hauling the heavily laden sledge. The explorers might, perhaps, be forgiven for thinking that Mawson was showing an undue favouritism as, with the exception of Mertz, all the members of this sledging team had been numbered among the pioneers who first set foot on the Adelie coast. They would soon learn, however, that the most innocuous comment or action could result in the immediate loss of his favour, no matter how privileged the transgressor might previously have been.

The sledgers had reached a point a little over one mile from the hut, at an elevation of 500ft, when Mawson ordered that the sledge be anchored before they walked back down the slope. The next day they recommenced their journey at noon, trudging back to where the sledge lay and then dragging it for another 3 miles, erecting flags as they went. The going was relatively easy, the ice being hard and marked occasionally by long-healed fissures. At the 3-mile point they stopped for some lunch and Mawson told Bickerton, Mertz and Hurley to return to the base; their work was done and the three men of the main team could be left to haul the sledge over the flatness of the plateau. As it happened, the weather saw to it that no one found glory on this occasion. By the time the support party reached the hut, a blizzard was beginning to blow and, with the same conditions prevailing the next day, Mawson and his team were forced back, their surveying work rendered impossible by the blinding drift.

With their return, the building work again took precedence but, at last, all the structures deemed essential by Mawson were complete and, much to Bickerton's satisfaction, attention could be turned to the construction of a shelter for the air-tractor against the western wall of the main hut. Work started on 18 March and progress was rapid: 'Thanks to the energies of all, an excellent garage was quickly built, which was probably larger than most buildings on the Continent, measuring 35ft long and 10ft wide, 10ft high in front and 5ft at the back. The top was covered with the machine's casing. The walls were comparatively snow-tight; but not so the roof. A night's heavy drift meant a day's shovelling for three men. The door was subject to some discussion; but, before anything could be done, the heavy drifts of April set in, and in two days a huge snow ramp formed in the lee of the garage, effectively closing the entrance.'[8]

Before the onset of the drifts, the machine had been dug from its icy tomb and then pushed, shoved and generally coerced into its new home. From now on, access to it could only be gained via the side door of the hangar, connecting with the main hut and workshop. Unfortunately, soon after the hangar's completion, the expedition members discovered that 'the garage roof made a short cut to the stores at the back of the hut'; 'being nice and springy to walk on'[9] it quickly became a public thoroughfare and Bickerton was constantly showered with dislodged drift-snow. Nonetheless, working in what he termed the 'business end' of the hangar, he could continue with the work of converting the battered aeroplane into a functional air-tractor. But his modifications could not be properly tested until the weather eased sufficiently for the main door to be unblocked. 'Consequently, any contrivance fitted to the machine had to wait till the summer until it could be tested.' With characteristic understatement, he noted that 'This was awkward.'[10]

It now appeared that the gales that had lashed the *Aurora* shortly after her arrival were not the result of freak conditions. In the days when the hut was nearing completion, the wind had picked up considerably:

> we realised we were at what must be the windiest spot in the world. This proved to be so and we hardly had the hut up before it began to blow hard day and night and this with the exception of 3 days went on for 8 months… . It made the cold much more intense, it tore our clothes and tents, blew away our property, walks were no fun and conversation outside impossible. It made simple occupations difficult and difficult ones collossal [sic]… . It made up [sic] keep in the hut

more than was good, and in every conceivable way made our life more difficult than it should have been. The wind was a pestilence from which we were never free.[11]

The blizzard carried before it huge, billowing clouds of drift-snow, scoured from the surface of the plateau above. Every gap between the planks of the walls, roof and floor of the hut served as an avenue through which the drift might pass and the men became obsessed with making their bunks weatherproof. Rags were stuffed into every crevice and tarred paper glued across each crack in the boards, and yet still the snow would find some so-far undiscovered route into their quarters. The chimney also became regularly blocked with snow and the men took turns to clamber on to the roof to scrape away the accumulation of snow and ice. There was no hyperbole in claiming that the AAE had discovered the windiest place on earth, though there was remarkably little satisfaction to be gained from the boast. Their discovery made prisoners of them all. Writing to his sister, Bickerton jocularly called Cape Denison a 'breezy hole' but, for all his assumed light-heartedness, he found it impossible to disguise the oppressiveness of the conditions and admitted that the 'weather here is beyond the limit'.[12] Following the late disembarka-tion from the *Aurora*, it had been planned to start the sledging expeditions at the first opportunity after the completion of the huts. Now they were forced to accept that they must abandon any hopes of long-distance travelling before the return of spring, though they still hoped that gaps in the weather might allow them to undertake some closer-range work.

Inside, life took on a semblance of order and routine. While Mawson had some privacy in his 6-ft cubicle, the rest of the men slept in bunks lining the walls. 'At times,' Bickerton admitted, 'when everybody was in the hut at once the crowding was bad. There was only one place where a thing could be left and found again with certainty by the leaver, and that was his bunk. Anything put elsewhere would be in someone's way and would get moved, when it would be in the way of another person, and so on. And this could happen all in a few minutes. Often at the end of a day one's bunk would be piled high with the articles one had dealt with during the day. Fortunately during the night the floor could be used for various bits of gear and the bunk made habitable.'[13]

Bickerton's bed lay in the south-east corner of the hut, below Mertz and in company with Madigan and Ninnis. In compliment to its two English residents, they christened the spot 'Hyde Park Corner' and suspended a carved wooden sign bearing this inscription from the ceiling. They also named their bunks, Bickerton opting for 'Arcady', though Ninnis, at least, could never decide whether the name was meant satirically. Over the next few months, Hyde Park Corner would become a favourite spot for gossiping and conviviality. Family, friends and sweethearts were all discussed and the men shared their plans and hopes for the future. Bickerton found it 'simply marvellous how it cheers one up to think of these things and make elaborate plans to carry out after our return to civilisation'.[14] As might be expected of four young men – at 28, Mertz was the oldest by five years – they also indulged in a certain amount of horseplay. On one such occasion, lying on each other's bunks, Bickerton and Madigan decided to establish whether they could push up the planks, mattresses and recumbent figures above them. According to his wont, Mertz had nailed his planks down and Madigan found them almost immovable. Ninnis, on the other hand, had failed to engineer his bed to the same exacting standards and he recorded that, at Bickerton's 'first hearty push, his feet and my bunk planking and mattress vanished ceilingwards, amidst a roar of tumultuous laughter'.[15]

All four men soon became fast friends, but Bickerton and Ninnis, as the only Englishmen in the hut, shared a special bond. For all their popularity as individuals, it sometimes seemed as though they came from a world apart and they naturally gravitated towards each other when reminiscing about a home for which none of their other companions could have the same affection. Unlike Wild and Gray, in his journal Bickerton makes no slighting references to 'colonials', but he does occasionally refer to a lack of shared experience: 'they are always asking about London. They can't grasp that London is such a large place, and are awfully surprised when I say I haven't been to certain buildings they have heard of. The other day they asked me about the British Museum: I told them all I knew, and casually mentioned that although I had passed it innumerable times I had never been inside. They were absolutely flabbergasted. Today they wanted to know all about theatres.'[16] With Ninnis, there were no such obstacles to overcome and, whenever they wanted a sympathetic audience for their homesick musings, the two men turned to each other, often taking the opportunity of lulls in the weather to stroll to the meteorological screen positioned some distance from the hut.

Meals were eaten communally at a long table with benches on either side, and cooking was undertaken according to a rota, one man acting as cook while another served as mess-boy. Hannam's position as chef par excellence remained unchallenged, but many of the men exhibited a keenness to emulate him, and soon each had his own speciality that might be looked for with either anticipation or dread. If Hannam sat proudly at one end of the culinary spectrum, then Leslie Whetter soon came miserably to inhabit the other extreme. The New Zealander's ineptitude brought wry smiles to some, disgust to others and inevitable despair to his allotted mess-man. Bickerton thought him 'so beastly clumsy it is an eyesore to watch him'[17] and, in his fumbling hands, even the simplest meals became a nightmare of foul smells and inedible, mud-coloured mush. More troubling, perhaps, was the obvious decline in relations between Mawson and Whetter, or 'Error' as he had come to be known. It was becoming clear that their leader had little time for incompetence or laziness, and he attributed both to the hapless physician. Furthermore, he had begun to demonstrate a willingness to criticise openly and showed little regard for personal feelings.

Inevitably, bathing must be a public business. In the early days of the expedition, Mawson and Percy Correll had both tried the icy waters of the bay, Mawson when trying to retrieve a lost crate of what was mistakenly thought to be essential parts for the stove, and Correll for the pleasure of a bracing swim. Neither man, rising from the water with the ice forming on his skin, had seen fit to repeat the experiment, nor had he recommended it to his companions. Instead, personal hygiene was served by a small, folding canvas bath, filled with water warmed on the stove. Not that this procedure was devoid of discomfort, as Bickerton discovered one evening when the sponge he was using, and which he had laid down for a moment, imme-diately froze to the consistency of rock. He admitted that 'Cleaning oneself and one's clothes were occupations I loathed heartily. I am not normally a dirty man, but here cleaning entailed such discomfort and physical labour that once every 18 days sometimes seemed too often to bare one's skin to the cold air, and dabble it with water which cooled so quickly, and strain one's fingers trying to wring out shirts and underclothes as thick as tweeds. Plenty of water would have made this easier, but getting hot water from ice is slow.'[18]

The men usually took their baths when they had been rostered as night watchman, when their main duties were to attend to the stoking of the fire and to take instrument readings as required. In the silence of the night, 'with a leg thrust into each oven, while the amateur washing dripped on to the red hot stove,'[19] the solitary watchman might also observe the eerie beauty of the aurora polaris, a phenomenon caused by solar winds bringing high-energy particles into contact with the Earth's upper atmosphere, where they are converted into curtains and streamers of flickering light.

Murphy, deprived of his intended leadership of the third landing party, was given the responsibility of maintaining and monitoring the stores and he spent many hours rooting about underneath the hut and in the storeroom at its side. The job of descending into the 'cellar' to chip and hew until a frozen penguin carcass could be separated from its fellows was one of his least enviable tasks. It became even less enviable when his method of utilising the dogs for the retrieval of the meat had to be abandoned after one animal's skills in evasion were proven to exceed his own in pursuit and capture. His helter-skelter chase after the delighted animal, as it careered around the base with a leg of mutton in its mouth, was deemed to be one of the finest spectator sports yet identified in Adelie Land, and a 'championship' of no mean proportions. With his natural ability as a raconteur and an unfailing wit, Murphy had become one of the most popular members on the staff and a regular at Hyde Park Corner. But the characteristics that made him a boon companion led Mawson to consider him too frivolous for the real work of the expedition and, besides the role of storeman, little real responsibility came his way.

For the main part, the dogs remained tethered outside. Their thick, shaggy coats gave them sufficient protection from all but the most severe cold, and once the temperatures began to fall dramatically, they could be brought under cover of the veranda. Despite their occasional fierceness and tendency to fight when bored or distressed, the dogs were friendly and responded warmly to any affection bestowed on them. Working on the air-tractor, Bickerton found it 'cold and lonely in the garage, and I welcomed the proposal that it should be used as a maternity home for the dogs, and from then on I always had someone to talk to while working'.[20] Sometimes, too, he and Ninnis would simply stand and watch 'their funny little antics and tricks that never pall'.[21] He was able to repay the dogs for their affection and good company one morning when a huge sea elephant lumbered down to the boat harbour where all but the pregnant animals were tethered. The sea elephant's intention of launching itself into the water had been replaced with an interest in the dogs and its curiosity rapidly turned into aggression. There had been just time enough for Bickerton to crash through the veranda and the workroom and snatch up a rifle and cartridges. Frank Wild believed that the sea elephants were essentially harmless, but Bickerton took no chances and the animal's carcass was quickly added to the stores beneath the hut.

As the blizzards gained in intensity, it became necessary for anyone venturing outside to arm himself with an ice pick and crampons. Herein lay another problem: too few sets of crampons had been brought. Those designed for 'normal' Antarctic conditions didn't give sufficient grip, and of the more successful type bought in Switzerland, there were insufficient pairs. When the crampons had been ordered, it had been intended that they would be used primarily during the sledging expeditions, to enable the men to progress across hard, slippery ice when pulling heavy loads. No one had anticipated that they would be needed to enable them to walk against the wind within a foot of their own front door.

In an attempt to address the shortfall, Bickerton now became a 'crampon cobbler', working up different designs with varying lengths of spike and strap. Any model with spikes less than an inch in length soon proved inadequate, its wearer quickly finding himself bowled over and then blown across the ice, arms and legs flailing, until hut, rock or other obstacle stopped his progress. On 16 March, Bickerton and Hurley had relieved Madigan in taking meteoro-logical readings but, as they left the hut, the wind knocked them both over, rolling them again and again despite their stocky builds. On another day, Mawson had been blown over eight times while skinning a seal. For warmth the men preferred wearing finnesko – reindeer-fur boots from Lapland stuffed with *sennegrass** for insulation – but since these boots had no firm sole, attaching the crampons proved difficult,

---

*   A grass from Scandinavia.

particularly when tight straps hindered circulation and invited frostbite. Even with good crampons, walking was immensely difficult, demanding that the pedestrian lean in towards the wind at an angle so acute that any sudden calms were likely to result in his falling flat on his face. The only alternative was to crawl on hands and knees, or to slither snake-like. The novelty of the conditions, however, did offer some opportunities for pleasure. After their experience on the 16th, Bickerton and Hurley had picked up packing case lids and then sat on them, allowing the wind to blow them across the ice in a series of terrifying but exhilarating races, their upright bodies acting like sails.

While the wind made every task hazardous and exhausting, the drift-snow was blinding. Writing to his sister, Bickerton told her, 'we get snow drift so thick that you can't see your feet, and 90 mile an hour blows are quite frequent[;] our highest for one hour was 104 miles an hour and the average for the whole year is 50. Imagine yourself travelling at 50 miles an hour for a year.'[22] On more than one occasion, when a strong gust knocked a man over within a few yards of the door of the hut, he regained his feet only to find himself totally disoriented, unable to determine whether he was moving towards safety or towards the freezing bay. As the hut was buried deeper in the drift, it became even more difficult to locate, and a man might, quite literally, stand upon his sought-for shelter without knowing it. Bickerton and Madigan became accidentally separated from Hodgeman on one excursion and, despite the shouts of his companions, the architect was lost for hours.

With the walls around them groaning with the strain, each man turned to his allotted task, some with enthusiasm, others with increasing frustration. All, however, had one characteristic in common, as Bickerton wryly observed: 'If you talked to anyone about his job he would hold your interest to the very best of his ability and end by saying that he wanted a hand the next day to shift and open some heavy cases. Why not come along?'[23]

Webb, his shortness of temper worsened by the incarceration, took readings at the shed-like magnetograph house each day. To reduce the effects of magnetic disturbance, the magnetograph house had been constructed a quarter of a mile from the living quarters and, no matter how appalling the conditions, he spent hours crouching over the delicate instruments, his breath condensing around him and turning to an icy rime on the walls. Madigan's equipment had also been located away from the hut, on small outcrops of rock, and every day, often accompanied by Bickerton, he fought his way to the screens to take his readings. Frequently, he had to hang on to their framework to prevent himself being blown away like a discarded rag. As meteorologist, he monitored a series of instruments that recorded temperatures, wind direction and speed. He also measured the amounts of drift-snow, though Bickerton believed that few instruments could match the hangar's 'efficiency as a drift gauge'.[24] The anemograph, which measured wind direction, and the anemometer, or 'puffometer' as it came to be known, which recorded gust velocities, fascinated the men. Each day they asked Madigan for his readings, discussing them like prisoners obsessed with the idiosyncrasies of their gaoler. And each day, the magnetician and the meteorologist struggled into their protective clothing and disappeared into the blizzard, finding their way by the aid of various recognisable landmarks or orienting themselves against the direction of the wind, which remained pretty constant. The temperature seldom rose above 0°F (-18°C) and their fingers were often frostbitten, as a result of removing their mittens to record figures or change recording paper. Within a few seconds of leaving the comparative warmth of the hut, their faces became completely hidden by the collection of snow, ice and frozen mucus that collected inside the shallow, funnel-like hoods that protected them. On their return, these ice masks had to be carefully thawed and pulled away, piece by piece, to avoid damage to skin and eyes. On 27 March, Bickerton and Madigan became completely disorientated on a trip to the meteorological screen and, when they finally found their way back to the shelter of the hut, their features were hidden by ice masks that weighed several pounds.

Correll served as the instrument maker, his duty to make repairs to the scientific equipment damaged by accident or climate. Men like Mertz, Ninnis and Hodgeman, who had no specific scientific duties, became deputies to the scientists. Hurley, meanwhile, fought a constant battle with the wind and drift in his attempts to capture the expedition on film. He would disappear into the tiny darkroom to develop the plates and then pass them round for comment: portraits of men and penguins, of the construction of the hut and, most challenging of all, of the blizzard itself. Often his inventiveness was focused on new ways to obtain good photographs but, as he soon established himself as the unrivalled joker of the pack, it was also frequently directed to novel means by which to surprise, entertain and, not infrequently, irritate his companions.

When not assisting Madigan, Bickerton spent every available minute in the hangar. The dogs kept him company, but he also became a master of delaying tactics: 'Anyone coming in to perform some small duty got little assistance from me. I tried to make it difficult for them to carry out their project, or forget it altogether. I frequently succeeded, and gained company thereby.'[25] With the propeller resting against one wall, and the wheels of the undercarriage lying on top of a pile of rubbish on the other side, this was his world, the place where his contribution to the success of the AAE was to be made. Shackleton had already taken a motorcar to the Antarctic, and Scott was equipped with tracked motor sledges, but this was the first aeroplane, or air-tractor; if it proved effective it might have a profound effect on future expeditions. Before it was loaded on to the *Aurora*, there had been little enough time to modify the wrecked monoplane. The broken wings had been removed and the fabric of the fuselage torn away, but its conversion had proceeded no further.

If Mawson's outlay on the machine was not to be written off entirely, it was important that Bickerton should complete his alterations before the sledging season arrived. The first priority was the laborious process of hammering out and straightening the machine's lengths of tubular-steel frame: 'It was some little while before the 30ft of the machine were all sound, or as sound as it was possible to make them down here. Owing to a shortage of a certain sized tubing, some of the joints had a somewhat "gadgety" appearance.'[26] Bickerton wasn't too troubled by this; now that the machine's arena was to be purely terrestrial, streamlining and aerodynamics were no longer pre-eminent considerations. Other matters, however, were far more worrying:

> Several small things were done which might be altered at the last moment. But there was one thing that troubled me greatly.
>
> When it became evident that the wind would not allow the sea to freeze, the only remaining field for the manoeuvres of the aero-sledge was to the South. We knew that for the first 3 miles there was a rise of some 1,400ft, and in places a rise of 1 in 3½.
>
> I thought the machine would take this all right (without any load), but it would not be safe to attempt without some means of preventing a headlong rush down hill, should at any moment the power fail.
>
> Suggestions were not lacking. It would undoubtedly involve a good deal of work. This, together with the fact that tests would be impossible until too late to make alterations, made it essential that whatever was eventually decided upon should be the best we could do. There was quite enough left to chance already.[27]

Without effective brakes, a downhill rush could only end in a collision with the huts and the stockpiled stores or, at worst, a plunge into the icy bay beyond.

Eventually, he selected a winning design. Made partly from pieces of a broken vice, it consisted of two hardened drill-bits, one being fitted to the rear end of each of the sledge's two skis. A man would sit on each of the aeroplane's ski-runners and, when ordered to do so by the pilot, rapidly turn a crank handle to drive the drill into the ice. The drills wouldn't stop the sledge dead, but they should generate enough drag to retard its progress gradually. The two brakes were of different sizes owing to the limited supply of material and 'The result', Bickerton noted, 'was not elegant, but looked strong and reliable.' Their operation also posed certain difficulties: 'To work them, a man would have to sit on each runner. As these were narrow, and the available framework to hold on to limited, the function of "brakesman" had acrobatic possibilities.'[28] Nevertheless, the enthusiasm with which the novices had already taken to the bruising occupations of skiing and tobogganing might give confidence that volunteers would not be slow in coming forward.

Four

This Breezy Hole

And through the drifts the snowy clifts
Did send a dismal sheen:
Nor shapes of men nor beasts we ken –
The ice was all between.

Samuel Taylor Coleridge,
The Rime of the Ancient Mariner

For all his ingenuity, there was little hope of Bickerton's being able to test the air-tractor for many months. With the close of the Antarctic autumn the winds increased in velocity and the drifts grew ever thicker. Since March, the average wind speed had been 55mph and for fourteen days in May it averaged 75mph. Bickerton later noted that: 'People fond of statistics may like to know that day and night for 2 years the recorded wind averaged 50mph with maximum 116mph for 3 hours and gusts up to 280. The number of calm days in 2 winters was 9. It was an absurd place of course for anyone to go and live, but no one could tell us that.'[1] In his journal, Mawson commented that anyone who had been subjected to the blizzard for only a few minutes might willingly exchange it for hell, 'and chance

his luck'.[2] On those rare occasions when the wind ceased altogether, usually as a result of its having temporarily lifted to a
higher altitude, the silence was eerie and quite bewildering.
Bickerton even found that 'We got so used to the noise it made
that if a lull came at night everyone woke up.'[3] As soon as a lull
was identified, the hut and its vicinity became a hive of frantic activity as all attempted to complete tasks that the gales had
rendered impossible. Specimen-gathering was enthusiastically
pursued and, despite the loss of the whaleboat, which had been
swept away on the ice-sheet to which it had been tethered,
Hunter and Laseron spent any time available in dredging the bay
for examples of marine life. Bickerton joined one of their parties
and, with beginner's luck, he helped to dredge up two entirely
new crustaceans and a worm, though the name *bickertoni* was not
added to the scientific nomenclature of Antarctica's fauna.

The erection of the wireless masts was another task that could
be completed only in calm weather. Until they were raised,
Hannam, as wireless operator, was redundant. The AAE carried
wireless equipment to the Antarctic for the first time and all were
anxious for the experiment to be a success. Besides, Ainsworth
and his team on Macquarie Island would be waiting for news of
the expedition and their job was then to forward any message
to Australia. Silence might be interpreted as disaster. In January
1904, Scott had been furious when the Admiralty decided to
send the *Terra Nova* to relieve his ice-bound *Discovery*. The last
thing Mawson wanted was to be 'rescued' in a similar manner.

The first job was to identify a location for the masts that
provided sufficient projections of solid rock to act as anchor-
ages for the stays. Work had begun with Bickerton and a team
of six sinking 'dead men' in the ice for the southernmost mast.
There were two masts, each broken down into three segments.
The lowest portion of each would require secure foundations,
and then additional stability would be provided by a network of
stays. At first, these were made of hemp, but the erosion caused
by the friction of the drift was so great that they soon had to be

replaced with steel wire. The usual schedule of scientific work could not be interrupted, but all lent assistance as soon as their primary tasks were completed.

The work was more difficult than anyone had imagined. Stoically accepting what Ninnis described as 'the rough part of gadgeting the wireless',[4] once again Bickerton found himself in the unenviable position of transporting sticks of blasting gelignite in the pockets of his Burberry trousers. These could then be thrust into niches of the rock to blow out the foundations. When the rubble was cleared from the new hole, the first section of the mast could be pushed into place and then secured with lumps of rock. When bolting the sections of mast together, it became necessary to work without gloves or mittens and frostbite became a commonplace. As foreman, Bickerton was particularly at risk, moving among the other men, constantly removing his mittens to check that bolts were sufficiently tightened and stays tautened adequately. For all the chaff that might ensue when a man was seen scraping at his face, in the mistaken belief that his frozen cheek was a lump of ice, frostbite was taken very seriously: no one was willing to lose fingers or toes, ears or nose.

The work on the masts continued throughout the winter,* whenever a lull permitted. As soon as it was recognised that the wind had dropped there was a mad rush for equipment and Burberrys. As the masts grew in height, it became necessary to rig a boatswain's chair, so that a member of the party could be swung up to tighten the higher bolts. More often than not it was Bickerton who made the ascent, working in temperatures between -9°F (-23°C) and -18°F (-28°C) and braving the 30mph winds that repeatedly knocked him against the mast. As McLean pointed out, in making these attempts, they felt lucky in 'escaping with frostbites and the knowledge that we were very much

---

*   The Antarctic winter runs, roughly, from the beginning of May to the beginning of August.

out of condition for climbing'.[5] Sometimes Bickerton would spend hours suspended in the frigid air, dangling 75 or 80 feet above the ground, looking down upon 'the old hut itself with its pile of accumulated filth' and the 'cheery little boat harbour'.[6] Section by section, the masts grew until the height reached by the boatswain's chair was exceeded; then he clambered to the top using climbing irons manufactured to his own design, constantly in danger of becoming tangled like a moth in the complex web of cables. Mawson was pleased with progress: he noted in his diary that Bickerton was giving 'good service' and, in his published account of the expedition, even called him 'the hero of all such endeavours'. But, in such conditions and with interminable interruptions, they couldn't hope to complete the masts for many months.

Slowly but surely, the hut became cocooned as the wind-borne snow gathered in thicker and thicker drifts. This at least meant that the men's accommodation was better insulated, and the interior temperature easier to maintain at a constant, if rather chilly, 40°F (4°C). It also provided an opportunity to increase the available storage space, as tunnels were dug around the hut. Bickerton and Whetter both proved to be natural sappers, enjoying the extension of a network of tunnels that came to be known as the 'catacombs'. Throughout the winter months, entry to the hut could only be gained through one such tunnel and every day it had to be cleared of minor snowfalls. The ice on the inside of the four windows was now several inches thick and, if anyone extinguished the acetylene lamp, the interior of the hut darkened to an obscure gloaming.

Except in the lulls, no one ventured outside unless it was absolutely necessary. Fuel and ice must be brought in and the scientific observations continued without interruption; otherwise, the 24ft square hut, the adjacent workshop and the hangar became the centre of their existence. Listening to gramophone records or chatting, the men concentrated on preparations for the sledging season. They modified the sledges, and Mertz showed the others how to apply to the runners a special preparation that he used on his skis to reduce their friction on the ice and snow. Hours were spent in sewing food bags and stitching harnesses, upon which lives might one day depend. If a man plunged into a crevasse – a fissure in the glacial ice, varying in width, often hundreds of feet deep and hidden by a thin crust or 'lid' of ice – only the strength of his needlework would stand between him and entombment.

Ninnis said of Bickerton that 'he has never been known to have an idle moment, unless he be reading poetry in his bunk at night.'[7] When not working on the tractor, he plied a needle and thread or helped Correll with the repair of instruments. On other days he manufactured an anvil for the workshop and a carpenter's plane to replace one that had been lost. He also assisted with the taking of meteorological and anemometer readings. In the hangar, work progressed well and Mawson seemed satisfied, perhaps buoyed up by the expectation of recouping some of the kudos lost when the monoplane had fallen to earth. On 15 June, the occupants of the hut were deafened by an all-pervading scream that vibrated through the air: Bickerton had at last managed to start the air-tractor's engine and, according to McLean, had it 'working at a fearsome rate'. The doctor even opined that 'The results should be good when we lay depots for spring sledging.'[8]

It became increasingly vital to find occupation for the men. From the days of Captain John Ross, trapped by Arctic ice for four winters between 1829 and 1833, previous Arctic and Antarctic explorers had learned the importance of keeping their ice-locked crews active. A routine of sometimes monotonous and mundane tasks was probably better than the destructive effects of total inactivity. This was perhaps part of the reason behind Mawson's emphasis on the importance of maintaining the scientific observations, though he also believed passionately in the value of the work and feared that a sedentary lifestyle might increase the risk of scurvy. It was unfortunate that his manner, often sneering and sarcastic, undermined the good sense of his resolution. Despite their admiration of his seemingly boundless energy and strength of will, Mawson did little to command the genuine love that Shackleton inspired. D.I. (*Dux Ipse*, or 'the leader himself') was the name given to him by the residents of Hyde Park Corner, though it was only ever used behind his back.

Crucially, the men also proved willing and able to occupy themselves, devising entertainments that amused as well as tired them. In the evenings, one of the non-culinary chores allotted to the cook was to provide some form of amusement, and comic songs, rhymes and limericks became a mainstay. Each dwelt on some well-known eccentricity of one or other member of the expedition: Hannam's astonishing capacity to put on weight, Hodgeman's uncanny ability to remain upright in the worst gales, and Bickerton's sanguine expectation that he would 'fly his motor sledge some day'.[9] Then, one of the men might tell a story, confident in the knowledge that his companions would cheer him on his way: 'At the smallest hint of drying up a shower of questions would be called, mostly designed to draw the speaker into talking of his private life. If anything said was approved the applause was terrific, if it was disapproved suggestions were offered for a change of subject.'[10] Some read – a personal favourite brought from home, or a volume from the expedition library, in which Polar journals and general literature were to be found aplenty. Bickerton's tastes varied from works on exploration to the comic verse of Hilaire Belloc, a lifelong favourite.

When not reading or playing bridge, another of his favourite occupations, Bickerton passed his time in conversation, often with Madigan, Mertz and Ninnis. They also recited extracts from the letters they had received before leaving Hobart and, having listened to those written by Madigan's fiancée, Bickerton told the meteorologist that 'if he married anyone who wrote like that he would never be at home so that he could get the letters'.[11] As their intimacy grew, they exchanged details of their various romances, though Madigan noticed that Bickerton was more confided in than confiding. Perhaps it was this willingness to be a listener, without demanding an audience in return, which made him so popular with his companions; Madigan called him 'easily the best fellow in the hut'. But, for all his apparent imperturbability and self-reliance, Bickerton had his own doubts and anxieties. Privately, and in moments of particular boredom, tiredness or frustration, he questioned the motives that drove a man to the Antarctic:

> Why does he do it? I don't know, I don't even know whether the reasons are selfish or unselfish, probably the former, but a selfish man is no good here. He can't be selfish to come and behave unselfishly when he gets here. Does he come, because he thinks it will do him good? I doubt it; if a man wants to improve himself he can do so at home. Yet I think this can improve a man if he is capable of improving himself. It is a queer mixture of 'every man to himself' and 'share and share alike' here: each man must keep himself to himself, but anyone who does not realize his duty to others is an impediment, a curse and might easily become a danger. It seems to me that games like this need the highest class of men that civilisation can produce: yet one has no right to expect to meet them here. A flaw in one's character will nowhere become so glaringly apparent as here, it even shows itself to him. That is something that does not occur elsewhere.[12]

Cooped up together for months on end, it was inevitable that there would be mutual irritation and frustration, sometimes leading to confrontation, sometimes to introspection and self-doubt. In later years, Joe Laseron would look back on the expedition and claim that 'there was not one quarrel, nor even one serious case of friction among our members.'[13] But Laseron's survey was taken through rose-tinted spectacles. Certainly, at times, even the ostensibly stoical Bickerton felt frustrated with both himself and his peers: 'Sometimes I wish I had not such a variable nature. I do a thing one day which I know to be right and the next day the very recollection of the thing makes me furious. I feel inclined to shoot that ★★★★. I didn't mean that at all, I meant [*sic*] this, that, and so on.'[14] A trivial incident or remark sometimes threatened to become more serious, until offended feathers were smoothed by disinterested spectators. It was vital that frustration or irritation were overcome; in his own journal, Ninnis acknowledged that succumbing to such feelings 'is fatal down here'. Bickerton admitted to having quite seriously plotted the murder of one of his companions – almost certainly Hannam – whose snoring seemed set to challenge the volume of the blizzard itself. Earlier in the year, Murphy had even opted to sleep in the freezing workroom rather than be subjected to it. Some found a release for such feelings in their journals, but Bickerton remained doubtful about the value of diarising: 'Diaries are rotten things really: you can't put down all you would like to. If I had had this book at 6 yesterday evening and nothing to do I would have let myself loose on a literary effort that I should have removed in the sober moments that followed.'[15] His attitude remained essentially unchanged for the rest of his life. Sometimes, he would assiduously record the details of each passing day, only to decry the value of such efforts before throwing down his journal in disgust. Overall, there was more solace to be found in his pipe.

Despite the occasional irritability, however, laughter was also common, the festivities which were produced on the slightest occasion going a good way to defuse the tensions of eighteen active men, locked from month's end to month's end in the same cramped square of ground. Every man's birthday was an acknowledged feast-day, during which his friends 'tried to invent some new dish, drunk his health and told him he was a good fellow'.[16] It became essential that there should be at least one every week, though this might necessitate premature ageing and the acceleration of time: 'Once a month we had a birthday, regardless of whether there really was one or not. The curious thing about these birthdays was the general wish to do something unusual to one's appearance. Shaving and hair cutting would be done then and clothes brought out which had not been worn before or for a long time. I achieved some success in this way, as I found I had brought by accident a stiff shirt of civilisation. It was not at its best, and was collarless and studless, but as no one knew I had it the element of surprise was mine.'[17] Every event worthy of notice was marked with a celebratory dinner and the bedecking of the hut with banners and ribbons. As the months passed, the latitude allowed in the selection of events became ever broader: Swiss Confederation Day, the anniversary of the *Aurora*'s sailing from London, the lighting of London by gaslight, were all duly marked.

The most extravagant dramatic production attempted was a comic opera: *The Washerwoman's Secret*. 'Admission free, children half price', the printed programme announced. Much of the comedy was due to Hurley's inexhaustible supply of drollery, but Bickerton, Laseron, McLean and Correll contributed with all their might. Bickerton – whose 'fine sense of humour'[18] had been remarked by Madigan and whom McLean considered a 'never-failing fund of humour'[19] – played the role of village idiot and lolloped about the kitchen-stage interrupting the soliloquies of the other performers with a barrage of irrelevant questions and commentary. Ninnis observed that, 'smoking a cigarette through his nostril and squinting in the most horrible manner ... [Bickerton] was really funnier than anything I have ever seen, his expression being weird beyond belief'.[20]

He also doubled as stagehand and costumier, his masterpiece being the presentation of Laseron as the busty matron, Madam Fuclose, and Dad McLean as the heavily rouged heroine. His slight dimensions swollen with the judicious application of rolled towels and enormous, jutting breasts of the same material, Laseron barked his duets in a Germanic guttural that delighted the audience and, when the time came for his demise, sank majestically beneath the surgical saw of Hurley's Dr Stakanhoiser. To protect it from the boisterous, hammer-wielding surgery of the good doctor, Bickerton had placed a steel plate across Laseron's stomach, secured by the swathes of costume. At the critical moment, however, the plate became displaced, allowing Hurley's hammer to descend upon his victim's now unprotected abdomen. The Bavarian mask slipped instantly, and was replaced by a momentarily enraged Australian science graduate whose torrent of expletives would have made the ears of a female audience glow. All considered the performance a comic masterpiece.

At last, 21 June arrived: Midwinter's Day. Five months had passed since the *Aurora* sailed from Cape Denison. To celebrate, Hannam as cook, with Bickerton as mess-man, prepared a sumptuous meal. A carefully printed menu card listed the courses and advised the diners that 'During dinner, the blizzard will render the usual accompaniments – *The Tempest, For Ever and Ever* etc.' Despite a poor batch of bread, everyone proclaimed the meal a tremendous success. Bickerton proposed a toast to the men of the Western Base, while Madigan and Bage asked that glasses be raised to the *Aurora* and the Macquarie Island party. They rounded off the proceedings with a song from McLean and a performance from the improvised orchestra, in which Bickerton played the mouth organ. All were buoyed up in the hope that winter's end was now in sight. Soon, sledging would be a viable prospect, and the detritus of sledging harnesses and food bags become vital equipment instead of so much clutter. Over the next few weeks, harness-stitching was again reinforced, alterations to the sledges scrutinised and the process of distributing carefully weighed rations into the ready-prepared food bags began. But the preparations proved premature. Despite occasional lulls, the weather continued to forbid any attempt at sledging until the early days of August.

On 15 August the usual activity in the hut was suspended and
the men gathered round the long table, their attention focused
on Mawson. Along with Ninnis and Madigan, the doctor had
just returned after six days spent on the plateau, the longest
sledging journey yet undertaken by members of the AAE and
the first of the spring season of 1912. The expedition had begun
after lunch on the 9th, the fair prospects of the previous day
being somewhat tempered by a 40mph wind blowing into their
faces. That night, they camped about 3½ miles from the hut,
the men huddled in the unaccustomed narrowness of the tent,
the six dogs outside burying their eyes and noses beneath their
paws to protect them from the drift.

The next day, they stumbled across the sledge that Bickerton
had helped to drag up the slopes for the abortive surveying
expedition of the autumn and Mawson decided that this spot
would be a good position for a depot, where stores might be left
for future sledging parties. For the remainder of that day, and
most of the following, the three men hacked at the surface of the
plateau with axes and shovels, gradually carving out a shaft that
they then widened into a room beneath the ice. They christened
it 'Aladdin's Cave' and occupied the new tenement for the first
time on the night of the 11th. Moving on during the morning
of 13 August, they managed only 3 miles before the threatening aspect of the weather forced them to turn around; they had
too little food to risk being marooned by a blizzard and the crevasses which scored the area would make sledging in poor light
too hazardous. They stumbled back to the cave and then, with
no improvement in the weather, spent the best part of two days
trapped in its eerie, glistening depths. Eventually, shortness of
rations encouraged them to make an attempt to reach the hut,
only 5½ miles to the north, and they found it without accident.
As a foretaste of the conditions that might be experienced on
the longer sledging journeys, the trip had been discouraging,
but the men were now wound up to a high pitch of excitement and anticipation. For all the benefits of the scientific work

undertaken at the hut, many of them had originally volunteered so that they might explore the Antarctic interior, and that meant sledging, no matter what the dangers and discomfort.

Shortly after Mawson's return, they enjoyed an unusually long spell of fine weather: five days of sunshine and calm. The same frantic activity that prevailed during all calms quickly ensued. Every day groups of men could be seen on the southern ascent, their sledges piled high with essential supplies for Aladdin's Cave – supplies that would no longer have to be dragged all the way up the slopes by sledging teams bent on longer expeditions. The stockpiled food and fuel might also be vital for such parties on their return journeys, when they would be exhausted and probably short of rations. Hurley was everywhere, with stills camera and cinematograph, recording the assorted activities and the wildlife that now began to reappear after the worst of the winter. With the return of life, the rifles were taken down from their hooks and the stores of fresh meat and blubber were rapidly replenished. Throughout the winter the force of the wind had kept the sea in perpetual motion, the waves preventing the formation of any solid ice; now, in the calm conditions, the water became choked with a million tiny crystals that became welded to one another, forming a surface capable of supporting a man's weight. They dug out the dredging equipment and Hunter and Laseron were soon busy at the water's edge, trawling for marine life that they might then pickle and postulate over.

On 4 September, Bickerton decided to join one of the dredging parties, the last of the year. Their field of operations was the floe ice that the calm weather had allowed to form to the north. Walking on the rotting floe, dodging the puddles forming in the sun's heat, could be a risky business. All the time, it was necessary to gauge the thickness of the ice and its weight-bearing capabilities to avoid plunging through into the icy water below. But there were dangers more life-threatening than a mere wetting, as Bickerton and his fellow dredgers, Madigan and Correll, were to discover. As they reached the point furthest from the shore,

someone near the hut observed the tell-tale clouds scudding
northwards, caught in the grip of the hurricane as it prepared
to hurl itself down the cliffs and across the bay. The fragile sea-
ice must be destroyed by such an onslaught and three shots rang
out across the bay, warning the dredgers of their imminent peril.
Laseron had watched as the three retreating figures dwindled to
tiny specks in the distance; now he stood willing Bickerton and
his companions back to safety: 'It was literally a race with death.
Already a breeze was blowing, and an odd gust of greater violence caused the frozen sea to stir ominously. Nearer and nearer
they came, and harder and harder blew the wind. In a group
we all stood on the solid ice of the boat harbour, and anxiously
watched their progress. Slight cracks were already beginning to
appear in the floe, and it seemed as if they would never make
that last hundred yards. Now they were fifty yards away, now
twenty, then willing hands reached out to pull the cart across the
fast-opening gap between the sea ice and the shore.'[21]

It was a narrow escape. Had the three men broken through
the ice, there would have been no way to rescue them: the
whaleboat had disappeared long ago and any man venturing
on to the disintegrating floe must inevitably follow his friends
into the tossing waters of the bay. As they retreated to the hut,
the sea-ice disappeared altogether, sucked into the churning sea
and smashed into a million minute fragments. The momentary
glimpse of a real Antarctic summer was shrouded in the flying
spray of a wave-whipped ocean.

There were three further attempts at sledging in September.
Webb, McLean and Frank Stillwell, one of the expedition's geologists, set out on 7 September, followed on the 11th by Ninnis,
Mertz and Murphy, and by Madigan, Close and Whetter a day
later. Bickerton meanwhile stayed at the base, his attentions
focused on the completion of the air-tractor. The first sledging
party headed south, the second went south-east and the third
west. Their instructions were to return within a fortnight and

not to exceed a distance of 50 miles, in case the weather should close around them. All had returned by 26 September, having experienced varying degrees of success. Webb's party got no further than a point 111/2 miles from the hut, when bad weather forced them to return, after digging another depot-cave that they christened 'Cathedral Grotto'. Facing winds of around 70mph and temperatures as low as -17°F (-27°C), Murphy and his group managed 18 miles before they were forced back, their tent slit from peak to skirt before it was whipped away from around their heads, forcing them to sleep in the open. In similar conditions, Madigan's team managed to reach a point 50 miles to the west, despite frostbite and the need for constant repairs to the tent. Temperatures fell to -35°F (-37°C), and their helmets actually froze to their faces, needing to be cut away before they could eat. Their tent, too, was finally torn to streamers by the wind, and by the time they regained the hut, Madigan's frostbitten toes were so bad that he was lucky to avoid amputation.

In late September the wireless masts reached a height of 90ft, sufficient for effective transmitting. Earlier in the year, McLean had noted that 'Bickerton had the coldest time of all',[22] and on another occasion, after hauling him up the mast, 'the wind came down in hurricane gusts swaying the mast and making his job pretty uncomfortable.'[23] Despite the increased stature of the masts, however, Hannam's repeated attempts to raise Macquarie Island were met with a stubborn silence. In fact, Arthur Sawyer, the operator there, could hear at least some of the increasingly plaintive calls from Cape Denison, though they were usually reduced to disjointed phrases and often produced more confusion and uncertainty than reassurance. He also transmitted regularly, but none of his signals was received. In the absence of any acknowledgement, the transmissions from Cape Denison became more and more arbitrary, the operators sending any message just to practise their Morse code. Sawyer's anxiety grew as he continued to receive mere fragments, some formally reporting the progress of the expedition, others referring to jokes that had backfired or failures in the kitchen. Although his real responsibility was the maintenance of the equipment, rather than its use, Bickerton regularly took a turn. Over time, his hesitant tapping improved but he never achieved anything approaching real confidence in his own proficiency and he felt that he would have immense difficulty in interpreting any incoming messages. His practice was effectively curtailed on 13 October, when 'we had a gust of wind, which instruments showed to be 210 miles an hour and the mast bit the dust.'[24] To Bickerton, who had expended immense amounts of both time and ingenuity on the erection, the still-upright southernmost mast was left a galling 'monument of wasted energy'.[25]

Although, by early October, the weather showed few signs of moderation, with the sledging season on their doorstep, the time had come to dig out the hangar and release the air-tractor, which had been locked behind a wall of snow and ice since April. Excitement at the prospect of the excavation was somewhat dampened by a public row which blew up between Mawson and Whetter on 3 October. Bickerton must have known, as did everyone, that relations between the doctor and the New Zealander had been declining for some time; it was simply unfortunate that the aeroplane provided the long-anticipated spark. Whetter had been smarting under Mawson's frequent jibes and increasingly depressed by the monotonous drudgery of jobs like ice collection; when he was selected to dig out the hangar, his temper snapped and a host of grievances were aired at last. These included a commonly held belief that Mawson was consistently overworking his staff, even going to the lengths of inventing chores if there was nothing productive to be done. Later in the day, with an ill grace, Mawson announced that working hours would be reduced and the Sabbath observed, but the tension remained palpable. Nonetheless, work continued on the excavations and Bickerton was able to report that 'The aero-sledge was brought out of the garage on October 6th and anchored on the glacier.'[26] The unrelenting boisterousness of the weather, however, meant that 'For a month after the machine was brought out only on one day could an attempt be made to start the engine.'[27]

At last, the weather began to improve; outside, doe-eyed seals gave birth to pups, while skuas and petrels soared overhead. On 12 October, they spotted the first penguin. Although the wind still averaged 57mph, the periodic calms lasted longer and the sun, which now shone for 24 hours a day, felt warmer on their faces. Mawson decided to confirm the details of the sledging parties. There were to be four main expeditions, all to set out in November. 'This', Bickerton knew, 'was the most serious work of the expedition'; each party would be 'equipped with all that fore-thought and experience could devise, to map, examine and record. No one knew what would be found and hope was high.'[28] Mawson himself would take the dogs and, travelling at high speed with Mertz and Ninnis, head for the far east; Bage was to take Hurley and Webb to the south. An eastern coastal party was to consist of Madigan, McLean and Correll, while Bickerton was to lead a party to the west. Hodgeman and Whetter would accompany him and they were to take the still-untried air-tractor. There would also be two supporting parties: Murphy, Hunter and Laseron to assist Bage in the early stages of his journey; Stillwell, Close and Hodgeman to support Madigan's eastern team. When the support teams returned, Hodgeman would join Bickerton, while Stillwell mapped the near-eastern coastline with Laseron and Close. The only man to stay permanently at the hut would be Hannam.

According to Ninnis, speculation had been rife regarding the make-up of the sledging parties. On 29 September, he claimed to have heard, 'unofficially', that Bickerton and the air-tractor were to accompany Mawson and he repeated the assertion on 10 October. The final decision to send the machine west instead may have been the result of Mawson's increasing scepticism over its reliability. Given the cost of the aeroplane and the labour expended upon its conversion, it must be granted an opportunity to prove itself. However, by sending it in a direction which had already been at least partially surveyed by the *Aurora* when landing Wild's team, and by Madigan, Close and Whetter during September, Mawson wisely minimised the impact its likely failure would have on the overall results of the expedition. The choice of the inexperienced Bickerton as the party's leader may seem strange but, so far as sledging was concerned, there was little to choose between the members of the AAE: some had undertaken very brief journeys in the preceding months but, to all intents and purposes, they were all novices. That Bickerton was originally included in the Far Eastern Party indicates that he enjoyed Mawson's confidence; now that the opportunity to prove the air-tractor's utility had become, to some degree, the *raison d'être* of the Western Sledging Party, he, as the machine's mechanic and pilot, became the obvious choice for leader.

Bickerton's journal makes it clear that, when discussing the expedition with Mawson, he proposed an entirely different course from that eventually followed. He suggested that, instead of seeking to return to the Main Base, he should be allowed to continue westwards, clinging to the coast, with the intention of rendezvousing with the *Aurora* as she steamed to pick up Wild's party. Such a plan, he thought, would have allowed them to cover a much greater expanse of uncharted territory and opened up the possibility of an encounter with Wild: 'If both of us, that is, his E[astern] party and our W[estern] party were to have set out with the idea of being picked up by the ship we might easily have met.'[29] Unfortunately, as Bickerton expressed it, 'my ideas were nipped in the bud.' Almost certainly, Mawson thought the plan far too risky since it depended not only upon the timely arrival of the *Aurora* but also upon the coastline to the west being suitable for an embarkation from the ice. It was probably just as well, since Wild's party had been landed a full 1,500 miles to the west, much further away than had been anticipated, and the meeting envisaged by Bickerton would have been impossible.

The formal letter of instructions Mawson handed to Bickerton was both detailed and specific. Taking the air-tractor, he was to 'proceed with it stearing [*sic*] west or as near west as you can, making as extended a journey as you can but returning to the hut by 15th January 1913'. His most westerly target should be Porpoise Bay and, during the journey, his team was to make a detailed route survey and take frequent declination and meteorological determinations, geological and biological observations, and notes on the character of the surface. The note ended with a stark summary of the limited measures that would be taken in the event of the Western Party's failure to return by the stipulated date: 'Should you not arrive at the hut by the date of the departure of the relief vessel, which will not be earlier than Jan. 15th or later than a few days after, she will steam west keeping in touch with the coast and looking out for you. If no sign of you the ship will go back to the hut scanning the coast on the way back. Then she will steam for Porpoise Bay and look for you for the last time.'[30]

Although Mawson referred to the contingency of the *Aurora*'s picking up Bickerton's team, in exactly the same way that his own Magnetic Polar Party had been rescued by the BAE's *Nimrod* in 1909, there was no mention of any provision for leaving a relief party. In the event of the western sledgers' failing to rendezvous and the *Aurora*'s subsequently failing to locate them by the time of her departure, their fate would, to all intents and purposes, be sealed.

As well as whatever doubts Mawson and he might harbour concerning the likely efficacy of the air-tractor (and, in his letter, Mawson included additional instructions 'Should the aeroplane not be available to you'), Bickerton was certainly concerned at the appointment of Whetter to the western expedition. After their very public quarrel, there could be no doubt regarding Mawson's views of the New Zealander's worth and the appointment of a team member who had been openly criticised for sloth might fuel the demoralising belief that Mawson had low expectations regarding the likely success of Bickerton's party. Perhaps to mitigate these concerns, at some point in the days immediately preceding their departure, Bickerton and Whetter reached an 'agreement'. Unfortunately, there is no note of the terms of their contract but Bickerton would later express his satisfaction both with it, and with its effect on Whetter's behaviour over the coming weeks. He had no reason, however, to question the appointment of his other companion. Alfie Hodgeman, or 'Uncle' as he was commonly known, was a popular member of the AAE. Madigan thought him 'a quiet, conscientious, hard working good fellow liked by all'.[31]

The date settled on for the first departure was 6 November and, on the evening of the 5th, there were toasts and speeches, jokes and stories. Wagers were made in chocolate over which party would travel the furthest, who would return the soonest and who last. The men were all wound up to a pitch of excitement they had not known since Hobart sank in the *Aurora*'s wake. On the eve of their plunge into the frozen heart of the Antarctic continent, they discovered that ten months of incarceration had done nothing to dampen their ardour; it might even have increased it, with the months of frustration adding fuel to their natural curiosity. They all turned in early, so that they might be fresh in the morning. But the 6th dawned with blizzard conditions and driving drift-snow. After an abortive attempt the next day, Murphy's party finally made a start on the morning of the 8th, followed shortly afterwards by the teams led by Madigan and Stillwell. Emotions ran high as the sledging parties left, one by one. 'Before sledging began,' Bickerton admitted, 'we all had known each other a little too well, the flow of ideas had grown sluggish and any discussion of local affairs was monotony.'[32] But, having spent so many months locked within the same few square yards of hut, the men had also, by degrees, become mutually dependent. Inevitably, there had been arguments and peevishness but now, at the moment of parting, they came to understand the strength of the bonds that had been forged. They also understood the very real risk that some of them might not return. On the *Discovery* expedition, one man had died while out sledging and, though the men of the AAE did not yet know of Scott's recent disaster, within the week a search party would discover his frozen corpse and those of Dr Wilson and 'Birdie' Bowers; the bodies of 'Taff' Evans and 'Titus' Oates would never be found. Madigan, in particular, could not conceal his emotion as he parted from Bickerton, and he admitted that 'The farewells at the hut were very affecting. I was dry-eyed through all the partings in Australia, but could not keep back tears when I said goodbye to Bick.'[33]

The parties led by Bage and Mawson both got away on the afternoon of the 10th, the doctor's dog team setting out last. Bickerton volunteered to put on a harness and hauled with Bage's team until they reached the 3-mile post. Here the four men shook hands, each wishing the others well; Bickerton then walked down towards Mawson's party, which was rapidly approaching, the dogs pulling well in the absence of drift. Again good wishes were exchanged and soon all six men had disappeared over the crest of the ice-slopes. Bickerton's own journey could not begin until Hodgeman returned from the east; in the meantime, he would occupy himself working on the air-tractor and dragging stores up to Aladdin's Cave.

Five

Westward Ho!

And look where mantled up in white,
He sleds it like the Muskovite.

Charles Cotton, *Winter Quatrains XXXIII*

Bickerton knew that in the days following the accident in Adelaide, the newly christened air-tractor had been widely viewed with disfavour. The crate was too bulky, its contents too fragile, and it 'had fared badly on the voyage from Tasmania to the Antarctic'.[1] A year later, however, attitudes had changed for the better. From the moment that it was dragged from the hangar and anchored on the ice, the 'Grasshopper' had been looked upon with interest and even enthusiasm. If nothing else, its maiden voyage would break the monotony of hut life and there were debates about its likely performance. Bickerton himself acknowledged that 'I had always imagined that we should be most handicapped by the low temperature; but the wind was far more formidable. It is obvious that a machine which depends on the surrounding air for its traction cannot be tested in the winds we experienced in the winter. One might just as well try the capabilities of a small motor launch on the Niagara rapids.'[2]

The inescapable reality was that, if the prevailing conditions of Adelie Land had been understood before the expedition, no one would have countenanced the use of an aeroplane. Bickerton's tests soon revealed that on a windy day with sun and a temperature of 30°F (−1°C) the engine could be turned only with considerable difficulty, owing to the thickness of the oil. Only on a calm day and with the temperature higher after an hour or two of sun, would it swing well enough to permit starting: 'It was not until November 15th that the engine worked outside, and, being calm and sunny, it needed no more stimulant or energy than it would in a decent climate. There were only three of us at the hut at the time (Hannam, Whetter and myself), all the others being out sledging. Having ascertained that the oil and air pumps were working satisfactorily, we fitted the wheels and air rudder, and a few manoeuvres were made in the vicinity of the hut.'[3] These tentative exercises quickly revealed that, on snow and ice, the wheels were worse than useless and he quickly discarded them. Otherwise, everything seemed in order. The time had arrived to put the Grasshopper to the test.

The first experiments were designed to test the brakes that Bickerton had manufactured earlier in the year. Running the air-tractor a couple of hundred yards up the ice-slopes to the south, he turned it for a glissade homewards. No doubt to the relief of both brakesmen and pilot, they discovered that 'the machine was soon brought to a standstill when in full career.'[4] They repeated the experiment 'from higher up the slope, with the same result'.[5] Satisfied that the risks to life and limb had been mitigated so far as possible, a few days later, Bickerton and Whetter tried a sortie to Aladdin's Cave: 'The engine was not running well, one cylinder occasionally missing, but in spite of this, and a 15mph head wind, the mile between the 2 mile and 3 mile flags was covered in 3 minutes.... . We went no farther, and luckily so. Soon after we got back it was blowing over 60mph.'[6]

Over the next few days, in lulls of any duration, they made further trips to the Cave and, on each occasion, deposited more essential stores. Meanwhile, no matter what the weather conditions, the routine work of the hut must not be interrupted. In Webb's absence, Hannam performed the duties of magnetician, while Whetter undertook Madigan's meteorological work. They also continued to sort stores and gather eggs and meat in case the *Aurora* failed to reach Commonwealth Bay.

On 27 November the two supporting parties returned: Stillwell, Close and Hodgeman from the east and Murphy, Hunter and Laseron from the south. Murphy and his companions had staggered 73 miles in support of Bage's southern party. In high winds and unremitting drift their daily progress was at times reduced to an average of only 3 miles, for an amount of effort that left them practically exhausted. The frequent need to remove their misted-up goggles had also resulted in snowblindness and, at one period, two out of the six men were stumbling along in complete and painful darkness. On the 22nd, after a valedictory feast of hoosh, a thick, porridge-like soup made from pemmican,★ plasmon biscuit and water, the two parties had separated. Bage, Hurley and Webb continued their trek southwards, while Murphy, Laseron and Hunter turned towards home, managing to cover 17 or 18 miles a day in improving weather conditions. Stillwell's and Madigan's parties, having covered a distance of about 46 miles, separated on the 19th. Stillwell's team then followed a course to Mount Hunt, the summit of which had presented a fine panoramic view, incorporating the sweeping curve of Watt Bay and, to the northeast, the polished surface of the Mertz Glacier Tongue. Next, they had laid a course for the Madigan Nunatek, which they discovered to be a serrated crest of blackish rock, 2,400ft above sea level. Conditions were generally fine, as they followed the coastline westwards towards the huts, and they took the opportunity to chart the shoreline and the off-lying islets. In comparison with the southern support party, they had had an easy time of

---

★   A fine-powdered beef with 60 per cent added fat.

it but benign climatic conditions and the more fruitful field of operations allowed them to boast a disproportionate degree of useful work.

As their own departure approached, Bickerton and his companions found most of their time taken up with last minute preparations: 'As is usual, just before a journey of any sort, our memories suddenly became active, and we found all manner of things that must be done, which we had not previously thought of. Hodgeman, who had only just returned from a trip, had all his private packing to do, besides the duties involved in passing the office of meteoro-logist from his shoulders on to Hunter.'[7] On 2 December a last preliminary trip was made to Aladdin's Cave with a 700lb (320kg) sledge in tow. The 'small crevasses repeatedly caused overturns'[8] but one of the great advantages of the air-tractor was the length of its skis, which allowed the machine to straddle even medium-sized crevasses. If the weather held, they intended to start the next day. If conditions were unsuitable for the machine, they would abandon it and proceed by foot.

On the 3rd, the day started windy, but it calmed by mid-afternoon and at 4 p.m. farewells were said and Bickerton, Hodgeman and Whetter 'left amidst a spiriting demonstration of goodwill from the six other men then at the hut. Arms were still waving violently as we crept noisily over the brow of the hill, and the hut disappeared from sight.'[9] Years later, Laseron would recollect his envy as the machine effortlessly breasted the slope; in describing the departure to Percy Gray some weeks later, however, Murphy found it more risible than enviable: '[Bickerton] took everything except a collapsible boat which they did not happen to have at the hut! He hung all these extraordinary articles on the rails of the machine, boots, old bits of iron, hammers, clothes etc... . The other chaps who weren't going, hung all sorts of other things round, carrots and lumps of coal, etc!'[10]

The engine pulled well, but the load had to be lightened on the steepest stretches, and Hodgeman and Whetter dismounted to walk on either side. All five cylinders were firing evenly and the misfire experienced earlier seemed to have settled down. With 400lb (180kg) of hauled sledge, supplies and equipment, besides the weight of the three men, Aladdin's Cave was reached in about an hour. Three 100lb (45kg) food bags and 12 gallons (55 litres) of oil were added to the load, along with the sledge loaded with benzine brought up the previous day. But, after a good start, their problems were about to begin: 'After a few minutes spent in loading up, our cavalcade of machine, 4 sledges and 3 men moved off. The going was slow – too slow – about three miles an hour on ice; this would probably mean no movement at all on snow, which we might expect soon. But something was wrong. The cylinder which had been missing a few days before, but had since been cleaned and put in order, was now missing again; and the engine speed had dropped more than it should in proportion … and we did two miles in very bad form.'[11]

At 11 p.m., with the wind rising, they decided to camp, 'feeling none too pleased with the first day's results'. When the aeroplane had crashed in Adelaide, one of the cylinders had been smashed. It had been replaced, but there was a risk of more deep-seated damage, which the conditions of Adelie Land were now making apparent. Such a fault could only be identified by stripping down the engine. Even if the day's calm conditions continued, however, Bickerton knew that performing such an operation would be a tall order. And then, supposing he could find the seat of the trouble, making suitable repairs was another matter entirely. He decided that it would be best to proceed to Cathedral Grotto, 11½ miles from the Main Base, and there remove the faulty cylinder. He would only be able to complete the job if the weather held; if it did not, then they must abandon the machine and continue ignominiously on foot, all the improvements and modifications he had engineered over the preceding months simply so much wasted effort.

'After several futile efforts',[12] he managed to restart the engine at 4 p.m. the next day and by five o'clock they were under way.

The motor's pulse remained uneven, with the faulty cylinder spurting oil and giving no compression. Although pulling power was reduced, the lack of compression might be interpreted as a good sign since it was a symptom of broken piston rings, a fault that could be remedied in a couple of hours by redistributing rings from the healthy cylinders. They had sufficient tools to complete this operation once they reached the Grotto but, after covering only 3/4 of a mile, disaster struck:

> the engine, without any warning, pulling up with such a jerk that the propeller was smashed. On moving the latter something fell into the oil in the crank case and sizzled. The propeller could only be swung through an angle of about 30°. We did not wait to examine any further, but fixed up our man hauling sledge which had not yet touched ground and depoted [*sic*] all except absolute necessities.
>
> We were sorry to leave the machine. We had never dared expect a great deal from it, and it had not surprised us in an alarming manner. But the present situation was disappointing and it is not pleasant to have to admit this at the very outset of a journey, when everything is wanted to keep up spirits.[13]

It took another 45 minutes to reach Cathedral Grotto on foot, where they again went over their equipment and further reduced the weight, arranging the surplus food bags and other items so as to make a landmark that would be discernible from the south. Everything would now depend upon a combination of muscle and determination. If Mawson's doubts about the machine were justified, however, it was a relief to Bickerton to acknowledge that his concerns over Whetter seemed unfair: 'W. entirely different man, enthusiasm over machine when going no less than my own and disappointment when left; has not yet shown signs of old self.'[14] They also found a note from Bage in the Grotto, 'wishing us good luck. The message cheered us, devoid of incident and badly written though it was' and Bickerton admitted to finding it 'nice to think that we were not quite alone in this dismal place'. Despite the odds rapidly mounting against them, he hoped that they might 'make some sort of show tomorrow' and the events of the following day, 5 December, would go some way towards justifying his optimism. By its close, he and his companions would have made Antarctic history in an entirely unexpected manner.

The day started clear, with a wind of about 25mph, and by 9.30 they had stowed their gear and were under way. Whetter and Hodgeman were both reasonably accustomed to man-hauling; for Bickerton, though, who had spent all of his available time in the hangar, it was a new experience, and an exhausting one: 'by lunch time I felt I could do no more.'[15] To avoid slipping and falling, every step had to be carefully judged and, always, there was the dead weight of the sledge to be dragged across the uneven surface. In choosing a route to the south-west, his main aim had been to get beyond the ice that was riddled with crevasses, their lids frequently being rotten. The journey was tiring enough, without the additional anxiety of finding oneself breaking through into a bottomless, icy chasm, with nothing but a hand-sewn harness to prevent a plunge into infinity. About 6 miles from the grotto, the surface changed to *sastrugi* and, after lunch, they headed due west. They had proceeded about 240yd, Bickerton now feeling energised by his ration of tea and plasmon biscuit, when they spotted a strange, black object lying on the snow: 'we picked up a meteorite approximately 5" x 3" x 31⁄2" [13 x 8 x 9cm] covered with a black scale, internally of a crystalise [*sic*] structure, most of the surface rounded except in one place which looks like a fracture, iron is evidently present in it. It was lying about 21⁄2" [6cm] below mean surface and did not appear to have been there long, probably only a month or so.'[16]

Although a member of one of the most common subgroups of meteorites, the 1-kg olivine-hypersthene chondrite picked up by Bickerton and his companions is unique in that it was the very first meteorite to be found in Antarctica – the first crucial step in establishing the continent as the world's richest meteorite field. The next Antarctic meteorite would not be found for another forty-nine years, by Russian geologists mapping Novolazarevskaya, their base on the southern spur of the Humboldt Mountains in 1961. Correct in identifying their find, Bickerton was wildly inaccurate in determining its terrestrial age. Geologists now estimate that the Adelie Land Meteorite fell to earth some 70,000 years ago and that, prior to its discovery, it may have been transported many hundreds of miles with the gradual movement of the ice plateau.[17]

For the remainder of the day the conditions remained pretty consistent: clear, mostly free of drift, with a steady wind. Every now and then, they caught a glimpse of Commonwealth Bay, a few large bergs glinting in the waters at its western edge. Halting hourly, they would rest, chat and eat a few raisins. Whetter, who had been suffering from haemorrhoids for some time, seemed to be subsisting on a starvation diet, taking little but water. He had 'brought some lime juice and spent most of the day conceiving schemes to keep a supply in the thawed state'.[18] Hodgeman, meanwhile, was 'most conscientious', taking 'meteorological observations every three hours religiously'.[19] Despite the obvious discomforts and hard work, all seemed pleased with their progress after the disappointment of the previous day. The *sastrugi* continued uninterrupted, but there was a noticeable, though gradual, rise in the land. By the time they camped at 8 p.m., another 12 miles lay behind them and, aching muscles and tired mind aside, Bickerton continued to feel optimistic, even imagining the new discoveries that might fall to their lot: 'on the whole we have had excellent conditions, given more weather like this and we should do a fine journey in spite of the disappointment with the aeroplane. Tomorrow given good weather we should be over the ridge we are now on and see some fresh seas, which is exciting to a small extent. Who knows we may yet see a mountain.'[20]

In the morning, it seemed that the good omens had been deceitful: a 35mph wind buffeted the tent and thick drift obscured the landscape. They could only sit tight and hope that it might soon lift, releasing them to continue their journey. It was, Bickerton noted, 'a distinctly dismal outlook'. The noise of the wind was deafening, making normal conversation practically impossible. In an attempt to entertain his companions, Whetter tried to read aloud, but Bickerton found that 'although I could have touched W. with my hand I could'nt [*sic*] hear what he was reading: the wind was – and still is – flapping the tent so violently.'[21] Occasionally, they chewed some chocolate or biscuit, but they only attempted a proper meal at 8 p.m. The limited space in the tent made it necessary to store all the cooking equipment outside, and retrieving it from the sledge was not only time-consuming and arduous but also dangerous because of the risk of becoming disorientated in the blinding drift:

> The other two roll up the three bags and give the man who is going out all available room: everything has to be donned although the sledge is only 3 or 4yd from door of tent. It is very hard when outside to pass things in without passing in drift at the same time, but the worst of all is when the man comes in. As you enter through the spout you see the green floor cloth gathered off the floor and standing about 3ft across one corner, behind this the others have camped with all their and your property: all the rest of the floor is free to you and you brush the snow off yourself rapidly but being very careful not to move quickly or you shake snow over the green barrier. When your burberrys are off the others start reclaiming their ground while you continue to brush off snow in your corner. The whole process today including taking a temp[erature] outside must have taken half [an] hour; in fine weather it would have been a minute at most.

This shows the difference between calm and drift with a 60–70 mile wind.[22]

When he opened his eyes on the morning of 7 December, Bickerton found that he could easily distinguish the 'extra dark pencil' line that ran around the circumference of the tent, a tide mark indicating the height reached by the settling snow since they had pitched their tent. The wind blew as strongly as ever, and the drift made the world as opaque. Their stoicism was beginning to slip: 'The heat of our bodies', Bickerton complained, 'has gone through the reindeer bags and floor cloth and the snow below is melting and the inside of my bag is quite wet in places.' By 9.45 p.m. he admitted to 'getting sick of this' and tempers were beginning to fray: 'it's damned annoying, can't sleep, can't eat though we would like to, and can't move on, which we would like to do more. W. is going to mumble the *Virginian*★ aloud: no he is not, he and H. have quarrelled over the thing. H. says W. won't read loud enough, so they have torn the thing in half and each man now reads his own portion quietly.'[23]

While they remained inert, Bickerton decided they should be economical with the food ration, so they reduced themselves to one meal in every 24 hours, hunger doing nothing to support their equanimity. The wind varied between 30 and 70mph, and the temperature fell to -20°F (-29°C). Throughout the next morning and early afternoon, the conditions remained unchanged, and they followed the same tediously familiar routine.

At 4 p.m., Whetter undertook a reconnaissance and reported that the wind had veered to the east. This presented them with an opportunity: at least with the wind behind them, they could make some headway without the drift being blown directly into their faces. Having drunk some hot, sugary tea, they broke

---

★ A novel of the 'Wild West' by Owen Wister.

camp at 5 p.m. and steered west by south, using the wind and the direction of the *sastrugi* to guide them. The temperature had risen to about 20°F (-6°C) but there was no sun, and they could barely see a few yards ahead, but at least they were on the move. The going was tough, as the reduction in the wind's velocity had allowed the soft snow to settle. During their enforced confinement they had sought a name for the sledge, and had eventually decided on 'The Meteor'; at this rate of knots the name must have sounded like a sick joke. By 10 p.m., as the drift worsened, there seemed little point in continuing. It had taken an exhausting 5 hours to cover a mere 8 miles, but they felt elated. They also found that the absorption of large quantities of sugary tea made them feel giddy: 'The stuff seems to have gone to our heads… . Being so hot we have perspired in our burbs. And our fleece sheets are wet through, our bags are already wet through owing to lying in last two days. I have not been so tired for a long time – years – so the wet bag I hope won't affect me much. I still feel quite funny after the tea. I have been singing away like I have previously only in bathrooms in civilisation. Talking of baths, well there is no bath within something over 1000 miles.'[24]

The next day, 9 December, it blew harder and drifted thicker and they remained trapped. 'In the loud flapping of the tent, and incessant sizzling of the drift' they debated their prospects. In one week they had managed only a pitiful 31 miles. At that rate, even if they conserved their rations and delayed their return until 20 January, they couldn't hope to do more than 107 miles. 'A depressing calculation', as Bickerton had anticipated an absolute minimum of 150 miles. They could probably economise further and make the rations last until the 30th but such an extension of their journey must take them well beyond the scheduled date of their return. Everything depended on the weather: 'We were beginning to learn that though this season was meteorologically called summer, it was hardly recognisable as such.'[25]

Even inside their tent, they were not entirely protected from the weather. After their one meal of the day, at 6.15 p.m., Bickerton noted: 'Had food, smoke and a yarn, breath etc condensed and frozen on inside of tent and wind every now and then shakes it down in showers, while I am writing this it is falling in my open bag. Conditions outside same – no sign of change.'[26] The next day was Whetter's birthday: 'it will be about the rottenest birthday he has ever had,' Bickerton thought, 'or likely to have.' They celebrated the occasion with a meal of hoosh, washed down with strong tea, made with leaves that had done service only once before. Having also emptied a tin of chocolate, Bickerton seized the tin's lid and flattened down the edges. Once it was compressed to his satisfaction, he placed it inside his bag and sat on it – a metallic island in a sea of rank-smelling, soggy reindeer skin.

A little after 9 p.m. they took advantage of a slight improvement in the weather to continue their journey, 'glad to get out of our wet bags and move on once more'. The drift still clung to the landscape in a fluctuating sheet, sometimes 3ft from the ground, sometimes 30, but it had thinned. The surface was soft, making every step an effort, but every yard travelled was a yard gained. As the wind veered towards the east, they decided to hoist the sledge's sail for the first time. Gradually the soft powdery snow gave way to towering *sastrugi*, some 5ft high and made of hard polished snow, occasionally catching a ray of the sun which sat two or three degrees above the horizon. The sledge received violent jolts as it bounced across each ridge and then dived into the drift collected on the western side. There was bound to be a casualty and, at midnight, Bickerton noticed that the sledge meter had stopped working. These fragile instruments were trailed, like small bicycle wheels, about 2ft behind the sledges and were prone to damage. Repair was out of the question and, as they didn't carry a spare, they would be reduced to estimating their rate of progress. At 1 p.m., with 6 miles behind them, they camped and Bickerton volunteered to pitch the tent.

During their winter incarceration, the explorers had adapted their circular Willesden-drill tents so that they could be more easily erected in the prevailing conditions. They had sewn the tent covers on to the bamboo poles, reducing the need to fight with a large sheet of canvas in the gales, and making the process of erection more like the opening of a great umbrella. One man would climb through the funnel-like entrance and use his weight to stabilise the structure, while his companions anchored the poles and placed ready-cut blocks of ice on the external skirt. When there was little or no wind, the whole process could be completed in a few minutes. In a blizzard, it might take over an hour; even then, the results might prove distinctly unsatisfactory, as Bickerton now discovered:

> I had not yet tried my hand at pitching, which almost entirely depends on the man who is inside, while the process is going on. One day while we were all grumbling I said I would oper-ate at the next camp. Grunts of assent brought the argument to a close. When the time came, and I found myself alone in the tent, it seemed like a cathedral, so I patted myself on the back, called for the others to come in, and arranged myself in a corner, with an 'I-told-you-so' expression on my face, ready to receive their congratulations. Hodgeman came in first. He is not a large man, though he somehow gives you the impression that he is, but after he had been in the tent some time it seemed smaller. He looked around when half-way through the spout, and gave a grunt, which I took to be of appreciation.
>
> Then Whetter came in. He is of a candid disposition.
>
> 'Ho! Ho! laddie, what the dickens have you done with the tent?'
>
> I told them they were mistaken. But it was no good. When we were all inside I couldn't help seeing that the tent was much smaller than it had ever been before, and we had to huddle most uncomfortably.[27]

They spent the next day and a half in these cramped surroundings. The wind had increased to 60 or 70mph while the drift remained pretty constant.

Long periods spent holed up in the tent, interspersed, occasionally, with a half-day's travelling had left Bickerton feeling dispirited. Mawson had made it clear that nothing much would be gained by surveying the first 100 miles or so of their route. Instead, they should concentrate their observations on the region beyond that point. It now seemed that they would be lucky indeed if they managed even to reach a spot so far from the hut:

> This is a dismal rotten country…. Here are we in the height of summer and with every right to expect the best weather, bottled up in a 6ft circular tent in sopping wet sleeping bags and no prospect of a change. Even should it fall dead calm now, we should have use of the rottenest surfaces ever travelled over. Give us a fortnight real good weather and I ask no more, after that it can do what it likes…. If I had not been through a winter in Adelie Land I would say 'But the weather must change, this can't go on for ever' however, as it is, I know that in this country if you don't expect the worst throughout you are sure to be disappointed.[28]

On the morning of the 12th, the wind blew at 70mph, threatening to tear the tent into ribbons and fling it into the bay, 15 or so miles to the north. By early afternoon it had receded to a steady 40mph and they decided to break camp and press on in an attempt to conquer their misery and discomfort: 'clothes all frozen and full of snow, or as saturated sponges – Rotten.' By 4 a.m., they had covered 13 miles. All felt pleased, despite the sledge having been damaged during the early hours of the morning. At about midnight, with the sail hoisted, it had struck a large *sastruga* splitting one side of the bow. Then, a short time

later, Bickerton slipped on the ice and fell. The wind had filled
the sail and dashed the already weakened sledge into another
waiting *sastruga*, splintering the bow completely. Lowering the
sail, they man-hauled to the site of their next camp. Feeling
responsible for the damage to the sledge, which he blamed on
his failure to remove his finnesko and replace them with his
boots and crampons, Bickerton was further chastened when he
discovered that he had allowed the chronometer to wind down.
Now, until he could take a time shot by the sun, they would
have to rely on the accuracy of Whetter's watch to pinpoint
their longitude.

For the next 10 hours the drift continued unabated, but at
4 p.m. it lifted sufficiently for them to attempt the repair of the
broken bow. As usual in these conditions, the task took longer
than expected and the temperature plummeted to around 17°F
(-8°C) during the day and as low as -10°F (-23°C) at night. In
an attempt to keep warm, they 'pushed the nose of the sledge
into the tent and did what we could that way'. Like the brakes
Bickerton had made for the aero-sledge, the new bow was
something of a hotchpotch, made from four sections of a spare
bamboo depot pole lashed together with raw hide. Ugly perhaps, but strong and serviceable. When they turned in, they felt
satisfied that another hour's work would see the job completed
and enable them to continue their journey.

The next day, the 15th, the wind whipped around them at
60mph and the drift remained as persistent as ever. Bickerton
later remarked that 'the variety meteorologically known as
"light" had hardly been met with at all.'[29] Nonetheless, they
completed their repairs to the bow and broke camp at 8 p.m.
While they fumbled with the fastenings, a Wilson's petrel flew
silently about the tent, the only life they had seen for days. For
the first time since 5 December, the drift died away altogether
and Bickerton even thought the 'Travelling quite pleasant'.
Determined to make the most of the conditions, they pressed on
and, without the aid of the broken sledge-meter, estimated their

speed at a highly respectable 2 miles an hour. Camping at 4 a.m. on 16 December, they could congratulate themselves on having covered another 13 miles.

Over the next three days, progress remained rapid despite their having to traverse a *sastrugi* field that constantly threatened to overturn the sledge. On the 17th, Bickerton was able to record that, with the sail hoisted and a 15mph wind behind them, they had managed to cover a total of 17 miles, heading north-west by north. This was the fastest and furthest they had travelled since setting out from the Main Base and they ended their march with, at last, a view of the sea or, at least, of icebergs some 25 miles to the north-east. After another four hours of travelling on the 18th, they 'topped a ridge and about 90° of horizon suddenly came into sight, simply crowded with bergs some of enormous size'. Bickerton counted '70 clear and distinct ones' and, even in the far distance, the crazed, stepping-stone path of bergs continued, the distinctness of individual masses gradually giving way to a white blur. To the far west a spur of land could just be discerned, running out into the bay. In common with other explorers of the age, Mawson named various physical features of the Antarctic landscape after the members of his expedition and its sponsors. He would later call this spur 'Cape Bickerton,'* the most westerly point seen during the expedition. They camped at 1 a.m. on the 19th, hoping that the following day might present them with an opportunity to take further observations and photographs. In particular, Bickerton wanted to obtain a latitude observation, a procedure that had proved particularly difficult as the drift continually settled on the artificial horizon of his sextant, rendering it useless.

When they woke some hours later, however, the magnificent and tantalising vista of the previous day had all but disappeared.

---

*   Cape Bickerton, 66° 20' S, 136° 56' E, 5 miles ENE of Gravenoire Rock which marks the northern extremity of the coastal area east of Victor Bay.

The ninety-degree expanse of horizon had contracted to half that size, and nothing could be seen but a few of the nearest and largest bergs. The whole lie of the land appeared to have changed overnight: the day before, they had detected a distinct rise to the west and a comparatively steep slope towards the sea; now they seemed to be standing on a level plain with a barely perceptible gradient to the coast, and no obvious rise to the west. Attempts at sketching and photography had to be abandoned and worse was to come. At midday, as Bickerton sought to take his long-delayed latitude observation, Hodgeman called out that the chronometer had stopped working. When the chronometers were being distributed to the sledging parties, it had been discovered that there were insufficient to go round. According to Gray, 'Bickerton said anything was good enough for him' and had started his journey 'entirely dependent for his longitude on what is very little better than a [cuckoo?] clock!'[30] Certainly the chronometer now appeared to be living up to its reputation as there was no obvious damage and it had been treated with as much care as a 100-mile journey over razor-backed *sastrugi* would allow.

By 6.30 in the evening, they were under way. As they moved north-westwards, the miraging effect of the afternoon began to lift and the bay once again opened itself up to their puzzled eyes, as though it were playing hide-and-seek on a continental scale: 'The mirage effect at about 10pm … was most peculiar, some bergs grew to enormous size as you saw the real berg, it's [*sic*] reflection in the water and the mirage effect of both where the sea horizon disappeared behind the land it was distinctly bent up. The *sastrugi* comparatively close appeared much broadened and looked like a number of small crevasses.'[31]

Gradually, the horizon became visible from east-by-north to north-by-west.* To the west, pack ice was unmistakable, running out from the coast for about 20 miles; beyond it there was

---

* That is, from just north of due east; to just west of due north.

a clear blue water-sky. They had originally intended to march towards north-north-west but now, for the first time in days, they could see crevasses in that direction, forcing them to take a more westerly route. As the wind lifted, they raised the sail and progress was rapid. It became necessary to trim the sail constantly, as they ran at a slight angle to the course of the wind. Any gust catching them unaware might whip the sledge sideways, threatening to capsize it and yanking violently at their harnesses. Since the sledge-meter had been shaken to pieces, they had always erred towards an underestimation of the distance covered, but today, even by a conservative reckoning, in twelve hours they had covered 30 miles. There was, however, a downside to their situation. Upon further examination on the 20th, Bickerton decided that 'The chronometer is up the pole altogether.' The instrument's inaccuracy and the difficulty in taking observations in heavy drift meant that plotting their position became almost impossible. 'We don't know what the time is or where we are,' he confided to his journal at 8 p.m. 'I have just tried a latitude shot and worked it out, it puts us somewhere out in the sea.'

At 9.30 p.m. on the 20th they moved off, heading north-north-west. The landscape remained as confusing as ever. 'This is a weird country', Bickerton noted. 'The hills and gradients etc all appear different with different positions of the sun.' They were troubled even further when Bickerton 'stepped down a crevasse'. If they continued on their current course, they might find themselves in an area strewn with crevasses and would then waste precious time working their way back out and on to a more solid footing. There was also the impossibility of travelling through a treacherous crevasse-field in drift. They immediately altered their course to the west.

The hard pulling was beginning to tell on them all. They had covered nearly 100 miles in five days and Bickerton admitted to feeling 'more done after 10 miles than I have for a long time', and once they camped in the early hours of the 21st, Hodgeman slept twelve hours continuously. Bickerton's hopes of getting an accurate midday observation 'while the other blighters slept' were dashed by an increase in the wind, which now averaged 60mph, with thicker drift. He was also becoming concerned at the prospect of the return journey, as they would then be marching into the wind and their pace would inevitably be slowed considerably. In an attempt to avoid the worst of the blizzard, they would also need to travel during the day and rest at night, contrary to the routine they had been following for the last two weeks. The main disadvantage to this course would be that they would overheat during the day and freeze in their tent during the bitterly cold nights.

For four days they were kept captive, the drift hissing and the wind roaring between 50 and 80mph. With visibility reduced to zero and crevasses in the vicinity, there was no hope of moving on. Gradually, their bags grew more and more clammy and the atmosphere in the tent more oppressive, the smell of reindeer skin mixing unpleasantly with the odour of three men who had not enjoyed the luxury of washing for three weeks. Occasionally, one of them donned his Burberrys and threw himself into the white abyss, to attempt an observation or for a necessary bodily function; but for 23½ out of every 24 hours, they huddled together in misery. And with each day, as their desire for space and fresh air grew, the pressure of the accumulating snow pushed the walls of the tent in at them, inch by inch. On the 22nd, Bickerton had expressed his hope that 'we shall be able to do 200 miles', but by 8 p.m. the next day he was tormented by pessimism and self-doubt: 'Things are getting into the same miserable state as last drift, bags, clothes and skin slowly getting wet. The only bright (?) spot in the day is food time and that only comes once every 12 hours and then not a full meal. I'm feeling bored and tired ... I can't go on drivelling like this. I suppose I'm discontented. If I am, I realise that it is wholly and entirely my own fault. I keep on saying over to myself "things might have been so different". Perhaps I have "bitten off more than I can chew".'[32]

Relief came only with sleep and with the dreams that it brought: Bickerton dreamt of a Christmas dinner in which roast beef figured largely and 'the gratifying sensation of feeling money in my pocket'. Sleep also helped to build up their reserves of patience and endurance and on the same day that he dreamed of his roast dinner, Bickerton was again feeling optimistic, despite concerns about the thickness of the soft snow and the inevitable difficulty of hauling the sledge through it. On Christmas Day, in temperatures hovering around -4°F (-20°C), their celebrations consisted of drawing a Christmas tree on the frosty side of the tent. They also conjured presents for each other, and for the rest of the expedition members: 'a stocking full of nails for Hodge', presumably for further securing the roof of the main hut; 'a dumbbell' for the easily exhausted specimen collector, John Close; 'a tin trumpet' to serve in place of Hannam's now-defunct wireless transmitter; 'a hammer for X'; and 'an aeroplane' for Mawson. They augmented their Christmas dinner with a tin of pears, brought especially for the occasion, but 'the event was a failure as the pain of thawing them out in our mouths was not compensated by the novelty of the taste.'

As the wind gradually fell, they decided to move on. Before breaking camp, they raised the expedition's Union and Australian flags and Bickerton took some photographs: 'We had a boil up of tea before we left: the sun was shining on the tent and it was pretty warm inside and when the primus had been on a bit it got too hot for H. and W. H. dived out looking like a turkey cock while W. talked about mountain sickness, made investigations on his pulse and sat down a lot.'[33]

By midnight, they had managed another 13 miles. The hauling had been hard and dangerous work. They were in the midst of a field of crevasses, not particularly dense, being one every 100yd or so, but tiring work since all had to be alert: 'you may not see them but they are there just the same.' The placing of every footstep had to be considered and they must be prepared,

at any moment, to rush to the aid of a less-wary companion.
Again Bickerton felt dispirited, and with good reason:

> I had been thinking while coming along what a waste of time
> this all is. We are now on ground where we can do some good
> but have to turn back… .
>
> I have decided this shall be our farthest west camp. This is
> rather an important step, but I considered the matter a good
> deal and came to the conclusion that we can do no good going
> on… .
>
> If we could do another 60–100 miles we might do some
> useful work but another 20 or so would do no more than we
> have already done, has already been done by the ship once and
> will be again in the course of the next 6 weeks.[34]

As well as suffering the disappointment of an expedition baffled
by persistently adverse conditions – blizzards had confined them
to their tent for nearly half of the time – Bickerton felt unusually tired again. By the early hours of 27 December, the wind
had risen to 70mph and there could be no question of further
progress, either to add to the 160 miles that they had covered, or
in a homewards direction. But there were even more important,
and potentially devastating, factors to consider.

They were beginning to fall sick. First, Whetter admitted to
being unwell, debilitated both by the pain from his persistent
haemorrhoids and by the starvation diet they rendered necessary. Then Bickerton was struck down: 'At 5.30 I woke up with
a start for some reason feeling nervous and suffering ghastly
pains in the lower regions, this gradually got worse and it eventually turned out I had an attack of dysentery – what could
have caused it I don't know, but I sincerely hope not to have any
more. I still feel a bit weak but we hope to move on in an hour ot
[*sic*] two as we can't afford to stop here any longer whatever the
weather may be like.'[35]

Besides his immediate discomfort, he had every reason to feel anxious. Nine months earlier, Scott and his four companions had died on their return journey from the Pole, their progress so impeded by appalling weather and increasing debility that they had eventually run out of food and fuel. If any of the Western Sledging Party became seriously ill, their progress must inevitably slow and, if they were again assailed by impenetrable blizzards, they could find themselves facing Scott's predicament. For once, the bad weather proved a blessing, as it allowed them the best part of a day to recover, though the conditions in the tent became unpleasant in the extreme. On 28 December, they prepared to start on their long homewards trek but, in their weakened state, it took an hour and a half to repack the sledge. A slight thaw had melted the snow around the base of the tent; when it refroze it effectively welded the material to the ground, making it necessary to chip and hack at the ground flap before it could be lifted and rolled. Eventually, they

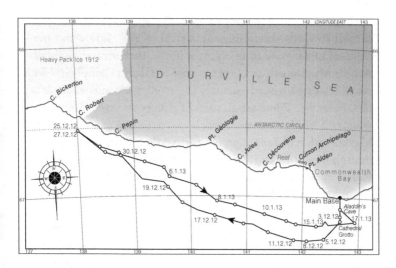

Route of the Western Sledging Party, December 1912–January 1913.

staggered off at≈4.10 p.m. The travelling conditions were also 'worse considerably than anything we have yet had by far'. When they again raised the tent, they reckoned on having covered 31⁄2 miles, and all acknowledged that their estimate was probably generous.

During the afternoon, both Whetter and Bickerton had experi-enced a strange, metallic taste in their mouths and they were concerned that it might be the precursor to another attack of dysentery. The next day, all three felt the same symptoms; 'H. had pains slightly, none of us could pull as hard as usual, we had repeated halts and travelled fairly slowly.'[36] Nonetheless, they managed to cover another 13 miles in a homewards direction. During their march, they picked up their outward tracks in a number of places, which at least revealed that their course was correct. Once camped, they discussed the possible causes of the dysentery. The pemmican seemed the obvious candidate and they agreed that, if they experienced any further ill effects, they would open a new bag and reserve the contaminated stock until last. When they camped at 11.15 p.m., their minds again turned towards the imminent arrival of the *Aurora* and her cargo of news. Pondering events at home, Bickerton thought of Aeneas Mackintosh and his betrothal to Gladys Campbell: 'We are all looking forward intensely to getting back and getting letters, news etc. There are all sorts of things we want to know. I wonder if Mack is married: will hope to see him soon.'[37] In fact, Mackintosh had been married for nearly eleven months and, though he didn't know it, Bickerton had already been nominated godfather to Mack's first child, Pamela. By the time he laid down his pencil, Bickerton was feeling 'cold and tired' and he found that the 'sky looks bad'.

Fortunately, the indications of poor weather proved deceptive and on the 30th, instead of the predicted blizzard, they enjoyed a 'ripping day, hardly any wind'. They travelled 8 miles and then reoccupied their camp of the 20th. Most importantly, Bickerton finally managed to obtain a decent time shot; this meant that, at last, they had an accurate chronological rate and could determine their longitude. At 8 p.m., while he busied himself with taking an observation for magnetic declination, Whetter and Hodgeman decided to walk towards two strange-looking peaks that were just visible about 6 miles to the north-west. The weather was ideal for such an expedition: there was hardly any wind and a coloured corona danced around the sun. All the conditions seemed to promise a period of fine weather, so progress might be rapid over the next week. With its usual contrariness, now that they were returning, the climate had decided to show its gentler aspect.

Upon nearer inspection, Whetter and Hodgeman found that the pyramidal mounds observed from the camp, were snow ramps on the lee side of wide, open crevasses. Each ramp stretched for some 200yd or so, and rose to about 25ft in height. In essence, the mounds were like enormous *sastrugi*, with a 10ft overhang on the windward side, the whole apparently caused by a south wind blowing into a 30ft crevasse. Back at camp, Bickerton was waiting with a surprise:

> I am in the way to see the New Year in, in a novel manner, the others are not back yet but are in sight about 3½ miles off. They, by the bye, are quite out of it as they both fondly imagine that today is the 30th so did I, but I discovered the error when I began writing this. It is weird to think of the line of noise that is travelling round the world, now the line crosses me in a few minutes but not noise. The only noise I hear is wind and that is nothing new. I have had enough of it to last me a very long time. In 9½ hours old England will begin adding its screams of welcome to the moving belt of noise... .
>
> Here they come, they are just 16 minutes late for the new year.[38]

Later, waking from a long sleep, they were faced with a new phenomenon: a snow-blind day. All traces of the sun had vanished from the sky. 'The result', Bickerton later recalled, 'was that you could see nothing but your feet and hands, the sledge and your companions. It was like living in a spherical tent made of sheets, except for the wind. Such days were an outrage to our senses. I have on these days stood looking straight overhead and slowly brought my eyes and head down searching hard but unable to see anything until I saw my own feet. There was no background or foreground. One could even stand with a large block of wind-packed snow in one's arms and see no outline to it except where it crossed one's clothes.'[39] If forced to experience such conditions for long, he thought, 'you would soon go mad'.[40] The inevitable disorientation could also make travelling extremely hazardous, as crevasses and even less-lethal obstacles like *sastrugi* became invisible and impossible to avoid.

After another hard day's march, the drift again descended and sealed them into their tent. Bickerton laboured over a New Year's pudding, which all agreed to be 'excellent and had quite a homely taste'. The drift continued uninterrupted until 3 January, and the New Year started in damp sleeping bags and boredom. On the 3rd, the sun reappeared and the drift was insufficient to prevent their moving on. For three hours Bickerton steered towards a large snow-bank in the distance, similar to the ones Whetter and Hodgeman had examined on New Year's Eve. As they approached it, the sledge struck one of the partially hidden *sastrugi* at an awkward angle and overturned, spilling equipment and upsetting the weight distribution. The three men

> unpacked the sledge and moved wearily onwards, when suddenly coming round the bank a wonderful [?] view opened up showing rocks and barrier edge... . The view was grand, the sun was just setting and the sky over the sea was heavily overcast but clear over the land. The cloud bank was light – rose at the top and deep red further down and all the sea and lower part of cloud were purple. The sea was a fine deep purple and studded with bergs, some just tinted by the sun

and some not. It was impossible to see the horizon the cloud
and sea merged one into the other. I proposed H. should make
a crayon sketch, but he said it was beyond him. Certainly if it
was truly represented no one would believe it.[41]

Bickerton even thought, 'This spot is probably where D'Urville
landed and drank his bottle of port to the cries of "Vive
la France".'

After a few hours' sleep, however, they woke to an even-
coloured, snow-blind day and the previous day's view seemed
like a dream. In this light it would be too dangerous to attempt
a descent to the coast: even the large crevasse that lay only 10ft
from their tent was invisible. Nevertheless, they decided to risk
some local exploration. Roped up, they proceeded carefully,
pushing the handle of the ice- axe into the snow every few feet,
to detect any rotten-lidded crevasses. The ridge that they had
walked round the previous evening lay alongside a large crevasse
about 60ft wide and running north-west to south-east. There
was a good firm bridge of hard *sastrugi* snow, its gradient sinking by about 40ft in 100 and ending in a vertical cliff of névé
snow and ice. Under it they found some caves which, on a sunlit
day, would have been glistening in blues and turquoise; today
they were featureless holes. Investigating the bridge, Bickerton
narrowly avoided calamity: 'There was a large hole about 40ft
across in one place where the snow bridge had fallen in. I was
standing on a firm bit of bridge looking over when W. started to
follow me, he sat on the edge of the crevass [*sic*] where there was
a step down and sounded the bridge with his foot, immediately
about a ton of snow fell, the portion I was on I expected to collapse too as it was now as far as we could see a beam supported at
one end. For some reason unknown it held and I wasted no time
in getting off.'[42]

Although Bickerton glossed over the incident in his diary, it
could have been fatal. Had the snow-bridge given way, he would
have hurtled into the crevasse, his only hope the strength of the

rope which tethered him to Whetter. Had the New Zealander also fallen, then the fate of all three men would have been sealed. They broke camp shortly afterwards and continued their march, crossing a number of old crevasses, one of them 35ft wide. Although sorry to leave the shore without photographing its magnificence, they had agreed that it was better to proceed while the weather held.

For the next few days, the weather remained largely calm and, for a while, sunny, making pulling hot work. They covered reasonable distances, though all were finding that they tired easily, probably as a result of the natural depletion of their reserves of energy and the residual effects of the bad pemmican. On the 6th, Bickerton discovered that yet another vital piece of equipment was malfunctioning: the sextant's artificial horizon seemed to have developed a distortion, creating 'a huge bulge on the image'. The fact that he was dependent upon a sextant for determining his latitude may be another indication of his willingness to accept substandard equipment. Scott had introduced the more effective theodolite for use in the Antarctic, its attachment to a stable tripod making reference to a horizon – whether artificial or actual – unnecessary. On the other hand, Mawson had already remarked on the poor quality of the theodolites and, on 4 August 1912, had noted his intention of complaining to the manufacturers, Messrs Carey and Porter. In an attempt to make allowance for the flaw, Bickerton started to take two separate sets of observations, one with each side of the artificial horizon.

The disappearance of the sun for extended periods reduced the shadowless landscape to a featureless void and their exact course became more and more difficult to determine; often the *sastrugi* offered the only guide to direction. They also discovered that the interrupted days and the travelling at unusual hours was confusing their timekeeping again, and their diaries showed different dates. The disparity caused friction between Bickerton and Hodgeman, each being too stubborn to admit defeat, while Whetter seemed completely baffled. Tempers shortened with exhaustion and a general weariness of the journey, and on the 9th, with the temperature at -4°F (-20°C), Bickerton expressed his frustration in his journal: 'Just worked out time shot, all to blazes, the wretched turnip of a chronometer has altered its rate, anyway I hope it has, because if not we're in the soup, beastly cold feet going to bag.'[43] The irritation, despite their daily progress, was general. All three were tiring easily and they shared a fear of being incapacitated by illness.

On 10 January, they awoke to find the sun blazing. The ground drift soon cleared up and they made good progress. Continuing the next day, they talked of the sight that would meet their eyes when they finally reached the hut: 'Coming over the hill we shall see the jolly dirty old ship, then the screen, then the top of the wireless mast … then the old hut itself … and perhaps the motor boat alongside and a crowd of fellows shoving off boxes for all they know. One of them will spot us, and call the attention of the others, boxes would be dropped, a rush by both parties, we coming down thirsting for welcome – they coming up overflowing with it. The questions from us, thick and fast, vigorous hand shakes, a meal, a smoke, a comfortable lounge, a yarn, and then for a quiet corner and letters.'[44] But, Bickerton thought, the weather conditions would probably spoil the dream. They would tumble down the ice-slopes in the stinging drift and blunder into the hut before anyone knew of their return. He was also becoming increasingly anxious about his inability to take observations and his resulting failure to precisely pinpoint their position. His diary becomes a dialogue in which optimism and doubt vie for supremacy, one moment confidently asserting that their remaining week's rations would see them through the 50 or so miles to the hut, the next recollecting that it had sometimes taken as much as twelve days to cover that distance.

The 12th heralded another 36 hours of captivity. The wind had already accelerated to 40mph and was gradually increasing in ferocity. Despite his attempts to prop himself against a deeply rooted ice-axe, Bickerton found it impossible to take an observation and he was soon forced back into the tent, 'sadder and no wiser'. The next day the wind had dropped to 35mph and the drift had decreased in obscurity. At 1 p.m. they broke camp and managed, so far as they could estimate, 5 miles in four hours. Their course was as difficult as ever to determine, but Bickerton was again feeling optimistic: 'I fancy in the present state of affairs we instinctively walk towards home: if ever a man had any homing instinct surely it would show itself on an occasion such as this.' Every hour or so, they rested, sitting or crouching in the lee of the sledge to have 'a clack'. The rest of the day and the following, they spent fighting their way through the drift, tripping and falling over the ridges of *sastrugi* and desperately trying to keep on a constant course despite being unable to 'see more than eight yards in any direction'.

On the 14th, they came in view of what they took to be Commonwealth Bay, though the image was distorted upwards by the effects of mirage. Camping in the early hours of the morning of 15 January, the memory of the view began to trouble Bickerton:

> When I got into bag I started thinking about the bay we had seen open up a few hours previous, and it struck me that the point we saw might be – and looked like – the Western point of Commonwealth Bay and the Bay the other side of it. This gave me a bit of a shock as it meant we had perhaps another 40 miles to go. I got up straight away and finding drift negligible went out to have another look at the view, but the whole thing had disappeared and I could see nothing, so I came back feeling rather worried, all the more so as it was getting overcast and it appeared that once again we were once again [*sic*] going to be done out of a lat. shot.[45]

They started at 4 p.m., all quietly anxious, but each vocally expressing his confidence that they were no further from the base than they had originally thought. With every step he took, Bickerton thought the expanse of water below them looked less and less like Commonwealth Bay. In the hope that they might be able to recognise the shoreline or, possibly, the shape of some of the bergs, he proposed that they should leave the sledge for a while and walk northwards. When, after 3 miles or so, nothing stood out with sufficient clarity, he determined that they should continue their rapid march, at least until they recognised a landmark:

> We hadn't been on this tack 1/2 hour when H. with a grunt darted back to the sledge and hauled the glasses out of the instrument box[.] 'Yes it is,' he yelled, 'it's the aeroplane'. Now when ever we have been looking before for anything we generally have to humour old H. while he points out all manner of unlikely objects. Consequently I had my doubts this time, but when I got the glasses myself I could have jumped for joy, there was the poor mouldy old thing as plain as anything, about 15 miles off. Let joy be unconfined, tonight we blow out the whisky from the medical outfit. Tomorrow with luck we will be at the 111/2 mile hole in 3–4 hours from here and the hut in the evening, then for the ship, letters, news and all good things the world can provide except a few which will come later. I'm in bag now for a peaceful glorious sleep and I don't care what happens.[46]

This day marked Bickerton's twenty-fourth birthday, and there can have been few more welcome birthday presents. The sight of the air-tractor confirmed their position and enabled them to plot an accurate course for home; the nightmare scenario of having misjudged their location by a margin that would have rendered their rations insufficient to support the return journey receded from their minds.

The next day the good omens continued, when Bickerton at last managed to get a latitude observation, enabling him to work out the declination and check their dates, which remained rather uncertain. The drift was thicker than it had been for some days but they were determined to continue, unwilling to slow their pace when they knew themselves to be so close to home. Throughout the day the ground sloped gradually downwards towards the bay and they travelled in the same overall direction as the crevasses which they knew stretched across the area. This was dangerous work, because it meant that all three men and the sledge could find themselves on a rotten lid at the same time; if one broke through, the whole lid might collapse, swallowing them all. The previous day, allowing for the effects of mirage, they had estimated that the air-tractor lay no more than 15 miles from their position, but they had travelled 16 miles due east without any further sign of it. The drift made visibility very poor and, afraid of missing it altogether, they decided it was better to camp, and wait for clearer conditions before proceeding any further.

Confusion seemed to be the order for the day on 17 January. By the time they camped in the early hours of the morning, the drift swirled around them like thick curtains, revealing momentary glimpses of the path ahead, then concealing it totally. Anxious to get on, in the afternoon Bickerton walked for about half a mile from the tent, hoping to find that the dense drift was localised: it was not. He then suggested that they might as well head due north rather than stay put and the others agreed. To be so near, and yet so far, it would be intolerable merely to sit still, impotent victims of so mindless a phenomenon as drifting snow. They hauled the sledge beneath a featureless sky until, at 4 p.m., Bickerton saw a dark, flickering speck some distance ahead of them: a depot flag, fluttering in the light wind. At last, it must be Cathedral Grotto, 11½ miles from the base. Once again, they cheered and slapped each other on the back, trudging with renewed vigour towards the tiny symbol of civilisation. But the lie of the land seemed unfamiliar, and when they reached the flag it didn't belong to the Grotto, but to some smaller intermediate depot that none of them recognised. Their joy gave way to puz-zlement, then to disappointment and, finally, to frustration. Hodgeman and Bickerton sounded with the ice-axe, to reassure themselves that the Grotto's entrance wasn't simply snowed in, and then decided to follow old tracks which led from the depot in a north-westerly direction.

Bickerton's frequent trips to Aladdin's Cave with the air-trac-tor had made him very familiar with its immediate surroundings and, after half an hour or so, thinking that he recognised a size-able snow-mound, he took the binoculars from the instruments case. He soon found a black spot in the centre of the snowfield: Aladdin's Cave, a mere 5½ miles from the hut. Whetter, who had been 'looking longingly round to the north-east at intervals' looked next and confirmed Bickerton's assessment. Excited by their discovery, Bickerton and Hodgeman 'felt inclined to drop the sledge and run, we were in such a hurry to get there: old W. was more staid.' Somehow, they had managed to skirt round the Grotto altogether and advance further and faster than any of them had realised and the confusion over the position of the air-tractor probably resulted from a miscalculation of the effects of mirage. Breathless but elated, they reached the oasis at 10 p.m. A heap of stones and equipment stood like a sentry at its entrance – shovels and cases of biscuits and benzine – all piled high to make an obvious landmark in the wilderness. At the top, a pickaxe had been balanced with an orange on one of its spikes, glowing like a beacon and proclaiming the arrival of the ship:

> We flung off our harness and dived at the cave. The entrance is practically a vertical shaft just big enough for one man, so traffic was rather congested. However, I got there first and slid down and found Alladin's [*sic*] Cave acting up to its name. In the centre of the floor was a food bag, the top covered with oranges and pineapples artistically arranged, on the shelf was a hurricane lamp covered with notes from earlier arrivals. The cave is not quite high enough to stand up straight, and is about

> six feet square. When I saw all this I let out a shout and the
> others soon came on top of me. We then set about to make
> more noise than one would imagine the little place capable
> of containing.[47]

After eating their fill, they squeezed back through the entrance
and put on their harnesses again. On the way down, they
diverted further to the west than was absolutely necessary,
simply to see the heart-warming view of the *Aurora* lying in the
bay: 'An instantaneous cure for snow blindness'.

Bickerton's prediction of 11 January, that they would sneak
into the hut, unheard and unseen, proved true: 'At 1.30am
(on January 18th) we got to the hut; all was very quiet and
we sneaked in and all three stood in the doorway of the large
hut unnoticed, some were asleep and some reading in bed, we
shouted "Rise and shine!" at the top of our voices, and each man
was out of his bunk like a Jack-in-the-Box. I still have only a
confused idea of what followed. I remember eating strawberries
and cream, drinking tea, smoking cigars and talking at a break-
neck speed all the time.'[48] After breakfast, he took the launch
out to the ship, where she rode at anchor in the bay, awaiting
only the return of the remaining sledgers before she could turn
her ironclad bows homewards.

Six

Hope Deferred

Engineering provides at least some pleasant toys for an intelligent child.
I specialized in wireless because of its mystery. And here I am. Voilà!
Arnold Bennett, *The Strange Vanguard*

Bickerton and his companions could feel proud of their achievements. Although their progress had been hindered by terrible weather, sickness and the failure of the air-tractor, they had still succeeded in exploring 160 miles of territory to the west of the AAE's Main Base. Moreover, albeit by sheer good fortune, they had taken the first step towards establishing Antarctica as the world's richest meteorite field, a benefit outside even Mawson's comprehensive programme of study. By the time of their return, of the four main sledging parties, only one remained unaccounted for: Mawson's. Bage's Southern Party had headed roughly towards the Magnetic Pole and, despite snow-blindness, insufficient provisions, appalling weather conditions and temperatures as low as -25°F (-32°C), it had reached a point 301 miles from the Main Base before turning back, arriving safely on 11 January. Madigan's Eastern Coastal Party had returned only a few hours before Bickerton's, having climbed Mount Murchison and Aurora Peak, crossed the Mertz and Ninnis Glacier Tongues and conducted a detailed survey of the coast, attaining a point some 280 miles from the hut. There was no immediate anxiety over Mawson's Far Eastern Party, although it seemed surprising that he, with the advantage of the dog teams, should have failed to meet the deadline that he had imposed on the other parties.

In fact, in some quarters at least, the greatest concern had been for Bickerton, Hodgeman and Whetter. From the deck of the *Aurora*, which had anchored in Commonwealth Bay on the morning of the 13th, the arrival of Madigan's party had been seen, but high seas had made it impossible for a boat to be launched and the crew had remained in ignorance as to the identities of the return ing sledgers. Percy Gray had expressed the hope that it might be 'Bickerton and Co. as they are worst off; they have been out now 43 days and only took 40 days [*sic*] stores'.[1] Gray's letters make it clear that he believed Bickerton foolhardy in his willingness to accept substandard equipment and it would be, he thought, 'an act of providence if he arrives safely'.[2] Whetter, too, as one of the party, admitted that their delivery had been 'a narrow squeal'.[3]

Over the next few days the expedition staff were kept busy packing equipment and ferrying it to the ship, so that they might all depart immediately upon Mawson's return. Captain Davis, meanwhile, as second in command, grew increasingly anxious. As the season advanced, the risk both to the ship and to Wild's party, waiting for delivery some 1,500 miles to the west, grew, and the urgency of departure increased with every passing hour. Davis had decided that in the event of Mawson's failing to return by 30 January, a relief party must be left at Cape Denison to undertake searches for the missing men while the *Aurora* steamed westwards to pick up Wild's team. Conditions permitting, he would return to embark the party before heading back to Hobart.

On the 22nd, he published the names of the men selected to stay. Madigan was appointed leader, with the rest of the party composed of Bickerton, Bage, McLean, Hodgeman and Sidney Jeffryes, an employee of the Australian Wireless Company, who would replace Hannam as wireless operator. As leaders of the sledging parties, Bickerton, Bage and Madigan made obvious choices for the relief party. A wireless operator and a doctor must, of course, also stay, and a sixth man, Hodgeman, would permit two sledging parties of three men each. If the Western Base Party was successfully rescued from its precarious position on the ice-shelf and a return to Cape Denison proved practicable, then Wild would be asked to take charge of the relief party.

Percy Gray thought it 'awfully bad luck on the chaps who stay behind here' but he also believed that 'For chaps like Bickerton who are more or less independent, it does not much matter.'[4] Examined from a purely worldly view, his assessment was probably accurate. Although Bickerton found that the 'thought of another winter was deadening',[5] the delay was not likely to damage his prospects: he possessed a private income and he could easily demonstrate to any prospective employer that he had continued to hone his engineering skills, albeit in rather unusual surroundings. This was not true for some of his companions. His particular friend, Madigan, knew that he was jeopardising his Rhodes Scholarship by requesting a second postponement, while Bob Bage might lose promotion by his continued absence from the Royal Australian Engineers. This being the case, the 'volunteers' were driven more by loyalty to their friends than by enthusiasm for their task. Madigan wrote that 'I am losing much by staying here another year, but I am a member of the expedition, and I cannot desert it when it needs me.'[6]

In writing to his sister, Dorothea, Bickerton adopted a less self-sacrificing tone: 'I have heaps to say and no time to say it in. You will know what has happened before receiving this, Mawson went out sledging & has seen fit for reasons best known to himself to stop out longer than was expected. Unfortunately the ship cannot remain here more than a day longer now as there is the other base 1200 miles to the West. So the only thing to do is to leave a party in this breezy hole for another year. It is a rotten game & a rotten place but nevertheless has to be done by someone.'[7] His letter veers between pragmatic nonchalance and ill-suppressed frustration, assurances that 'We won't have such a bad time' and that 'it is quite possible we may enjoy ourselves more than last year' being interspersed with fears that 'you will have ceased to talk about me by the time I get back.'[8] He also voiced his irritation at Davis's decision to leave Hobart 'just before a mail came in, which is rather annoying for us who are stopping another year', a disappointment which must surely have rankled after the near desperation with which he and his fellow sledgers had looked forward to the receipt of fresh mail.

While the postbag was much lighter than had been hoped for, it did, however, bring fresh entertainment in the form of Dorothea's newly published novel. *The New Wood Nymph* traces the romantic and emotional trials and tribulations of its young heroine, Eve Waldron, but it is most interesting for its vignette of Bickerton himself – fictionalised as Eve's friend, 'Theo'. Madigan and McLean both read the novel and may well have recognised Theo's 'endless fund of energy' and 'his evident relish of every detail of camping out'. In particular, they must have smiled at the description of Theo's easy-going attitude to his future career: 'Theo had been trained as an engineer, but he had not yet got a job. He seemed very cheerful without one.'[9] Whatever the amusement of his friends, however, Bickerton seems to have accepted his place in the novel without a qualm. He told its author, 'I like it awfully and congratulate you,' and went on to hint at his desire for female company with the request that 'if you come across any "Eves" you can introduce me on my return.'[10]

Such light relief must have been welcome as, with each passing day, the certainty of disaster increased. On 20 January, Bickerton, Madigan, McLean and Stillwell had retrieved the air-tractor from what McLean called its 'lonesome post on the plateau'.[11] They pushed the machine back towards the hut, and the following day, Hurley filmed Bickerton at the controls as he steered it down the ice-slope behind the hut. Then, on 25 January, in poor conditions, Hurley, Hodgeman and McLean set out towards the east in the hope of running into the returning sledgers. They laid additional depots, stocked with biscuits, sugar and fresh oranges, but saw no sign of Mawson and his companions and they returned on the 30th. Meanwhile, the *Aurora* sailed eastwards, firing rockets and watching for any signs of life – all to no avail. The process of landing supplies and of gathering fresh meat continued whenever weather conditions permitted and it became increasingly clear that the ship's departure was imminent. Davis had intended to sail on his westerly course no later than 30 January, but in the event, he stayed until midday on 8 February when, after hurried goodbyes on board, Bickerton and his five companions 'climbed to the rocky hill to wave goodbye to the ship'.[12] According to McLean, 'We were all heartily glad when she was out of sight.'[13]

'At half past four the same day,' Bickerton later recalled, 'a man appeared coming over the hill to the south; this was Mawson, the only survivor of the missing party.'[14]

With sixteen dogs, Mawson, Ninnis and Mertz had set out on 10 November. Their intention had been to map the coastline to the east of the point likely to be reached by Madigan's man-hauling team, from whom they separated on the 17th. Their usual practice was for Mertz to take the vanguard on skis, with Mawson and Ninnis following with the two dog sledges. In this style, and despite poor surface conditions, they made fairly rapid progress. On average, they covered more than 10 miles per day and charted the coastal features as they went. On 14 December and some 311 miles from the Main Base, somewhat to his surprise, Mawson had observed that he was crossing the lid of a crevasse. Although they had encountered numerous crevasses during their journey, they were now on a smooth, even surface, some distance from the much-rougher and decayed ice of the coastal regions, where crevasses were common. He called a

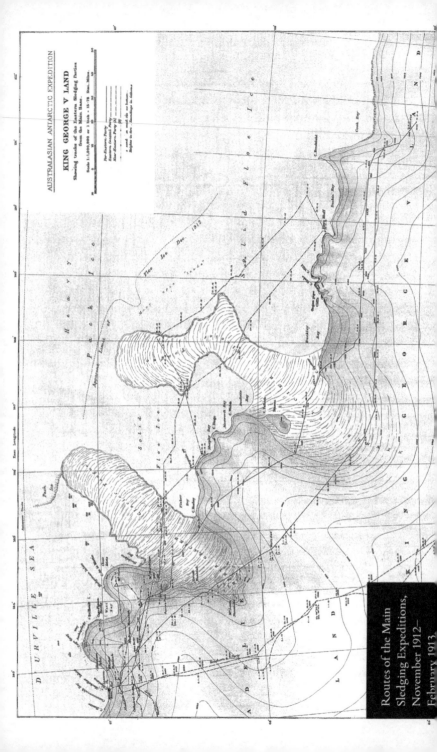

AUSTRALASIAN ANTARCTIC EXPEDITION

KING GEORGE V LAND

Showing tracks of the Eastern Sledging Parties
from the Main Base.

Scale 1:1,000,000 or 1 inch = 15·78 Stat. Miles.

Far-Eastern Party
Eastern Coastal Party
Near-Eastern Party (A)
" " (B)

Routes of the Main
Sledging Expeditions,
November 1912–
February 1913.

warning to Ninnis, who acknowledged, and continued on his way. A few moments later and in response to an anxious look from Mertz, Mawson had turned round to discover a barren and lifeless ice field: Ninnis had disappeared. Retracing their steps, they discovered that the lid of the crevasse, which had supported the weight of Mawson and his eight dogs, had crumbled beneath that of Ninnis's team, sending man and dogs hurtling hundreds of feet to their deaths.

As well as being horrified by this unexpected catastrophe, Mawson and Mertz now found themselves in a most precarious position. Believing that the leading sledge faced the greatest risk, Mawson had distributed the supplies and equipment unevenly. Well-intentioned though this decision had been, it now meant that the best dog team, all of the dog food, the bulk of the provisions and the majority of essential equipment had all been lost in the soundless depths of the crevasse. Having spent hours calling into the echoing void, the two survivors had no choice but to accept the inevitable. They read the burial service, took careful measurements to determine their exact position and then considered the options open to them. Essentially, there were two. The first was to make their way down to the coast, where food in the form of seal and penguin meat might be obtainable and then work their way back to the Main Base across the sea-ice. This would mean travelling longer distances and over uncertain surfaces. Alternatively, they could manage with the food they already had and, taking the shorter inland route, travel back towards the base at speed, shooting and eating the dogs as, one by one, they collapsed from exhaustion and malnutrition. They opted for the latter course. This meant that they would have the advantage of covering ground with which they were already familiar, but it would also necessitate reducing their food intake by approximately two-thirds.

Suffering from weariness and depression and with their daily ration cut from over 2lb (0.9kg) of rich sledging ration per man to 14oz (0.4kg) of mostly dog flesh, inevitably the men began to weaken. By the 29th, Mertz, in particular, was rapidly declining in health and spirits. His waterproof Burberry trousers had been lost with Ninnis and, as a result, his legs were continually damp and increasingly uncomfortable. He also began to lose skin, which simply fell away from his legs and groin; the flesh beneath was red-raw and every step became a torment. Mawson experienced similar symptoms, and it may be that, as well as suffering the effects of exhaustion and a poor and inadequate diet, the two men were being slowly poisoned by the excessive quantities of vitamin A in the dogs' livers they were eating. They struggled on for days but, when Mertz succumbed to dysentery, they had no choice but to call a halt. Delirium succeeded and, in the early hours of 8 January, the affable Swiss died in the wretched surroundings of their makeshift tent.

Weakened by his trials, alone but with at least a greater quantity of food, Mawson now faced a solitary trek of more than a hundred miles. On each day that the weather permitted movement, he managed to stagger a handful of miles on bloody feet from which the soles had become detached. An exemplar of scientific rigour and objectivity, each night he also continued to add to his meteorological notes. By 17 January, two days beyond the date of his proposed return, he had attained a point halfway across the Mertz Glacier Tongue, and by the 28th, he was just 20 miles from his destination. He crawled through the entrance of Aladdin's Cave on 1 February but then remained blizzard-bound for a week. This involuntary break in his journey gave him time to recuperate and to gorge himself on the supplies left by the other sledging parties, but it also, he knew, reduced the already-slim chance of his finding the *Aurora* riding at anchor in the bay. When, at last, the blizzard lifted, he could clamber out of the ice-cave and complete his three-month-long expedition: 'the rocks around winter quarters began to come into view; part of the basin of the Boat Harbour appeared, and lo! there were human figures!'[15]

Bickerton was the first to reach the bedraggled scarecrow as he stumbled down the ice-slopes to the south of the hut, and

Mawson must have presented a startling sight. His hair and beard, dyed blonde by the sun, had been coming out in clumps; he was badly sunburned and frostbitten; sores on his lips and nose were suppurating; and he had lost many pounds in weight. For weeks, the members of the expedition had been debating the possible fate of their leader and his two companions but, in Bickerton's words, they had 'little imagined that he was trudging along all by himself with nearly 100 miles back, X in his bag in the open and Ninn at the bottom of a hole no one knows how deep'.[16] Now, the priority in everyone's mind was to call back the *Aurora* so that she might rescue them from the miserable prospect of another year in the Antarctic. Jeffryes, the new wireless operator, sent a briefly worded recall message over and over, the ship's lack of a transmitter making the repetition essential. Then, all they could do was wait. Within a few hours, it seemed to Bickerton that the prayers of the impatient men had been answered: 'The next morning found the ship back. At first there was too much sea to get a boat over, and we tried to be patient. We looked at the sea, the wind instruments and the barometer and the ship. Every lull brought hope and every gust might be the last. If only the wind would drop ever so little a boat could fetch us. In the evening the barometer began to fall and we knew the captain would notice it too, and a little later the wind increased and the ship left and we were left to ourselves for another 10 months.'[17]

The last hope now remaining to them was that the *Aurora* might be able to pick up Wild's team and then make another attempt to reach them. With the passage of each day, however, the hope receded further and further, and it was small consolation to admit that this had been a 'necessary decision by the captain as we had another party to be relieved and it would take him a week to reach them with the season already late'.[18]

With all hope of an early relief now gone, it was natural that the thoughts of the seven castaways should turn towards their missing companions. Mertz and Ninnis had been popular with all of their fellows and the survivors' diaries and letters are full of tributes. Leslie Whetter had thought them 'two of the best chaps I ever knew'[19] while Hannam considered them 'two of the finest fellows it has ever been my pleasure to meet'.[20] Bickerton did not commit to paper his own thoughts on the deaths of his particular friends, but Madigan's journal gives some impression of the impact of their loss: 'Of the four happy members of the Hyde Park Corner ... only two remain. Bickerton and I sleep in the old corner – how desolate it seems – I have heard Bick sobbing under his blankets – and their terrible end, I cannot write of it.'[21]

In the journal he kept religiously up to the time of the departure of the Far Eastern Sledging Expedition, Ninnis left ample evidence of the warm friendship which had existed between the four residents of Hyde Park Corner. He had also recorded their intention of meeting after their return to civilisation: 'This evening the four of us were discussing the rags we would have at home next year, when Madigan arrives in England to go to Oxford and when Mertz will come over from Switzerland ... when we hit upon the happy idea of taking a turn as supers in a theatre for a bit and having a mighty rag (until we get the sack). It should be top hole sport; we must do it.'[22] He also noted that he had 'Registered a bet with Bick tonight that the dogs will cover more distance than his aeroplane.'[23] Ironically, of course, Ninnis would have won his wager by a margin of some 300 miles, but there can be little doubt that Bickerton would have been more than willing to pay the agreed forfeit of a fine dinner and a theatrical performance had he only been able to enjoy them in the company of his dead friend.

Despite their grief, there was little option but to settle, once again, to the routine of life at Cape Denison. Although Mawson claimed that 'there still remained useful work to be undertaken', even he could not deny that their 'prospects were decidedly duller than the previous year'.[24] In mute acknowledgement of the fact that the majority of the expedition's work had already been completed, the new routine was altogether more lax than that of the previous year. The men rose later and, with breakfast stretching between 9 and 10 a.m., it was often 11 a.m. before the real work of the day began. Scientific observations continued but their frequency was reduced. Madigan took charge of the fresh team of dogs, which had been presented to the expedition by the triumphant Amundsen in Hobart and brought south by the returning *Aurora*. When not tending Mawson, McLean concentrated on bacteriological work; Jeffryes operated the wireless; Hodgeman assisted Madigan with the meteorological work and began the preparation of maps and plans for publication; Bage undertook the jobs of magnetician, astronomer and storeman; and Bickerton divided his time between assisting Bage, serving the wireless and mechanical odd jobs.

For all his attempts to find useful occupations, however, Bickerton could not deny that the second, enforced year was oppressed by a gloom that only custom rendered tolerable: 'The hut was not so cold the second winter and we were not so crowded.... . But the wind was unvarying as ever, the food we knew too well in every possible combination, and we felt badly the need of occasional entertainment with people not subject to our routine or monotonous climate. We came to accept our life as the normal and an effort of the imagination was needed to see oneself in a world supplied with grass and friendly weather and modern plumbing.'[25] Some members of the expedition were more successful than others at keeping the blue devils at bay. Fretting at the extended postponement of his Rhodes Scholarship and increasingly critical of Mawson, Cecil Madigan, at least, often sank into depression and irritability and, in such conditions, despair could be contagious.

The labour expended on the wireless in the first year of the expedition had led only to vexation: the many hours spent on raising the masts had produced nothing but static and interference, culminating in their eventual collapse. When it had become clear that a relief party must be left, Captain Davis had given orders for the erection of a single mast, manufactured from the wreckage of the originals, and standing 115ft high. They also raised a short stay-mast to windward. Now, Bickerton found that hopes for the successful operation of the wireless offered some compensation in the prevailing misery: 'The great thing of course is the wireless, you may get a message from me before receiving this. Last year although some of our messages got through we never knew it as we, for some unknown reason could not receive.... Now the undamaged mast is fixed up by the sailors from the ship, & we also have another operator.'[26]

At first, he allowed Jeffryes to take the lead in all wireless-related matters and the new recruit proved conscientious in the exercise of his duties. In fact, Jeffryes had volunteered for the post of wireless operator in 1911 but Mawson had rejected his application. Upon his second attempt, he had been appointed by Conrad Eitel. The decision was to prove profoundly misguided, with dire results for the men marooned at Cape Denison. Nonetheless, on 21 February, wireless communication was at last established with Macquarie Island – Ainsworth and his whole team having volunteered to stay and continue to man the wireless station – and Mawson patriotically seized the opportunity to request permission to name the newly discovered territory King George V Land. Two nights later, they learned the fate of Scott's Polar party, a bulletin that must have seemed particularly poignant given their own recent losses. Messages continued to be exchanged regularly, though, according to McLean, 'we take things very quietly and scarcely think about the fact that it is the first time any Polar expedition wintering has been in wireless communication with the outside world.'[27]

Bickerton once again revealed his prowess as a 'master of many trades'[28] and occupied himself with a variety of self-imposed tasks. He constructed an ice-melter for the stove; rigged up an electric bell to facilitate communication between the main hut and the wireless room; and repaired the anemometer, the gramophone and the kitchen clock. On one occasion, he even acted as dentist, inserting a filling for a fully conscious McLean. He and Bage also dismantled the engine of the air-tractor and stood 'in their glory covered with grease and admiring the many "beauties" of this latest French type of aeroplane engine'.[29] Their dissection revealed that the machine's calamitous seizure had resulted from the connecting rod having fouled the revolving drive shaft. One of his most essential jobs was repairing the expedition's typewriter, which was receiving severe punishment as the erstwhile sledgers began the process of writing up their diaries, ready for inclusion in the official account of the expedition. The machine also became a mainstay of their home-made entertainment.

During the first year of the expedition, the literary-minded McLean had proposed that they produce their own magazine, along the lines of Scott's *South Polar Times*. The name chosen for this periodical was, appropriately enough, the *Adelie Blizzard*, but its production had been short-lived. Now, with fewer distractions and a greater amount of free time at their disposal, McLean revived the *Blizzard* as a monthly publication, with the men contributing articles, poems or illustrations according to their particular talents. While Mawson laboured over his verses and Hodgeman, as expedition draughtsman, produced the covers, Bickerton concentrated on the internal illustrations and comical advertisements. Perhaps the best of these latter, was that for his 90hp Blizzard '(1913–14 Racing Model) Single speed forward. No reverse. Air cooled. Never overheats. Special pattern forced draught carburettor. A standard car of this model holds all World's Records from flying mile to twelve months inclusive. The car that did 91.56 miles an hour for 48 hours. Still as good as new. Reliable.'[30] The reason for the sale: 'Owner desires to give up racing, leaving country.'

Although the contributions to the *Blizzard* were made anonymously, it is possible confidently to attribute a number of pieces to Bickerton.[31] The largest is a humorous composition entitled

'Cornered!'. Purporting to be an extract from his diary, the essay describes how a reluctant Bickerton is chased by McLean for a contribution. Curiously, since the tale is both well written and entertaining, when McLean was preparing the *Blizzard* for its intended publication in later years, he dismissed 'Cornered!', noting in his diary that 'Bickerton wrote this, I know, out of good nature – something to help fill up the May number. He would be the last to wish it put in. Now, we have plenty of much more readable matter.' Perhaps, on this occasion, the doctor's admiration of Scott's *South Polar Times* and his desire to compete with it, resulted in his taking the *Blizzard* a little too seriously. Bickerton's last recorded contribution was a rhyming 'Adelian Alphabet' composed in partnership with Bob Bage, in which

A is Antarctic where I'm writing this rot,
B is our Bay; a more definite spot.
C is the Cold which tries to frost-bite you,
D is the Drift which we find here 'in situ'.[32]

More poignant are the definitions chosen for M – 'the Messages others must spurn' – and for N – 'the Nothing they send in return'. Poignant because Bickerton appears to have received only a meagre handful of wireless communications through-out the second year. So rare an event was a message from Leslie Whetter, in which he admonished Bickerton to 'Buck up old man',[33] that the recipient, 'who had resolved not to smoke during the month ... considered, with our approval, that he had sufficient justification for breaking out'.[34]

On 8 June, the topgallant and the top of the mainmast were carried away by the unremitting gales and, for a time, communication with Macquarie Island was suspended. Instead of repairing the damage in the usual manner, Bickerton and Bage decided to adopt a novel means of overcoming their dif-ficulties, with the Australian engineer leading their attempts to 'invent a kite to fly at the end of about 200 feet of sounding wire, which will thus act as an aerial'.[35] McLean observed that 'We don't feel very confident that it will stand the tremendous gusts'[36] and events quickly justified his pessimism. Their first design, constructed from discarded boxes, was quickly thrown down and smashed and its fate was soon shared by another model made from carbide tins. When their last design – a tin propeller – also failed, Bickerton 'wondered why they had taken so much trouble'[37] and resigned himself to the more prosaic method of clambering up the dismembered mast to unravel the tangled aerial wires. Soon, however, the mast-smashing gales outside the hut would pale into insignificance when compared with the tempest about to be unleashed on the men inside.

For some weeks, eccentricities in Jeffryes' behaviour had become more pronounced, and on 11 July, McLean admitted in his journal that there were 'undoubted signs of delusive insanity'.[38] In such a confined space, with few opportunities for either exercise or distraction, the impact upon the rest of the expedition members was profound and it was to become even more so when Jeffryes' delusions became increasingly paranoid. Madigan recorded the symptoms in more detail: 'Jeffryes seems to have had enough of me, but to our horror, this evening he went up to Bickerton and asked him if he would be his second if he did any shooting. Bick tried to pacify him.'[39]

The next day, he and Bickerton 'put away all the cartridges.... Jeffryes has no firearms and can't get any now.' Innocent conversations which in no way bore upon the wireless operator were interpreted as insults and slights, resulting in uncontrolled ravings and accusations. In later years, Bickerton described a typical outburst to one of his friends. It had started with Jeffryes accusing him of plotting his murder: 'He accused him at breakfast before them all. The Doctor had a talk with him and advised [Bickerton] to argue with him as though he were sane and try and prove calmly that he had not made any attempt to kill him. There was a long argument and then the madman asked "Would you swear on the Bible that you did not and will not try to kill me". [Bickerton] of course said yes bring me a Bible. "Would you swear on your mother's Bible". Yes if I had it. "Swear by all you ever held truest and dearest". Certainly I would. "Well even if you did all that I wouldn't believe you".'[40]

One day the wirelessman even threatened to resign from the expedition and the situation was only defused when Mawson half-humorously pointed out that such an act would necessarily result in his relinquishing all claim upon AAE accommodation and supplies. He also refused to attend to his personal cleanliness and Bickerton was reduced to washing his soiled garments and bed linen while the deranged man sat scowling and muttering to himself on his bunk. No one was immune to the impact of Jeffryes' condition and normal intercourse became practically impossible through nervousness and the dread of sparking another outburst.

The fluctuations in Jeffryes' condition – his rants were interspersed with periods of apparent rationality – encouraged Mawson to allow him to remain in charge of the wireless when, on 5 August, repairs to the mast allowed communications with Macquarie Island to be re-established. When it was discovered that he was sending reports of his companions' madness, however, he was relieved of his responsibilities. By this time, the conditions in the hut appear to have been weighing particularly heavily upon Bickerton. As in the previous year, he had taken the leading role in the work on the masts – McLean noted on 5 August that he was 'in great fettle, climbing all over the jury-mast'[41] – and he urged Mawson to give him the job of wireless operator, presumably to ensure that he remained productively occupied. Perhaps in recognition of the role that he had played in facilitating the continuation of wireless transmissions, and in spite of the fact that Madigan's command of Morse was superior, Mawson acquiesced. Aware that his wireless skills were somewhat deficient, Bickerton tried to improve his efficiency by practising using a buzzer with Madigan and Bage.

Although responsibility for the wireless meant occupation, it also brought with it an assortment of frustrations. In particular, magnetic disturbances and the presence of St Elmo's fire, a form of electrical discharge causing the items affected to glow with a pale blue light, often meant that messages could be neither sent nor received. It was also necessary for the wireless operator to keep unsociable hours, since the signals from Macquarie Island tended to be at their strongest at twilight and during the night. Bickerton did not send many messages under his own name; the records kept by the Macquarie Island relay station show only the briefest of messages sent to his uncle in Plymouth, to Frank Wild (now in England), and to Johnnie Hunter, asking him to bring 200 cigars on the return voyage of the *Aurora*.[42] His reticence, however, is perhaps largely explained by Mawson's determination to levy a charge for the sending of any personal messages. Although justified by the parlous state of the AAE's finances, this decision, which, it should be stated, Mawson applied equally to his own communications, did little to endear him to his companions.

Matters were made even worse by what some, particularly Madigan, perceived as their leader's cavalier attitude to the deaths of Ninnis and Mertz. In fact, although Mawson called the loss of his sledging companions 'a thing which is always liable to happen; a risk which is part of the game and inseparable from pioneering in ice covered land',[43] his apparent offhandedness may well have resulted rather from a wish to contain his own intense emotions than from actual callousness. Either way, his manner of dealing with the tragedy did little to diminish the tension, and the atmosphere in the hut became increasingly dissonant.

While some disagreed with Madigan's views – there is, for instance, no criticism of Mawson's actions or attitude in McLean's diary – there is clear evidence that Mawson's relations with Bickerton took a downward turn. Restless and energetic in temperament, the engineer's belief in the need to keep 'our hands busy all the time and our minds as active as possible'[44] would have accorded well with Mawson's modus operandi, and this sympathy is reflected in his inclination to take sides against the insouciant Whetter during the row over working conditions. But, like Ernest Shackleton, and in spite of the assistance he lent to Bage in his magnetic observations, Bickerton had no real affinity with the scientific preoccupations that drove Mawson. In May, the latter had complained in his diary that Jeffryes had 'no conception of scientific analysis. Both he and especially Bickerton have such unsuited tempers for polar exploration that I think it would be unwise to take them properly in hand and try to force the wireless research.... Bickerton likes doing the things he likes to do.'[45] A few days later he had again taken up the theme, expressing his frustration that he couldn't 'get him or Bickerton to take the subject up scientifically', finding their supposed reluctance 'another argument in favour of scientists for everything'.[46] In Bickerton's defence, Mawson had chosen to recruit him and, while he naturally showed a preference for 'doing the things he likes to do', these things included many long, uncomfortable and often dangerous hours tending the wireless masts, without which no amount of scientific rigour in usage and interpretation would have been of the slightest use.

Relations between the two men continued to fluctuate; by early August, Mawson was willing to acknowledge that 'To Bickerton is due all credit'[47] for repairs to the masts but, by the end of October, Madigan noted that Bickerton and the 'almost intolerable' Mawson had 'not been hitting it off lately'.[48] However, besides the mildly ironic suggestion of a Christmas-wrapped 'aeroplane for D.I.'[49] and the reference to a disagreement over the objectives of the Western Sledging Party, there are no criticisms of Mawson, either real or implied, in Bickerton's writings. Nor did Mawson, outside his diary, ever voice his reservations concerning Bickerton's unscientific approach, and in later years, the two men met and exchanged cordial letters. Even Madigan, one of the most critical members of the AAE, later worked with Mawson in the Geology Department of the University of Adelaide, indicating that, once removed from the peculiar and intense atmosphere of Cape Denison, differences which once seemed insuperable had been satisfactorily resolved.

To break the monotony of their existence, the members of the relief party left the hut whenever weather conditions permitted. In late June, Bickerton introduced McLean to the pleasures of racing on packing-case lids, in a manner that he and Hurley had perfected the previous year, and on 20 August, they tried a new sport: 'Coming back to the Hut I met Madigan and Bickerton going for a slide to a steep snow-slope along the western cliff ... we had some really exciting slides down an almost sheer drop of thirty feet, ending in great drifts of snow out of which we could pick ourselves, only to climb up some steps cut with an ice-axe and start again. Bickerton, Madigan and I formed a linked trio and hurtled down at lightning speed. It is quite the best sport I have had for a long time.'[50]

At other times, they played football and tried out the superior Norwegian skis which Mawson had decided to distribute among the men. The frequency with which Bickerton is mentioned in McLean's journal indicates that the two were forming an increasingly close friendship, and when McLean was night watchman, Bickerton often stayed up until four or five in the morning, talking of the *Aurora* and their return to civilisation. The growth of this particular friendship no doubt owed much to the absence of Ninnis and to the increasing moroseness of Madigan, though Bickerton, too, had his moments of depression. One day he told Madigan that he felt they would never again feel young, or light-hearted, or happy, and on another, he and Charles Sandell, on Macquarie Island, exchanged gloomy wireless messages, Bickerton sending 'This place is awful!' and Sandell replying, 'So is this – Hell!'[51] The atmosphere became less oppressive when the weather allowed them to go for walks around the bay, the discovery of a new and beautiful vista being, Bickerton thought, 'like a new kind of drink when you are thirsty!'[52]

With the passing of the months, it was inevitable that the *Aurora* should once again become the central topic of conversation. As the wind dropped, Bickerton and McLean anxiously watched the ice forming along the coast and discussed the possibility of its rendering the bay inaccessible to the returning vessel. At midnight on 15 November, Bickerton heard the Macquarie Islanders transmit the words 'Ship goes' and all agreed that the word 'today' must have been lost in the ether. A few days later, he asked Sandell to transmit the message 'O.K. by the yard' when the *Aurora* arrived at Macquarie Island. Still haunted by the thoughts of the bay becoming ice-bound, on 2 December Bickerton tried to blow up the harbour ice using sticks of dynamite, with precisely the same degree of success that his attempts to treasure hunt with dynamite had enjoyed on Cocos Island two and a half years earlier.

As they waited for their salvation, preparations were made for a final sledging expedition intended to retrieve the instruments cached by the Eastern and Southern Sledging Parties the previous year. Bickerton, Bage and Madigan began trials with a small receiving set to be carried on the expedition so that time signals could be transmitted to the sledgers. Bad weather prevented the departure until 25 November, when, for the last time, Mawson, Hodgeman and Madigan dragged their recalcitrant sledge up the ice-slopes behind the hut. In their absence, Bickerton added the finishing touches to his last engineering project for the AAE: the construction of a memorial cross to Mertz and Ninnis, which he made from massive sections of the broken mast, bound and capped with brass. On 30 November, he and McLean raised the structure on Azimuth Hill and, to complete it, added a simple plaque manufactured by Hodgeman from a section of the kitchen table, and commemorating the 'supreme sacrifice' made by their comrades 'in the cause of science'. Mawson's belief that the structure was 'solid enough to last for a hundred years even in that strenuous climate'[53] proved accurate, as the vertical section of the cross was still standing more than eighty years later.

On 12 December, the sledgers returned, empty-handed but brimming with news: the *Aurora* was in sight! Over the next few hours, the men dashed about, unable to contain their excitement, their furious packing continually interrupted by excursions outside as they sought a glimpse of masts or funnel. Finally, they returned to their bunks, dazed with relief and happiness – all but Bickerton who, instead of retiring, attached a flag to the towering memorial cross and climbed the slopes to watch the ship's snail-like progress towards the shore. 'Something like smoke appeared on the horizon,' he recorded, 'then it appeared again and again at regular intervals. This was the ship.'[54]

Soon the hut was filled with fresh faces and excited chatter and more than a week was spent in packing the miscellaneous equipment and personal gear that had allowed the seven men to survive for their second, lonely year, and in ferrying it across to the waiting *Aurora*. Painfully aware of the expedition's mounting debts, Mawson insisted on stripping the hut of practically every item belonging to the AAE, no matter how redundant and valueless. High spirits abounded and the process of loading and stowing the multitudinous boxes, which even included the monoplane's smashed engine, was not devoid of humorous incident. The ever-risible Percy Gray particularly enjoyed the ceremony with which Bickerton and Madigan transported the last of this junk to the ship:

> They arrived alongside the ship going dead slow and took a sweep round the ship at the same solemn pace, – with every ridiculous piece of rubbish hung out all round the launch. A broken foot scraper was hoisted in the bow, and old kerosine [*sic*] lamps without any burners, pumps without any valves etc and high above all on an oar an old coffee grinder that they had never used because it wouldn't work properly.... . I

believe all hands were immensely tickled, and a smile was seen
even to flitter over the sorrowful face of [Captain Davis]![55]

On the 21st, as the loading neared completion, preparations
were made for bringing the remaining dogs aboard and Gray
witnessed another comical incident which, he readily admitted,
made him laugh 'till I cried'. In order to feed the dogs on the
voyage, Bickerton, Mawson and Madigan had used the launch to
transport a large case of seal meat 'simply floating in blood and
oil'. As the case was hoisted on to the *Aurora*, it was slung clum-
sily 'causing a perfect shower of slippery meat, oil, gore, etc,
to deposit itself over the unfortunate wretches in the launch'.[56]
Dripping in this foul mess, Bickerton then attempted to sling a
slab of meat from the launch on to the deck of the ship but, in
so doing, instead hit the unsuspecting Mawson. 'Nobody dared
laugh out load,' Gray noted, 'but I think we all came very near
bursting blood vessels.'

Despite such antics, and weather that veered from peaceful
calms to wave-whipping fury, the hut was eventually sealed
up on 23 December. The men wielding the hammers and nails
were Bickerton and Madigan, the last two men to leave the hut,
as they had been included among the first eight to set foot on
Cape Denison nearly two years earlier; 'afterwards,' Bickerton
noted, 'we left, blown away in a gale, violent even for that place
of winds. And no one has seen the place since. Life on the ship
seemed very good after the hut, there were so many people to
talk to and such a lot to say, but Adelaide, South Australia, was
better still.'[57]

Seven

Endurance

It wasn't as it had seemed at first, the end of one human phase and the beginning of another; it was in itself a phase. It was a new way of living.

H.G. Wells, *Mr Britling Sees It Through*

After an absence of nearly two and a half years, Bickerton arrived in England early in 1914. The return of the expedition received wide newspaper coverage and there were receptions in both Australia and England, but these naturally focused upon Mawson, whose epic solo journey across the plateau appealed strongly to the public imagination. Perhaps Bickerton's warmest welcome came from Dorothea's children, whose affections he earned with the gift of a valuable stuffed Emperor penguin. In presenting Bickerton with the bird, Mawson might have expected that it would be given pride of place as a prized Antarctic souvenir; instead, for many years, it would serve as a novelty Christmas decoration, with the children's presents being piled at its webbed feet.

Incredibly, the furore of welcome had hardly died away before Bickerton launched himself into the preparations for another

Antarctic venture, one that would become a byword for heroic endeavour against seemingly insuperable odds: Shackleton's Imperial Trans-Antarctic Expedition (ITAE). To all appearances, his extended sojourn at the windiest place on the face of the planet had done nothing to extinguish an adventurousness that was beginning to assume almost pathological dimensions.

Suffering from what appeared to be an aggravated form of scurvy, Shackleton had been invalided home from Scott's *Discovery* expedition and had then failed to reach the Pole on his British Antarctic Expedition. The ITAE – or *Endurance* expedition as it would more commonly be known – was his opportunity finally to achieve success in the Antarctic. His plan was to cross the continent from the Weddell Sea, via the South Pole and the Beardmore Glacier, to the Ross Sea, in a manner first proposed by the Scottish explorer W.S. Bruce in 1908. Although Shackleton made no attempt to disguise the essentially romantic notion behind the scheme – he called it 'the last great Polar journey that can be made' – there were also genuine scientific gains to be anticipated. Not least of these was the opportunity of establishing whether the great Victoria Land mountain range stretched across the whole of Antarctica. His plans included an extensive programme of scientific experiments and surveys but, while scientists were to be included in his staff, he also admitted to the Royal Geographical Society that, in choosing his men, 'in the main their function is to get through'.[1] The Austrians, under Dr Felix König, were planning a similar expedition, so there was also an undeniable element of imperial competition.

Shackleton suffered no shortage of volunteers for his expedition. Some 5,000 offered their services, their letters being pigeon-holed under the categories 'Mad', 'Hopeless' and 'Possible'. Faced with such competition, Bickerton owed his selection to two important factors, the first being his friendship with a number of Shackleton's most trusted colleagues, most notably Frank Wild. Upon his return to England in the summer of 1913, Wild had leapt at the chance of another expedition and

Shackleton immediately recruited him as second in command. He and Bickerton liked and respected each other: not only had Wild offered Bickerton a place on his proposed South Polar expedition, but on his previous venture in the Antarctic, in a letter dated 28 January 1912, Wild had noted his wish to include the English engineer in his Western Base Party: 'I am glad to say that I have a splendid party, all very enthusiastic and good workers; I should like to have had Bickerton but Mawson would not let him come.'[2] On being picked up from Queen Mary Land in February 1913, he had also told Percy Gray that Bickerton was one of 'the two fellows he most was looking forward to seeing'.[3]

Wild's high opinion of Bickerton would also have been reinforced by the latter's old friend and advocate, Aeneas Mackintosh, whom Shackleton had recruited to lead the Ross Sea Party that would lay depots between McMurdo Sound and the Pole. Besides Mackintosh's and Wild's liking for Bickerton, however, a second crucial factor influenced Shackleton's decision to recruit him. As well as 120 huskies, he intended to take with him a number of motor sledges, including one that would be driven by an aeroplane propeller. Although inventors such as Count de Lissek, René Legrain and Nivert had been experimenting with similar designs since at least 1909, Bickerton's recent experiences made him the world's foremost expert in the operation of such machines in truly Antarctic conditions and Shackleton recognised that his involvement might prove highly beneficial.

It is, however, uncertain whether Bickerton was recruited as a permanent member of the expedition staff or merely to act as an expert consultant whose involvement would end once the expedition sailed. The circumstantial evidence points towards his having been a full recruit. On 8 April 1913, from Cape Denison, Bickerton had addressed a wireless message to Wild, care of Conrad Eitel, the AAE secretary. In it, he requested that Wild 'Send a line when does Shackleton leave',[4] a question which seems more likely to have come from the hand of a volunteer

than from that of a mere consultant. Furthermore, in the innumerable newspaper interviews that he gave in the lead-up to his
departure, Shackleton referred repeatedly to his recruitment of
members of the AAE. In the *Morning Post* for 6 February 1914,
for instance, he stated: 'Applications have also come in from
members of Dr Mawson's present expedition, and two men
who are now with that explorer in Adelie Land will be included
among the scientific staff.'[5]

Of the members of the second-year AAE relief party,
Bickerton was perhaps the most likely to volunteer for another
expedition. Madigan was anxious to take up his long-deferred
Rhodes Scholarship to Oxford; Bage was under obligation to
return to the army; Jeffryes was insane; McLean had agreed to
work with Mawson on preparing *The Home of the Blizzard* for
publication; and Mawson would no longer consider serving
under another leader. Only Bickerton and Hodgeman remain
and there is no indication that Hodgeman was at any time connected with Shackleton's plans. The second of the two recruits
mentioned by Shackleton was Frank Hurley, who, at the time of
the interview with the *Morning Post*, had returned to Antarctica
on board the *Aurora*. The final piece of evidence to support the
supposition that Bickerton remained sufficiently enamoured of
Antarctic life to return on another expedition is to be found in
the letters of Percy Gray. On 16 January 1914, during the prolonged homeward voyage, Gray wrote that 'Old Bickerton is
the only one who really seems to enjoy the life, and he honestly
confesses he is supremely happy.'[6]

When trapped in his tent on the ice plateau in December 1912,
Bickerton had sworn that, 'If ever I come this way again it will
be the Ross Sea or nowhere'[7] and that 'if I do any sledging again
things will be different.'[8] Perhaps it was Shackleton's intention
to include him among the Ross Sea Party under Mackintosh's
command or, perhaps, given Shackleton's intention to take
the propeller sledge to the Weddell Sea, Bickerton's love of
the explorer's life was stronger than his previous predilection for

the Ross Sea. But other factors may also have motivated his decision to join the ITAE.

For all Mawson's no-doubt genuinely felt proclamations
regarding the AAE's unique scientific discoveries, he could not
deny that the performance of the air-tractor had been disappointing. In his soon-to-be-published account of the expedition,
he introduced Bickerton's sledging narrative with the words:
'Bickerton has a short story to tell, inadequate to the months
of work which were expended on that converted aeroplane. Its
career was mostly associated with misfortune.'[9] In an interview
with *The Times* on 2 January 1914, Wild was rather more enthusiastic, stating that the machine had been 'very useful', but he too
had been forced to acknowledge that the vehicle had eventually
been abandoned. Even Bickerton admitted that 'We had never
dared expect a great deal from it.'[10] Nonetheless, its failure had
been profoundly frustrating and it was impossible for him not
to believe that, as engineer responsible for the white elephant,
some at least would find him guilty by association. If, therefore,
the ITAE presented Shackleton with another opportunity to
achieve success in the Antarctic, it might also enable Bickerton
to redeem himself, though the experiences of the AAE and other
recent expeditions showed that pinning all his hopes for success
on untried machines entailed a great deal of risk. Whatever his
reasons, Bickerton agreed to accompany Shackleton to Norway
to test equipment.

The snowfield under the Hardangerjøkulen mountain near
Finse had been selected for the testing. As well as experimenting with the motorised sledges and sampling the rations they
intended to take to the Antarctic, the members of the Finse
party would use the round tents newly designed by Shackleton
and George Marston, sketch artist on the BAE. The party consisted of Shackleton himself, Wild, Bickerton, Captain Thomas
Orde-Lees – a Royal Marines officer who had been involved in
the design of the motor sledges – Harry Brittain, Marston and
another army officer named 'Fritz' Dobbs. They sailed on the

Wilson Line's *Eskimo*, which left Hull in mid-May, and then travelled from Kristiania* to Finse on the recently completed Bergen–Kristiania railway, arriving on Wednesday 20 May. Brittain, a friend of Shackleton's and a pioneer of skiing in England, knew the area well and had previously stayed in the hotel that was to serve as their headquarters.

A number of journalists attended Sir Ernest and he enthusiastically expanded on his plans and the use to which he would put the newfangled motor sledges. When the time came for the team to make their way to the glacier, Joseph Klem, the hotel proprietor, offered to take them up on reindeer sledges and they willingly accepted this novel means of transportation. The reindeer were bedecked with ribbons in Norway's national colours of red, white and blue to commemorate the country's Independence Day on 17 May, and the cavalcade presented a colourful spectacle. Only the weather spoiled the carnival atmosphere, with a strong wind carrying sheets of sleet before it. Nearly forty years later, Brittain remembered that 'It was terrible weather when we arrived there, a real blizzard,' but he admitted that it 'suited their ideas of trying out everything under what might be Antarctic conditions'.[11] At a point about 3 miles from the hotel they began the lengthy process of erecting the two tents, which were of a new hoop design and vaguely igloo-like in appearance. When folded, they formed a large 'D' shape and, according to Shackleton, it was believed that three men should be able to erect them with ease, even in high winds. One man would lay the folded tent flat on the ground, another would then throw snow on the snow-cloth or skirt, while a third pulled on a guy-rope to raise the whole structure. Despite the designers' optimistic claims that, in fair weather, a single man should be able to raise such a tent unaided, Brittain thought it 'a hell of a job ... with that hell of a wind blowing the whole time'.[12] Marston, on the other hand, considered the tents 'a great

---

* Now Oslo.

success',[13] though his opinion may have been somewhat biased by his role in their construction.

After an uncomfortable night on the glacier, the next day Bickerton, Shackleton and Orde-Lees returned to the hotel, leaving Wild in charge of a party that would 'camp out and make sledge journeys daily over the mountains in the vicinity'.[14] In the meantime, Bickerton and Orde-Lees were to begin testing the motor sledges on a frozen lake close to the hotel. The expedition would be equipped with three different types of machine, but only two were to be tested at Finse. These included the propeller-driven sledge and a 'motor-crawler' which was driven by Swedish-designed paddle-wheels and powered by a 9hp Coventry Simplex engine. The other machines – two heavy static tractors which would be man- or dog-hauled and then used to wind in heavily loaded sledges – would not be properly tested until they reached the Antarctic. The Motor Despatch Company of Southwark Bridge Road had manufactured the machines, to designs worked up by Orde-Lees in consultation with the Royal Aircraft Factory and the company's chief engineer, Albert Girling.

Ingeniously, all the Simplex engines had been equipped with small water cisterns, each with a drainage tap. When in use, the cisterns could be packed with snow, which would then be melted by the heat of the engine and thereby provide a constant supply of hot drinking water, negating the need to pitch a tent and light a stove whenever a brew was required. The same gadget could also be used as a hotplate and as a drier for damp clothes or sleeping bags. When Shackleton had appeared in front of a committee of the RGS in March 1914, severe reservations had been expressed regarding the usefulness of such contraptions. In a spirited if slightly disingenuous defence, Shackleton had replied that the sledges were designed primarily to help conserve the energy of the dogs and that, if and when they became a hindrance, he would immediately abandon them. Backed into a corner by the sceptical and determined probing of the committee members, he had also admitted that the machines helped to raise public interest in the expedition and, once interest had been raised, funds were significantly easier to come by. None of the machines was expected to travel more than 500 out of the 1,800 miles total, not least because it would be impossible to carry sufficient fuel for a journey of longer duration. Despite the doubts of the committee, he continued to assert that 'I am right to think it is worthwhile to try the machines because if I can do 200 miles on 500lb [227kg] weight of petrol … it will be a tremendous asset to me.'[15]

The propeller-driven sledge bore little relation to the converted Vickers monoplane that Bickerton had laboured over at Cape Denison and Shackleton had already told his critics that 'It is not an aeroplane; it is a sledge with an aeroplane propeller.'[16] Remembering the snail's pace of the AAE's air-tractor, Bickerton might also have raised an eyebrow if he had been privy to his leader's statement that 'Its function is to run at full speed.'[17] The machine was about 12ft long, with a 30hp Anzani-type aero-engine positioned at the rear within a metal frame that, in turn, supported the propeller unit and an uncomfortable-looking seat for the 'pilot'. A belt conducted power from the engine to the propeller and the machine was steered by means of pedal-controlled flippers mounted on outriggers. When Brittain returned from Wild's camp complaining that the beds were too hard, it was agreed that he, as the most expert skier in the party, should be towed behind the machines so that he could report on how they coped with the inequalities of the surface. It turned out to be 'a very uncomfortable job, not only because you were a few yards behind the exhaust, but on top of the evil-smelling exhaust oil was pumped on to you from time to time'.[18] Brittain was not the only spectator to be unimpressed by this new form of transport. As they started the engine, it 'made such a hideous noise that the reindeer wearing 17 May ribbons fled, frightened, into the wide expanse'.[19]

The performance of the sledges proved to be mixed. Shackleton believed that they would be able to haul a 2,000lb

(907kg) load at 5 or 6mph; but on the glacier, things didn't look so promising. There could be no doubt that the drive belts needed to be replaced with chains and it would probably be necessary to strengthen the whole design. If Shackleton felt at all disillusioned, he dissembled well, later telling a correspondent from *The Times* that 'the motor-sledges had worked excellently, both on rising and on falling ground, and the results were quite beyond his expectations.'[20] No doubt his primary concern was to prevent negative rumours finding their way back to Britain, since any adverse reports might dampen the ardour of prospective investors. At least one member of the Norwegian press who journeyed up the glacier to watch the demonstration was not so easily persuaded: 'Shackleton has constructed a new sledge prototype, characterised by the fact that the sledge is moved by an air-propeller in the same way as an aeroplane... . The propeller achieved an enormous speed... . The sledge, however, did not... . In the enthusiasm of the moment, Shackleton forgot that it was 4–5 [centi-] grades above zero when the sledge was tested. It is not certain that the motor will function as well in the Antarctic snow-desert when the mercury will sink to 30 grades below.'[21] Despite Shackleton's ebullience and Wild's belief that 'Both the sledge tractors proved satisfactory in their trial runs,'[22] some members of their team were as sceptical as the Norwegian journalist. George Marston, unhappy in his self-imposed separation from his wife and baby daughter, glumly predicted that 'Perhaps it will go for twenty min[utes].'[23]

Further experiments were attempted to test the controls. These proved more successful and, issues of strength aside, it was demonstrated that, by skilled manipulation of the pedals, the sledge could be turned round in its own length and its progress halted within the same distance. Once the pressmen had departed, Shackleton held a conference with Bickerton and Orde-Lees and it was agreed that he should journey to Paris at the earliest opportunity to obtain larger, stronger engines that would be necessary to push the machines across steep inclines or difficult surfaces. Bickerton, meanwhile, left for England with the other expedition members, but not before writing to the hospitable Joseph Klem to 'thank you for the courtesy, kindness and help you have given us; and to say that when the Expedition is over we hope to come again to the joys of Finse'.[24] By 27 May, the party was back in Kristiania, and preparing to embark on the *Eskimo*. Wild and Bickerton reached London just in time to attend Mawson's address to the RGS at Queen's Hall on 9 June, along with Davis, McLean, Hodgeman, Madigan and Gray. Antarctic exploration still enjoyed a wide appeal and even the trial expedition to Finse had been well publicised in the national and international press. Such ventures, however, were about to pale into insignificance when compared with events on the wider world stage.

Almost exactly a month after the return of the expedition from Norway, on the other side of Europe, in Sarajevo, Gavrilo Princip emptied his revolver into the Austro-Hungarian Archduke Franz Ferdinand and his wife Sophie. Across the continent, domino collided with domino as the Great Powers invoked treaties, issued ultimatums and mobilised their armies. By the beginning of August, the time ordained for the ITAE's departure, war seemed unavoidable. Shackleton quickly found his crew depleted by the inevitable recall of serving officers like Fritz Dobbs and Courteney Brocklehurst. In response to the rapidly worsening international picture, he volunteered both his own services and those of his men and ship but Winston Churchill, as First Lord of the Admiralty, and then the King himself ordered him to proceed with his Antarctic plans. Those plans, however, no longer included Bickerton.

On 16 July, eighteen days after the murder of the Archduke but a full week before the issue of the Austro-Hungarian ultimatum to Serbia, the *Morning Post* carried a list of Shackleton's personnel. The names of Dobbs and Brocklehurst are present but Bickerton's is not, implying that, long before the inevitability of war had become widely accepted, he had decided not to return south. His reasons for withdrawing are not clear but may lie in the uncertain performance of the propeller-driven sledges and the part assigned to him on the expedition. Even though the machines had been designed specifically for Antarctic work, rather than cobbled together as the AAE tractor had been, their utility seemed highly questionable. The intense cold had been one of the biggest problems when operating the air-tractor in the Antarctic and, even though the temperatures in Finse had been nowhere near as low, the sledges had proved temperamental. He might also have been concerned about the staffing of the expedition. Unassuming and with a keen sense of humour, Bickerton had a habit of slipping unobtrusively into the companionship of his fellows and the expedition staff already included two established friends, Wild and Mackintosh. Brittain thought Bickerton a 'very good chap' and Shackleton expressed himself as 'very satisfied' with all the members of the Finse party.[25] But Bickerton would have to work closely with Orde-Lees. The Royal Marines captain was something of an eccentric and preferred to work alone. Marston found him 'difficult' and Shackleton would soon be expressing doubts about his habits. How would the relationship function in the Antarctic?

Whatever the reasons for Bickerton's decision, he would not remain unemployed for long. On 4 August, as the *Endurance* lay at anchor in his hometown of Plymouth, Britain declared war. Three days later, Field Marshal Lord Kitchener, the Secretary of State for War, issued his 'call to arms' and asked for 100,000 volunteers to serve for the duration. The response was immediate and recruitment offices found themselves besieged by thousands of eager volunteers. Bickerton answered the call on 11 September, when, at a small, overcrowded office in London's St James's Street, he enlisted with the 16th (Public Schools) Service Battalion of the Middlesex Regiment. He was just one among 12,527 men to join the colours that day.[26] The fact that more than a month passed between the declaration of war and his enlistment indicates that, whether or not he was convinced of the inevitability of the conflict, he was willing to allow events to develop before committing himself; his resignation from the ITAE merely increased his flexibility. Certainly the expedition still absorbed some of his attention as, before volunteering, he had found time to wish his erstwhile companions on the *Endurance* well, and presented them with the thin-paper edition of the *Encyclopaedia Britannica*, which was duly added to the expedition's library. Having spent two winters in the Antarctic, Bickerton knew the value of the gift – he had relied upon it when writing his comical article for the *Adelie Blizzard* – and, during the ITAE, it would prove useful in more ways than one. In later years, Orde-Lees remembered it particularly: 'Mr Bickerton presented the thin paper edition of the Encyclopedia Britannica, one of the most useful gifts on the expedition and one for which we had especial cause to be truly grateful when marooned on Elephant Island.'[27] Shackleton himself considered it 'the greatest treasure'[28] among the few books salvaged from the library of the sinking *Endurance* and its worth was so keenly appreciated that some of its tattered pages were even brought back to Britain in 1917.

The 16th Battalion, the Middlesex Regiment was one of the new 'pals' battalions', the formation of which constituted perhaps the single most successful civilian recruitment incentive of the war. As well as helping to reduce the immediate pressure on the army's massively overburdened recruitment offices, the pals' battalions addressed the concerns of those men who felt unwilling to launch themselves into a military career among total strangers. The system reassured prospective volunteers that they would be able to fight with their friends and neighbours. Each recruit to these battalions shared a common bond with his fellows: membership of a club or a sports team, perhaps; residence in a particular neighbourhood; employment in a specific trade or profession; or, as in Bickerton's case, attendance at a public school or university. The system helped to swell the army's numbers and generated an intense camaraderie in the new battalions. In the months and years to come, however, it would be discovered that the advantages of such a scheme were more than counterbalanced by the disadvantages when, in one bloody action, whole communities could be wiped out.

In common with the nearly half a million men who had precipitately launched themselves into a military career since 4 August, Bickerton spent the next six months in drill practice, musketry and marching. Company training was succeeded by battalion and brigade training and, gradually, the mass of raw recruits was turned into something more closely approximating a fighting unit, though the lack of experienced NCOs and officers made the process painfully slow. As his proficiency grew, Bickerton was promoted, firstly to lance corporal on 1 October 1914 and then to corporal on 1 January 1915.

It was also around this time that he again met Douglas Mawson, who, on 29 June 1914, had been knighted for his leadership of the AAE. After a brief return to Australia, Mawson was in England en route to a lecture tour in the United States. From his training camp at Woldingham in Surrey, Bickerton wrote: 'Please excuse pencil but ink is scarce and makes such a beastly mess when upset. I'm sorry I can't get away today to say goodbye, but will look forward to seeing you on return. By the bye let me know when you are coming back and if you will stop at the Waldorf. I hope the American tour will be a success.... I have told all my friends that they are to buy our book and not to expect me to give it them.'[29] Trivial in itself, the letter reveals that, despite the tensions reported at Cape Denison by Madigan, Mawson and Bickerton had returned to good relations by the end of 1914. It was also during this trip that Mawson wrote to the Secretary of the Admiralty requesting that Bickerton and his fellow AAE veterans be awarded the prestigious King's Polar Medal. Sir George Reid, the Australian High Commissioner, had already raised the subject, but the matter had been overlooked in the immediate aftermath of the declaration of war. Writing from Regent Street on 21 December, Mawson stated that 'More than half the members of the land party … are now wearing khaki, either at the front or in readiness to proceed to the front, and the acquisition of the Medal would be of immediate value to them.'[30] His attempts to expedite the medal's issue met with little success. Although The Times reported on 10 February that 'the King has been graciously pleased to approve the award of the Polar Medal to the officers and men who took part in the Australasian Antarctic Expedition of 1911–14', Bickerton's medal would not be forwarded to the War Office until 2 December 1915. From the point of its receipt, he would wear the medal's distinctive white ribbon on all of his military tunics, though the war prevented the usual investiture at Buckingham Palace.

It was not long before Bickerton began to consider applying for an officer's commission, his ambition no doubt encouraged by his brother-in-law, the Reverend John Garrett Bussell, who was now serving as a captain with the Royal Sussex Regiment. Although a vicar, and assistant master at Marlborough College, Bussell revelled in the army life and had already fought through much of the Boer War. As a clergyman he might have chosen to serve as a military padre but, instead, he chose to fight, believing that he could lead more effectively by example than by prayer or sermons. Although the army was crying out for officers and NCOs, the disadvantages to the system of recruiting pals' battalions were beginning to show. In the early years of the war, men would be considered for a commission only if they were public school- or university-educated and, preferably, had been members of the Officers' Training Corps. As an ex-pupil of Marlborough, one of the country's premier public schools, and a student of the City & Guilds, Bickerton made an ideal candidate. Between August 1914 and March 1915, 506 Marlburians were granted commissions – the highest number from any of the major public schools. But, by enlisting with the 16th Middlesex, Bickerton had joined a battalion that was made up, almost exclusively, of men with a similar background. To grant a commission to every applicant would inevitably result in the battalion being denuded of a significant proportion of its fighting capacity. Already, by the end of 1914, 350 of its NCOs and other ranks – approximately one-third of the battalion's total strength – had been commissioned and another four New Army battalions with a similar demographic make-up faced the same quandary. Despite these problems, Corporal Bickerton completed his application for a temporary commission on 30 January 1915.

In his case, the wheels of military bureaucracy completed their revolutions well before restrictions were placed on applications from such battalions. Although he was not formally struck from the strength of the Middlesex Regiment until 1 May, by the end of April, Bickerton had received his commission and had paused to be photographed in Walsham's studio in Aldershot before joining his new unit. A crewman aboard the *Aurora* had once described him as 'that military looking cuss'[31] but, in the photograph, it looks as though his baggy uniform had been designed for a much bigger man, making him seem more like a schoolboy in fancy dress than a hardened Antarctic veteran. His request to serve with his brother-in-law had been granted and now he might look forward to seeing Bussell, who commanded A Company in the Sussex Regiment's 7th (Service) Battalion. The word 'Service' denoted that the 7th was a new battalion, recruited to augment the regiment's regular establishment.

With the rank of second lieutenant, or subaltern, Bickerton was to become a platoon commander serving under Captain Impey, the commander of D Company. Of the battalion's 1,100 men, A, B and C companies were made up, almost exclusively, of Sussex men, mostly agricultural workers. D Company, on the other hand, was an exception, consisting almost entirely of men drawn from the mining districts of Newcastle and Sunderland, and Bickerton, Oxford-born and Plymouth-bred, was to take charge of No. 15 Platoon, Geordies almost to a man. D Company had also enjoyed the dubious privilege of suffering the battalion's first fatality of the war, Private George having died of spotted fever at the end of January.

After further weeks of inspections and field exercises, by the end of May, the 7th Sussex was deemed ready for overseas service. The training syllabus introduced on 21 August had allowed six months to bring raw recruits up to an acceptable level of proficiency. It had taken the 7th Sussex over nine months but, in this, the battalion was in no way exceptional. Inexperience and lack of equipment had slowed down all the battalions of the New Army and some would not be ready until they had been in training for a year. The 7th Sussex belonged to the 12th (Eastern) Division, the second New Army division to be sent overseas – preceded only by the 9th (Scottish) Division, which had left for France on 9 May. Bickerton, along with fourteen fellow officers and 450 other ranks, left Aldershot by train at 7.20 p.m. on 31 May; by 10.40 the whole battalion was crossing the gangplanks on to the SS *Victoria*, an ocean liner commandeered for use as a troopship. The voyage was made without incident and the ship docked at Boulogne at 1 a.m. on 1 June.

A few days later, the battalion moved up to the front line around the battered town of Armentières on the River Lys. In late September 1914, at the time of the 'Race to the Sea', when the Allies and the Germans tried to outflank each other north of the River Aisne, the BEF had withdrawn to the area around Armentières. This had been the lead-up to the First Battle of Ypres. Since then, the town had been subjected to periodic shelling, and the cathedral and the area around the station, in particular, had suffered severely. It was here, on 28 June, exactly one year after the assassination of the Archduke Franz Ferdinand, that Bickerton suffered the first loss of the war that affected him personally: the death of John Bussell. Early that morning, Captains Bussell and Bowlby and Lieutenant May undertook a tour of inspection in an advanced and somewhat exposed salient. Bussell was in a particularly cheerful mood, expounding on the pleasures of the army life and remarking on the interesting features of this part of the trench system. Bowlby wrote: 'Three of us officers were walking together, myself in front, Captain Bussell about half a yard behind me, and a fellow called May about two yards behind Bussell. I had just gone down a small step, when a bullet whizzed just over my head, and caught the Captain, who was on the step. It was a mercy that he must have died absolutely instantaneously, and after he was hit he never spoke again.'[32] Bewildered by their companion's death, Bowlby and May 'had an awful time getting him away on a stretcher back to the dressing station'.[33]

The impact on Bickerton is likely to have been profound. In the Antarctic he had remembered his brother-in-law with affection and poked fun at 'the decent, whole hearted way you people take a holiday, bounce round two continents & take 1/2 a year over it. Lucky beggars.'[34] He had even suggested that they set out on 'a caravan toddle', upon his return. In applying for his commission, he had also deliberately chosen to ask for a posting to the 7th Sussex so that they might serve together. Now within four weeks of landing in France, Bussell was dead. As Bowlby phrased it, 'It was just a rotten bit of bad luck.'[35] Bussell was the first of the battalion's officers to be killed, and only the third fatality overall.

There are few records covering the remaining period of Bickerton's time with the Sussex Regiment and his service does not stand out from that of thousands of other anonymous trench officers. None of his letters survive from this period, but the battalion history paints a monotonous picture. Week after week, he and his fellows followed the same routine, their experiences tallying closely with those of the countless other 'Tommies' from Kitchener's New Army. They manned the front-line trenches for a few days and then, returning to their billets, relinquished the trenches to whichever regiment had been detailed as their replacement. Much of their time was spent in attempting to consolidate the trench system, making it, so far as possible, both defensible and comfortable. The land around Armentières had a high water table, and excavations soon filled with foul-smelling water, the marshy ground further polluted by the decomposing bodies of animals and men. Duckboards disappeared in the slime, equipment, clothing and boots soon became clogged with mud and, despite hours of back-breaking work, the trench walls remained prone to sliding down into the quagmire. Artillery bombardments were frequent and, since the British and German trenches were seldom more than a hundred yards apart, sniper fire proved a common hazard. Of comforts there were none, and even essentials were few and far between.

During late September, the battalion played a minor role in the disastrous Battle of Loos, the biggest British offensive since the start of the war. The plan was the brainchild of the French commander-in-chief, Field Marshal Joseph Joffre, and was designed to divert the attention of Germany and her allies from the theatres of Gallipoli, Brest-Litovsk and the Isonzo, where British, ANZAC, Russian and Italian forces had suffered severe setbacks during 1915. Joffre's strategy included the launching of simultaneous attacks by the British to the north and south of Lens and by the French in Champagne. While the British pushed eastwards across the Artois region, capturing the coalfields around Lens and menacing the German occupation of Lille, the French would forge on towards the Ardennes. Together, they would form the two arms of a pincer movement that aimed to pinch out the German salient between the Somme and Aisne rivers and, ultimately, challenge the tenability of the German positions on French soil. Overall, the plan was hugely optimistic. The 7th Battalion's job was a diversionary one, intended to gull the German High Command into thinking that the main assault was to be conducted at Houplines while, in reality, it would occur further to the south, around the mining village of Loos. In a tale that would become sickeningly familiar, the British lost 60,000 men in the battle, mown down by German gunners whose positions had survived largely intact a pathetically inadequate and short-lived Allied artillery bombardment.

Though Bickerton did not know it at the time, the casualties included his AAE friend Cecil Madigan, shot through the thigh on 26 September and invalided to England. The 7th Battalion's minor and distant role was reflected in its low casualty figures: three men killed and nine wounded, mostly in Bickerton's D Company. In the immediate aftermath of the slaughter, the battalion moved down to the main battlefield, taking up positions opposite Hulluch.

In the absence of waterproof capes, officers and men alike were soaked to the skin by the heavy rains of late autumn and tormented by the 'itch', a constant irritation caused by the breeding lice, and which no amount of scratching seemed to alleviate. Equipment rusted and clothes began to rot. Evil-smelling brown slime encased their feet and ankles, making every movement an effort. Standing for days in this putrid mire, a man would lose all feeling in his feet and legs; then his limbs would begin to swell and the numbness would give way to excruciating burning. The condition was named 'trench foot' and it bore distinct similarities to frostbite. In an attempt to prevent its spread, every day, Bickerton and his fellow officers undertook a foot inspection, checking for the tell-tale signs: the marbled skin and the blisters. Some officers hated these inspections more than any other job, watching a medical officer cutting away boots and puttees and trying to separate the rotten wool of socks from putrefying flesh. But, bad though it could be, Bickerton had probably seen worse, watching as Dad McLean had treated Mawson's ruined feet, with their blackened toes, the nails hanging off and the pus-oozing soles that Mawson had actually tied back on so that he could continue his solitary trek.

The battalion history for this period contains only two references to Bickerton. The first relates to his suggestion, during November, that an attempt should be made to bury some of the corpses of the men killed at Loos on 25 and 26 September. The sickly, cloying stench of decomposing flesh had become intolerable and the sight of the ragged remains sprawled, sometimes within a few inches of the trench parapets had begun to sap morale. Bickerton requested permission to bury some of the dead 'by scraping holes and rolling the bodies into them, after removing the identity discs'.[36] One of the men he selected for the burial detail later remembered the horror of that night, as Bickerton led them into No Man's Land: 'When the thick white mist gathered about us, we left the trench and roamed about over the rough ground, which was clothed in a stubble of dead, coarse weed and grasses, littered, too, with the implements and apparel of war…. . We wondered, as two of us reverently buried the leg of a Highlander, whether its owner was yet alive, it was so great and wonderful a limb, clean and full of strength. There were many parts to be buried, a right arm, and here a hand, clean amputations lying amongst the grass, with not another sign of those to whom they belonged.'[37]

While it went some small way towards improving conditions for the men occupying the trenches, Bickerton's action was, however, to result in bureaucratic criticisms being levelled at his burial detail. In their anxiety to bury their comrades and to regain safety, the amateur sextons failed to obtain exact map coordinates for each 'grave'! The second reference to Bickerton relates to the manner of his escape from the trenches – into an altogether different theatre of war.

Above, left: The explorer's father, Joseph Jones Bickerton. Energetic and ambitious, despite involvement in a minor electoral scandal in 1880, Bickerton rose to become a long-serving Liberal councillor and Town Clerk of Oxford.

Above, right: Eliza Frances Bickerton, the explorer's mother. Ten years younger than her husband and of a romantic disposition, there is some evidence to suggest that Eliza may have been responsible for squandering a portion of her son's patrimony.

Left: Frank Bickerton aged 4. This photograph was taken in 1893, the year before Joseph Bickerton's early death and the family's subsequent move to Eliza's home county of Devon.

Early in 1911, Bickerton and Aeneas Mackintosh, a veteran of Shackleton's British Antarctic Expedition, undertook a treasure-hunting expedition to Cocos Island in the Pacific. They sought a stash of pirate gold valued, in 1911, at £20 million. This is believed to be the only surviving photograph from the expedition.

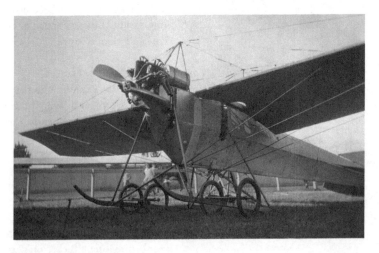

The Vickers REP monoplane: Douglas Mawson intended that it should perform the first ever powered flight in Antarctica but, within hours of this photograph being taken, the monoplane plummeted to earth during a test-flight in Adelaide, rendering its further use as an aeroplane impossible.

The explorer in his prime:
a portrait of Bickerton by
the official photographer of
the Australasian Antarctic
Expedition, Frank Hurley.
Hurley would later become
famous for his dramatic images
of Shackleton's *Endurance* in its
death-throes.

Bickerton at the controls of the Heath Robinson 'air-tractor sledge' at Cape
Denison in November 1912. A few weeks later, he piloted the machine during the
early stages of the Western Sledging Expedition.

Work on the metal fuselage of the air-tractor in the hangar at Cape Denison. From left to right: Robert Bage, Belgrave Ninnis and Bickerton.

The AAE's main hut during the almost incessant blizzard. Between January 1912 and January 1913, the average wind speed at Cape Denison was 50mph, with gusts of well over 250mph.

This photograph of Bickerton and an unidentified friend was probably taken in a reserve trench early in 1916, at about the time of his transfer to the Machine Gun Corps. The ribbon of his Polar Medal can be seen above his left breast pocket.

Bickerton at the controls of a Sopwith Pup. Having destroyed two enemy machines, including a Fokker triplane of the type made famous by Baron von Richthofen, Bickerton was seriously wounded in September 1917 and invalided home.

In May 1918, while serving as a test pilot at the Aeroplane Experimental Station at Martlesham Heath, Bickerton crash-landed a Vickers Vimy bomber. Here he is seen with his friend Lady Eileen Orde, recuperating from the injuries he sustained during the crash.

This portrait of Bickerton as 'The Explorer' was executed by Cuthbert Orde in Paris in 1922 – just after Bickerton's return from Nyasaland. Orde completed a number of portraits of his friend, four of which are known to survive. The whereabouts of this oil painting, however, is unknown.

Bickerton and unidentified friend on the veranda of his log cabin on Harry's Brook in Newfoundland, sometime between 1925 and 1928.

Bickerton at the wheel during a crossing of one of the many rickety river bridges en route to Karonga on Lake Nyasa, October 1932.

The cast and crew of *The Mutiny of the Elsinore*, a film based on Jack London's novel and made at Welwyn Studios in 1937. Bickerton, the film's editor, can be seen second from the left on the back row. His friend, Joe Stenhouse, master of the *Aurora* on Shackleton's *Endurance* expedition, is seated in the centre of the middle row, immediately behind the director.

Bickerton and his wife, Lady Joan, pictured at the 'Florida' night club in February 1938. Note the wounds to his left hand – the thumb is distorted after being nearly severed in an explosion during the war, while the little finger is a mere stump, the top having been shot off in September 1917.

Eight

Air War

The wanderers of heaven,
Each to his home, retire; save those that love
To take their pastime in the troubled air.

James Thomson, *The Seasons*

Like most infantry officers, Bickerton would have known that
there was a route out of the trenches, should he choose to
take it. The Royal Flying Corps was desperate for observers,
particularly men who knew the lie of the land, had some navigational abilities and, preferably, at least a basic understanding
of mechanical or aeronautical engineering. Simply by raising
his hand, any competent officer possessing such skills could be
snatched away from the mud and the disease and the stench of
ground warfare. This being the case, it might appear strange that
Bickerton should delay making his application until May 1916.
His reasons are unclear, but it may be that he was reluctant to
inflict an even less experienced amateur platoon commander on
the men of D Company. Such feelings were far from uncommon and the supposition is underpinned by the fact that he
made his transfer request almost immediately after his links to

the 7th Battalion were severed by a higher authority. The break
came when, with another lieutenant and 330 NCOs and other
ranks, Bickerton was ordered to join the newly formed 36th
Brigade of the Machine Gun Corps (MGC). Although it would
continue to act in conjunction with the 7th Battalion, essentially
the 36th Brigade would be a new unit and so any feelings of
obligation were effectively removed. Transfer to the MGC was
soon followed by a week's leave, from 28 April to 5 May, and it
seems to have been during this period that Bickerton completed
his application for the RFC. In doing so, he could be confident
that the shortage of aircrews meant that no commander, no
matter how sorely pressed, was permitted to stand in the way of
an officer wishing to volunteer.

Twenty-one months of combat experience had wrought
major changes in the modus operandi of the RFC. In particular,
the unarmed reconnaissance of the war's early months had been
replaced by a far more aggressive approach towards enemy aeroplanes. Both sides understood that air supremacy was crucial to
success and the work of Allied and German air forces alike could
be divided into two: reconnaissance for Army and Corps HQs
and artillery, and the interruption of similar activities being
carried out by the enemy. Also, despite the fact that demand far
outstripped supply, much greater discernment was being shown
in the selection of observers. Since it was essential that pilots
and observers work in successful partnership with the gun-
crews on the ground, spotting targets and reporting back on the
fall of shot, officers with a knowledge of artillery were considered particularly suitable. Bickerton had no such understanding
but he possessed other highly valued qualifications. He had
considerable practical experience of aero-engines, he was familiar with the trench network and might be expected to recognise
positions from the air, he had been trained in navigation by E.A.
Reeves of the RGS, and a year as chief wireless operator at Cape
Denison had given him a thorough grounding in the use of
Morse code. Suitably impressed, the RFC authorities accepted

his application, albeit on probation. If he proved suitably adept at learning the skills of the aerial observer, then his temporary transfer would become permanent. One fact that may have counted against him, however, was his weight. On enlistment in September 1914, he had weighed 11st 2lb (70.8kg), well over the maximum stipulated for an observer. Perhaps the rigours of trench life had reduced his bulk, or perhaps the RFC's desperation was making it more flexible; either way, for the time being at least, Bickerton could enjoy the extra three shillings per day that attachment to the RFC brought with it. His orders were to report, on 11 May 1916, to Major U.J.D. Bourke, officer commanding 10 Squadron, at the Chocques aerodrome, 3 miles from Bethune.

Formed on the first day of 1915, 10 Squadron had been in France since July of that year and had played an active role in the Battle of Loos. Now, as a component of the RFC's I Brigade, it was cooperating with First Army, undertaking close reconnaissance and artillery work for XI Corps. Since April 1915, the squadron had been equipped with two-seater BE2cs, designed by Geoffrey de Havilland of the Royal Aircraft Factory (RAF) at Farnborough. The letters 'BE' stood for 'Blériot Experimental' and indicated that the machine followed the tractor configuration favoured by the Channel-hopping Frenchman – much like the Vickers REP – with the 70hp air-cooled Renault or 90hp RAF engine positioned in front of the pilot and observer. The BE2c met all the criteria of a reconnaissance aeroplane: it was stable in the air, so stable, indeed, that its common nickname was 'Stability Jane'; it was comparatively strong; and it was easy to fly. Less reassuring for the airmen, however, were its other characteristics: lack of manoeuvrability, an agonisingly slow rate of climb – it could take an hour to reach 8,000ft – and poor defensive capability. Combined, these deficiencies, when opposed to the far-superior firepower of the Fokker Eindecker, or EI, and its more powerful successors the EII and EIII, had resulted in the BE2c being given another and altogether less attractive sobriquet: 'Fokker fodder'. Since July 1915 the Fokkers, with their forward-firing, synchronised machine guns, had cut swathes through the ranks of the BE2cs and the need to surround every reconnaissance machine with a swarm of escorts had stretched the RFC's resources to breaking point. This slow, inoffensive and vulnerable aeroplane was to be Bickerton's steed for the foreseeable future – or until he was killed in one.

A new observer's initiation into the RFC was essentially a baptism of fire. First, a few circuits of the airfield would serve to establish whether the volunteer could stomach being airborne. Then he must prove that he could orient his aeroplane in the screaming, freezing, violently vibrating void: Bickerton would later compare the 'horrid noise' of flying with 'going through an everlasting tunnel in a train'.[1] Determining his exact position – in order to report on the fall of artillery shot, note troop movements and undertake aerial photography – was far from simple. The ground below did not present itself with the clarity of a well-drawn map; instead, the surface was churned by the fall of a million shells, towns and villages were smashed to rubble, and trenches scarred the landscape. The movement of light and shadow across this bizarre confusion of mud, ruined houses and, far to the west, ploughed fields could make it even more bewildering; and roads, rivers, canals and railway lines did not always stand out with the anticipated clarity. Again, when contemplating the experience of aerial navigation, Bickerton later commented: 'If I wished to visit a country but was unable to do so, a good map of it would afford an excellent substitute for the journey, and I could spend much time with it. Now flying, you have both the journey and the map, but they are oddly mixed because the journey is nothing without the map. If the ground is dull or invisible … there is nothing but noise left, and the journey is as if done in one's sleep, as far as living experience goes.'[2] The ever-present threat of vastly superior enemy aircraft, however, and the risk of being hit by anti-aircraft (AA) fire, or 'Archie' as it was colloquially known, made the observer's experience over the Western Front more nightmarish than dreamlike.

In reality, most of the true observation in a BE2c fell to the pilot, who enjoyed much the better view, and the term 'observer' became something of a misnomer. The same held true if the object of the flight was photography: the position of the observer's seat, in front of the pilot and wedged between the upper and lower wings, making it necessary to place the mahogany-boxed camera next to the pilot. Even Bickerton's supposedly important understanding of wireless telegraphy became something of an irrelevance, as it was the pilot who signalled their observations. His primary function was to nurse the temperamental 47-round, drum-fed Lewis gun and watch for marauding enemy aircraft, to ensure that he saw an assailant before his bullets tore through the flimsy wood and fabric of the fuselage, and the equally vulnerable flesh and bone of its occupants.

There were, of course, some compensations for the dangers encountered. Not least among these was the quality of the accommodation on the ground. With the mud of the trenches still clinging to his boots, Bickerton now found himself inhabiting an entirely different world. The squadron enjoyed particularly good fortune in that its mess was housed in a decayed chateau, where meals were not only served with a selection of wines, but were also followed by liqueurs and coffee; where, between 'shows' – the euphemistic term for offensive sorties – he and his fellows could ride, play tennis and fraternise with the inhabitants of nearby Bethune. Death and mutilation remained ever-present but here, unlike in the trenches, there were means to aid temporary forgetfulness. Some parallels might even be drawn between the life of the explorers at Cape Denison and that of the pilots and observers of the RFC. In both situations, short bursts of intense and highly dangerous activity were interspersed with periods of comparative inactivity and even boredom. In the mess, there was the same predilection for sentimental gramophone records and rowdy sing-songs around a discordant piano. The fear and anxiety common to both environments were kept effectively at bay by noise and activity and, in moderation, by alcohol. One substantial difference was that the kind of high-spirited horseplay that Bickerton so enjoyed, and which Mawson had frowned on as being, presumably, at odds with the scientific seriousness of his expedition, was here almost actively encouraged.

It was also true that, in exactly the same way that many of Mawson's scientific staff possessed only limited practical knowledge of their chosen fields, the losses caused by the 'Fokker scourge' meant that many of the pilots and observers sent to replace the dead and wounded were woefully inexperienced. Often, new observers lacked even a rudimentary knowledge of the Lewis gun, their (and therefore also their pilot's) only means of defence. Fortunately, this criticism could not be made of Bickerton, as his months in the trenches had made him familiar with the standard weapons of the British infantry. Again, his period in the Antarctic would have served him well: a primary cause of failure in the airborne Lewis gun was the extreme cold at high altitude. As an engineer accustomed to the wayward behaviour of machinery in extreme temperatures, he probably had a better chance than many of remedying the gun's failings in the air. In some ways, the conditions he now experienced were an exact counterpart to those prevalent at Cape Denison. There, he and his colleagues had operated in temperatures often hovering around -40°F (-40°C) and in winds averaging between 40 and 50 knots; now, he worked in 70 to 80-knot winds at temperatures well below freezing. After long sorties at high altitudes, it had been known for pilots to be almost frozen into their cockpits and incapable of movement once they had been lifted out of them; the effects of thin air and the intense cold at high altitudes also made frostbite commonplace.

On 1 July, the Battle of the Somme began. With its strength raised to eighteen machines, 10 Squadron's role was to support diversionary attacks along the front, north of the main battle area, bombing enemy communications and troop concentrations, particularly on junctions, billets and ammunition dumps along the railway lines radiating from Lille southwards to Lens, Douai, Cambrai and Valenciennes. Disrupting enemy communications and preventing the transfer of reinforcements to the battlefront in the south was deemed so essential that bombing sorties were undertaken day and night. But, without escorts, the bombing often became more opportunistic than planned, and once their bombs had been released, the pilot and observer must fight their way back to Allied lines, struggling against the prevailing westerly winds in their underpowered BE2cs.

By mid-July, Bickerton was considered experienced enough to become guide to a new pilot recently arrived from England: a young Australian named Ewart Garland. While the allocation of this responsibility might be taken as a compliment, however, it also served further to reduce his chances of survival. As well as flying in an aircraft that had long ago been outclassed by the enemy, Bickerton must now trust his life to a pilot who had only put up his wings on 6 July and whose very first solo flight had taken place less than two months earlier. On 18 July, they took their first flight together over the trenches around Festubert and Aubers, though low cloud hampered Bickerton's attempt to increase Garland's familiarity with the area. Three days later, he guided Garland over the front line for the first time, the latter noting in his diary that they were '"Archied" fairly near'.[3]

On 27 July 1916, Bickerton qualified as a flying officer (observer) and his secondment to the RFC became permanent. A year earlier, the skills required by a qualified observer had been defined as: a comprehensive knowledge of the Lewis gun and the standard RFC camera; the ability to send six words per minute on the wireless transmitter with 98 per cent accuracy; and a thorough understanding of the cooperation methods between aeroplanes and artillery. Given the particular constraints placed on the BE2c observer, it might be doubted how much practical experience Bickerton could boast in some of these areas. Nevertheless, Garland thought him 'a most conscientious and original observer, who … on occasion, saved both their lives'.[4] Certainly, there could be no doubt about his meeting the final criterion: that of having completed at least ten flights over the lines. The constant action during the Somme had ensured that his quota had been more than filled and he had been extremely fortunate to survive long enough to stitch the distinctive – and derided – winged 'O' above the ribbon of his Polar Medal. How much pride Bickerton may have felt in his qualification is open to question. Despite the fact that, in two-seaters, the observer was responsible for shooting down most enemy machines, many still considered his role to be distinctly subservient to that of the pilot. In fact, so ambivalent was the prevailing attitude that many observers mockingly called their badge of rank the 'flying arsehole'. Whatever his own views on the subject, however, Bickerton could at least take some small satisfaction in the addition of a further two shillings to his daily pay.

A few days later, he qualified for another new piece of insignia: his first wound stripe. Flying at a steady 4,000ft for artillery spotting, aircraft were subjected to a constant barrage of AA fire and, even at 11,000ft, they risked being hit by splinters. Small lumps of shrapnel might pass directly through the fuselage and wings without doing much serious damage – assuming neither the crew nor essential controls or braces were struck – but a direct hit would be fatal. The more skilful German gunners could position their shot with brilliant accuracy, so that a pilot might be faced with an impenetrable wall of flak, forcing him to turn in a direction predetermined by the gunner on the ground. On 31 July, flying at 2,000ft with Garland as pilot, a shrapnel shell burst close to Bickerton's aeroplane. Splinters tore through the fabric of the fuselage and one piece punctured his flying jacket, wounding him in the shoulder. Fortunately, Garland was already beginning to reveal the pluck and aptitude that would eventually win him the Distinguished Flying Cross, and he evaded further hits by pushing the sluggish BE2c into a 120mph dive. Bickerton's wound was only slight and within a few days he was able to fly again.

A fortnight later, he suffered a second and altogether more serious wound. On 16 August, low cloud prevented flying and, instead of playing tennis, Bickerton, Garland and a few other officers turned their attention to the invention of a new weapon to be used against their opponents. Bickerton had already exercised what he later called his 'inventive brain' in the creation of a double Lewis gun, a weapon that Garland remembered as being both 'effective and dangerous'. But the new weapon was altogether less reliable; it consisted of a standard Very pistol into which Bickerton stuffed a quantity of gunpowder. 'Some high charges were fired', Garland noted, 'with success. Bickerton did the firing. After the 3rd he fired another which burst the gun. His face was shattered and both thumbs are lost. A small piece scratched me. But no one else was hurt.'[5]

In the Antarctic Bickerton had shown a distinct predilection for dangerous experiments, such as dynamiting the bay ice and lighting benzine cans before glissading them down the ice-slopes. He had also revealed a degree of carelessness. On one occasion he set fire to his own clothes, and on another he damaged the wireless motor with a badly fitted drive-belt. Finally, he had ignited an acetylene charge with a carelessly handled hurricane lamp, this accident leaving him, as McLean described it, somewhat scorched and shocked. But none of these mishaps had wrought much damage or come so close to justifying Gray's opinion of his foolhardiness. In the words of the subsequent medical board: 'he was handling a pistol-handled gun when it burst. Right thumb was nearly severed from hand... . Condition is much the same for left thumb but the cut is not so deep... . Soft parts were raised as a flap from right cheek but this has been sutured and is healing. There is a superficial wound on inner side of right upper arm and a few small

foreign bodies are embedded in conjunctiva without impair-
ment of vision.'[6]

Even a cursory examination at a field dressing station must
have revealed that Bickerton could not be expected either to fly
or to handle a machine gun for some months to come. Instead, he
was sent home from Boulogne on the SS *Western Australia*, arriving in Southampton on 22 August. A week later, he attended the
medical board at the 5th London General Hospital and learned
that he was to be incapacitated for two and a half months, calcu-
lated from the date he received his wounds. In fact, it would be
nearly a year before he returned to the front – but then it would
be as a fully qualified pilot and in charge of one of the RFC's
new single-seater scouts: the Sopwith Camel.

Bickerton spent much of his sick leave in London and took the
opportunity to meet up with a number of his colleagues from the
AAE. Douglas Mawson, who, since July 1916, had been working with the Explosives Supply Department of the Ministry of
Munitions, and Archie McLean, invalided home from France
with appendicitis, had been discussing the possibility of preparing the *Adelie Blizzard* for publication. Ironically, on the very
day that the exploding Lewis gun shattered Bickerton's hands,
McLean wrote to Mawson, suggesting that Bickerton might be
employed to produce a new illustration. Had the two men seen
the childlike scrawl that replaced Bickerton's usually small and
elegant handwriting when he completed the questionnaire for
his medical board on 30 August, they would quickly have dismissed the idea of his drawing anything. Bickerton met Mawson
within a few weeks of his return from the front and the latter
wrote to Professor Edgeworth David on 9 September describing
his injuries: 'Bickerton of the AAE is in London convalescing
from a nasty mauling – an antiaerial [*sic*] gun he was working burst – his face is knocked about and his two thumbs were
hanging off but seem to be joining on again though useless.'[7]
McLean, now living in a flat on the Ravenscourt Road, appears

not to have met Bickerton immediately; instead Mawson told him of their colleague's plight and McLean expressed his relief at hearing that 'his wounds were not serious'.[8] Shortly afterwards, he suggested that an artist should be employed to 'touch up Bickerton's drawings'.

A few months later, Bickerton again met the irrepressible Frank Hurley, who was preparing to take up a post as an official war photographer. Hurley recounted the meeting in his diary entry for 20 November 1916: 'I was delighted to meet my chum Bickerton during the evening, (of the Mawson Expedition) and with whom I dined. Poor old Bick has had his face sadly disfigured by the bursting of a machine gun. He is the same as when I knew him three years back.'[9] Mawson's and Hurley's words indicate that Bickerton may have been somewhat disingenuous when describing the cause of his injuries. Each appears to have been under the impression that he had been handling an anti-aircraft or Lewis gun when wounded; presumably he was too embarrassed to tell them that his injuries were, to all intents and purposes, self-inflicted. Hurley's shock at Bickerton's appearance, however, was not overstated. The English engineer had been one of the most handsome men on the expedition, but the burst of the Very pistol had left him with a jagged scar, running from beneath his right eye and cutting down towards his mouth; Vita Sackville-West would later romanticise it as a sword-cut. The wound interfered with the growth of his previously luxuriant moustache and made it necessary for him to trim it close. There were also tiny lumps of shrapnel embedded beneath the surface of his skin, like black freckles.

Hurley had recently returned from the ill-fated but undeniably heroic *Endurance* expedition; now he was in London to see to the expedition's photographs and to obtain prints of some of the AAE images. The two explorers dined together again three days later, and perhaps laughed at the unexpected uses to which Bickerton's parting gift of the *Encyclopaedia Britannica* had been put. As well as providing entertainment and settling disputes during the expedition's long months of imprisonment on Elephant Island, it had, just as importantly, served as toilet paper when all other supplies ran out. Another topic of conversation must certainly have been the fate of the depot-laying Ross Sea Party, led by Bickerton's old friend, Aeneas Mackintosh. But the conversation would have been limited to speculation. Not until January the following year would news filter through of the disaster that had overcome the expedition in general and Mackintosh in particular. Supported by the AAE's old ship, the *Aurora*, Mackintosh's party had wintered at Cape Evans and then made a lengthy depot-laying expedition during the summer months of 1915–16. One member of the expedition died from the effects of scurvy on the return journey and then, in an ill-advised attempt to cross the fragile sea-ice between Hut Point and Cape Evans on 8 May 1916, Mackintosh and V.G. Hayward had been swept out to sea and lost. Their bodies would never be found.

Throughout the months of recuperation, the injuries to Bickerton's thumbs gave him the most trouble and even two years later he would admit to still not having 'full use of hands for ordinary things'.[10] Despite the discomfort of his wounds, his facial disfigurement and the frustrating months of idleness, however, he had been lucky, overall. In August, the Germans reorganised their air force, introducing specialist fighter squadrons called *Jagdstaffeln* and, with the introduction of the new, more powerful and better-armed Albatros fighter, they again succeeded in wresting air superiority from the beleaguered RFC. The average life expectancy of an RFC pilot had been cut down to just three weeks, and since observers remained completely dependent upon the pilots, their chances were equally bleak. By the end of the Battle of the Somme, the RFC had lost 500 airmen and nearly 800 aeroplanes. In little over a fortnight, Bickerton had been wounded twice; had he not been invalided home the chances of his surviving a third time would have been slim indeed.

As a qualified Flying Officer, Bickerton was required to train as a pilot 'at the earliest opportunity'[11] and, in February 1917, he attended a 'special' medical board to establish his fitness for flying. Shortly afterwards, he reported to No. 1 School of Military Aeronautics at Reading to receive technical training, before proceeding, on 1 June, to the Central Flying School at Upavon in Wiltshire. There was certainly nothing unusual in his progression from observer to pilot; indeed, so common had the practice become that a major complaint within the RFC was that as soon as an observer became really good at his job, he disappeared to the Central Flying School. The scant chances of promotion or recognition available to even the most able observers also tended to make such moves welcome to the men themselves. It was even true that, by requesting a transfer to the RFC, Bickerton might have reduced his chances of promotion. Two years and three months after volunteering, and over a year and a half after being commissioned, he remained only a second lieutenant, the lowest commissioned rank. Had he stayed with the 7th Battalion and survived, he might have been a captain by now, even though the promotion might have resulted from his stepping into dead men's shoes.

Few wartime records of pilot training have survived the depredations of RAF 'rationalisation' and Luftwaffe bombing, so there is little evidence upon which to speculate regarding Bickerton's initial proficiency. But, after more than a year working on the Vickers monoplane both in Australia and Antarctica and months as an observer on the Western Front, he was already familiar with the structural features and control mechanisms common to most aeroplanes: the rudder pedals, the ailerons and longerons and, of course, the stick that operated the elevators. He now needed to obtain two certificates. 'A' was divided into two parts: the first consisted of a written examination on the theory of flight, RFC organisation, and artillery-cooperation procedures; the second part incorporated practical tests of his skills in aero-engines, rigging, Morse and machine guns.

Certificate 'B' covered actual flying. Passing out of the CFS with the full wings of a qualified pilot, he would also have been expected to obtain his Royal Aero Club Certificate, but the exigencies of war prevented many pilots from doing so and he seems not to have made the application. Instead, after a brief period as a temporary instructor at Upavon, he received a posting to 70 Squadron, joining it at Estrée Blanche on 21 July 1917.

Formed in April 1916 and equipped with Sopwith 1½ Strutters, in Belgium, 70 Squadron had been engaged in long-range reconnaissance, photography and offensive patrols. The squadron had suffered greatly in the previous months: their Sopwiths were outclassed, and the insistence upon aggressive tactics and the near exhaustion of the crews had all contributed to devastating casualties. On one day in March they had lost eight two-seaters in a single sortie. 'Bloody April' had followed, with more RFC casualties than in any month of the war. Now, the squadron shared an aerodrome with three others: 22, 66 and the famous 56. The last-named, with its Santos Experimental (SE) 5s was perhaps the most fêted of all the 'fighting squadrons', including in its ranks high-scoring aces such as Arthur Rhys Davids, James McCudden, Dick Maybery, and Leonard Barlow. With the camaraderie typical of squadron messes sharing an aerodrome, it is likely that Bickerton met at least some of these heroes of the RFC.

Bickerton's new squadron was the first to be re-equipped with the new single-seater Sopwith Camel, delivery beginning in June. This being the case, Bickerton probably doubled as a 'ferry pilot', delivering a new Camel as well as himself. To the battle-weary veterans of 70 Squadron, the new aeroplane would have been even more welcome than the novice. Inexperienced or not, however, the very fact that he had been chosen to join a scout squadron with 'one of the finest [records] in the whole history of the RFC'[12] counted for a great deal. As a rule, the scout squadrons received the very best in men and machines and, at the very least, his selection indicates that his trainers believed him to possess the makings of an effective scout pilot. These included a proven aptitude for flying, a level of physical fitness that would enable him to cope with the sudden and frequent changes in altitude and, most important of all, an aggressive single-mindedness. Scout pilots were seen to be the most glamorous members of the RFC and, statistically, they were more likely to receive rewards and recognition in terms of both medals and promotion. To balance the equation, their life expectancy was also the shortest.

Much smaller than the BE2c, the Camel looked snub-nosed and aggressive, perfect for a dedicated fighter. Most importantly, it possessed twin, forward-facing Vickers .303 machine guns. At last, the development of the Constantinesco interrupter gear meant that an Allied machine gun could be fired directly through the arc of a propeller, making attack far easier. The Camel also had an effective fighting ceiling of 12,000ft, a thousand feet higher than the BE2c's maximum ceiling, and it could operate successfully at even higher altitudes. In an arena where height was critical, this statistic gave additional reassurance. Many experienced pilots thought the Camel a joy to fly, with controls so light to the touch that it sometimes seemed that the machine had predicted the pilot's next intended manoeuvre. This responsiveness resulted largely from the concentration of weight in an unusually small space. The pilot sat immediately behind the engine, so that his body weight and that of his controls, engine, weaponry and 1,000 rounds of ammunition were all squeezed together. When coupled with the additional torque provided by the 130hp Clerget rotary engine, this meant that the Camel possessed an unparalleled ability to turn in either direction in a remarkably confined area and, if handled skilfully, with no loss of height. The ability to sustain tight vertical turns remained one of the crucial tests of the fighting pilot and, in combat, they would constantly try to turn inside each other in an attempt to get behind their opponent. However, if the turn was not handled properly, the Camel's nose had a tendency to dip suddenly, forcing the machine into a spin, with catastrophic results at low altitude. All in all, Bickerton's being chosen to fly a machine so prone to kill the inexperienced and unwary must be seen as further evidence of his competence as a pilot.

Many new pilots, with nothing to sustain them in combat but a few short hours' flying time and the experience of their comrades, demonstrated a certain reluctance to fly. Bickerton, in contrast, appears to have embraced his role as a scout pilot with enthusiasm. One senior medical officer reported not only that he 'enjoys flying' but that 'This officer appears to be particularly intelligent, alert and keen about his work.'[13] His enthusiasm for flying, particularly at low altitude, is also apparent in his later journals: 'now the wind has dropped we do 100mph at 1–2,000 feet; goats and chickens scatter. One hill, a small bun, stands out on the sea-like horizon. Although we did 12 hours' flying, the last part was exhilarating as we hurried between 100 and 110mph and were sometimes only 100 feet up, and the air was still.'[14]

Certainly, in the weeks leading up to the Third Battle of Ypres, there was no shortage of opportunities to fly in combat. The ground offensives began on 31 July and, on that day, Bickerton reported seeing men leading horses on the Roulers–Iseghem road. Swooping down to 200ft, he fired 140 rounds into them in a manner being duplicated by his comrades all along the front. Bad weather between 1 and 4 August reduced flying to a bare minimum but, on the afternoon of 5 August, he received orders to escort a flight of Martinsyde G100s, his role, to protect the lumbering, single-seater biplanes from enemy aircraft while they attacked German positions. Over Wercken, two Albatros-Nieuports fired on the formation, hitting Lieutenant Ellam's machine. Bickerton reported:

> I followed the leader in a sharp left hand turn on to an E[nemy] A[ircraft]. Enemy was attacking a Camel which was diving straight and emitting black smoke. I dived and got in

a burst at 100yd before he dived. I went down to see if the enemy attacked the Martinsydes, but he turned off.

I had then lost the formation. I kept about the same place for three minutes or so. A Camel then appeared about 1000 feet above me and another EA was a little below me. I got behind him and fired a burst at 100yd range. He had commenced to dive when I fired. He went down in a spiral nose-dive but I did not watch.[15]

Once engaged in combat, a pilot focused solely on the task in hand: that of downing his man while avoiding the bullets of his opponent. In this instance, while Bickerton followed the Albatros down to prevent a further attack on the Martinsydes, the rest of his flight reformed and flew eastwards with the bombers, leaving him isolated. After making his second attack of the afternoon, he was able to rejoin the returning Martinsydes, and followed them back to the lines. Still relatively inexperienced, he cautiously waited near the lines for ten minutes in the hope of meeting more of the Camel escorts, while retaining the option of diving back across his own lines in the event of an enemy attack. For the time being, discretion remained the better part of valour.

Throughout August, Bickerton and his colleagues were in constant action, supporting the Allied attacks on the ground. The unusually early August downpours frustrated their efforts, hampering air operations and reducing the ground around Ypres to a quagmire. On 14 August, a terrific storm crashed and thundered over the battlefield, but at 7.30 p.m. the next day, growing in confidence, he accompanied a flight on an offensive patrol 15,000ft over the Menin district. A classic British tactic was to fly east and then to watch the skies to the west, in the hope of catching marauding enemy planes as they returned, thereby cutting them off from their line of retreat. Following this method and approaching from the north-east, Bickerton now led an assault on five enemy aircraft. The safest means of attacking was to approach an enemy from his blind spot, firing in short bursts and then zooming away before the hunter became, in turn, the hunted. Bickerton's positioning seemed perfect: 'Being in front I came in contact first and approached to within 5yd of my man who was oblivious of my presence and was flying straight and throttled down. I got a good sight. The left gun was useless and the right gun fired about 5 shots and jammed.'[16]

Lieutenant G.B. McMichael fired a lengthy burst into the German aircraft as it turned away from Bickerton and across his own front, and both watched it spin into the clouds below. Had his guns not jammed, with ideal positioning and the element of surprise, Bickerton might have won his first victory, though his claim to have fired from a range of only 5yd may have been the result of inexperience. In the heat of battle, distance-perception often became distorted, leading pilots to believe that their targets were much closer than was, in fact, the case. Either way, the cloud cover made it impossible to determine whether, between them, he and McMichael had crippled or killed their opponent. The next day the squadron suffered a major loss when Captain Noel Webb, an ace with fourteen victories to his credit, was shot down and killed by Richthofen's lieutenant, Werner Voss, flying a Fokker triplane of *Jagdstaffel* 10. For the pilots of 70 Squadron, insult was added to injury when German bombers made a concerted effort to destroy their aerodrome, making repeated attempts to locate it throughout the nights of 16, 17 and 18 August. The droning of the Gothas' engines could clearly be heard, although there was some reassurance to be gained from the banks of searchlights and AA guns that defended the squadron's base.

Between 17 and 23 August, British and German forces fought bitter engagements around Hill 70, supported by intense air activity. At 8 a.m. on the 20th, Captain Dean led Bickerton's formation against eight hostiles west of Cambrai. Dean attacked an Albatros single-seater, but only managed a short burst before both of his Vickers machine guns jammed. As Dean turned away to clear them, Bickerton engaged another Albatros from 150yd but could observe 'no visible result beyond the EA diving'.[17] The rest of the German formation dived away while the Camels were still 400 or 500yd distant. Bickerton's first victory came two days later while flying Camel B3862 over the south-east corner of Houthulst Forest. Houthulst was the largest of the forests in the Ypres salient and an area so devastated by sustained artillery fire that James McCudden compared it with a farmyard of clay mud, much trampled by cattle. Captain Dean, again leading the formation, reported that the eight Albatroses that they had engaged constantly used the sun to their advantage, diving down on to the aeroplanes of 70 Squadron and then zooming back into the sun, effectively blinding the British pilots. As Dean swerved to avoid the fire of an Albatros D that had come to within 10yd of his tail, Bickerton engaged the enemy machine: 'They were 1,000 feet above and dived singly, using the sun to their best advantage on nearly every occasion. The EA did not come amongst the formation at all, but opened fire at over 100yd (except one), and then climbed off. Opportunities of firing were practically nil, but I fired at one EA who was climbing over me, after attacking the leader. I got a good sight, and deflection, and kept firing till I could hang on the propeller no longer, and fell in a spin …'[18]

With around one month's combat flying, and probably no more than that on the notoriously difficult Camel, Bickerton had now begun to demonstrate sufficient confidence to push his machine to its limits. He was also developing an aggressive attitude that brought him to the attack even when facing the disadvantages inherent in engaging an enemy above. Attacking upwards inevitably meant a lack of speed and a tendency to stall and spin. Having made the best of a very limited window of opportunity, he was rewarded with a confirmation of his kill in that week's RFC Communiqué. His success was perhaps even more laudable, as B3862, the machine that he used throughout much of August, was plagued by poor performance and was permanently retired from active service only three weeks after this kill.

Having drawn blood at last, that evening Bickerton patrolled again. Increasingly belligerent and devoid now of the novice's natural trepidation, he joined Camels from another flight of 70 Squadron and some SE5s in attacking a formation of enemy machines over Ypres: 'Four EA were hurrying East at about 11,000 feet, but owing to the tremendous number of machines attacking it was difficult to get near. I saw an SE send one down in a flat spin, afterwards bursting into flame. After returning to our patrol area, four EA attacked us – I got a good burst with both guns on to an EA who was firing on a Camel. He rolled right over and then spun. I watched him down about 7,000 feet, he was still spinning when I last saw him.'[19] Despite Bickerton's certainty that the Albatros-Nieuport was spinning out of control, however, the kill was not confirmed, merely being listed as an 'indecisive'.

In the Antarctic, Bickerton had been heavily involved in two ground-breaking experiments – with aero-engines and with wireless telegraphy – and with one major discovery: that of the continent's first meteorite. Now his turn came to make aeronautical history with the RFC. On 3 September, in retaliation for Allied night-time raids on their aerodromes, German Gothas attacked St Omer and targets around the Thames Estuary. Sixteen aircraft were scrambled in England and two in France, the latter piloted by Bickerton and Captain Clive Collett, a New Zealander and one of the squadron's best pilots. What made this operation remarkable was the fact that the Camel had never before been flown at night; indeed, the RFC authorities considered the type too unstable for such use. The raiders escaped unharmed but the operation served effectively to debunk the theory that the Camel could not be used as a night-fighter and, from now on, it would serve regularly in this role.

It was almost certainly the case that neither of the 70 Squadron Camels had been equipped with instrument lights and, throughout the sortie, Bickerton would have flown only by feeling, unable to read his speed, oil pressure or engine revs. Neither he nor Collett left any description of this pioneering experiment – Collett merely recorded in his log that the flight commenced at 9.10 p.m. and lasted for 55 minutes – but, in later years, Bickerton flew down the Nile at night in an aeroplane with an engine similar to that of the Camel. Then he noted that 'Taking off in the dark was impressive as the engine ... – a radial – blows flame from its twenty exhausts,'[20] and his experience in the Camel cannot have been any less impressive, if rather more nerve-racking. As well as the usual risks inherent in night flying, those of collision and disorientation, the Camel added its own particular difficulties. Its rotary engine was notoriously prone to failing oil pressure, a fault which could result in engine seizure and a forced landing, never an easy task and one rendered practically suicidal by darkness. The fact that Bickerton was chosen for this mission and that he completed it without mishap must be seen as a tribute to his increasing skill as a pilot and to his strong nerves. This impression is reinforced by the opinion of Cecil Jones, another 70 Squadron pilot, who remembered that 'Bickerton was a very tough character and wore the Polar Ribbon.[21] An extremely nice fellow, he commanded "A" Flight until wounded.'[22]

Over the next few days, bad weather continually interrupted flying but, on 8 September, the squadron's pilots flew their machines to a new base at Poperinge, the move being completed amid the noise and hubbub of a colossal bombardment. The following day Collett was invalided home after having his little finger shot off; since July, he had destroyed fifteen enemy machines, including three on the day he was wounded.[23] On the 10th, flying Camel B2342, Bickerton became embroiled in a battle over Roulers, a village dominated by the high ground of the Ypres salient. The risk of collision, with either friend or foe, constituted one of the greatest dangers in a dogfight and the fighting became so confused that he 'almost collided with a camel [*sic*] which was going down in flames and an enemy tri-plane close behind it'.[24] Bickerton immediately engaged another formation: 'we got in behind them and I dived on one firing a burst from 30yd range, and he disappeared under me. On look-ing under my tail I saw a machine bursting into flames, which I consider was the EA I fired on.'[25] Lieutenant Wheeler con-firmed the kill and noted the time as 5.40 p.m. Overall, most pilots on both sides seem to have felt a certain camaraderie with their opponents. Even in the heat of battle, there was enough humanity to feel very real sympathy for a man trapped inside a burning aeroplane, his choices reduced to either throwing himself from his cockpit without a parachute or being burned alive. Bickerton's terse combat report, completed immediately after landing, is devoid of emotion, but if he felt any sympathy it was likely to have been tempered by the spectacle of one of his own colleagues suffering the same horrific fate only a few minutes earlier.

During the late morning of 20 September, he took up B2342, which seems to have become his regular machine in place of the recalcitrant B3862, in company with another Camel flown by Lieutenant Booth. The day before, in an attempt to sup-port an attack being made by the Second and Fifth Armies, 70 Squadron had cooperated with 10 Squadron of the Royal Naval Air Service in the first organised bombing operation to use the Camel. Bickerton's job was to continue the work, straf-ing German troop positions all along the Ypres front. Crossing the trench line to the west of Houthulst Forest, he and Booth picked up a solitary Sopwith Triplane, belonging to the RNAS and presumably separated from the rest of its formation, and they continued towards the forest together. 'Enemy machine-gun fire and AA fire were fairly active,' Bickerton reported, and later in the day Lieutenant Wilson noted that 'Archie' in this area was 'very accurate'. As Bickerton swung this way and that, trying both to confuse the German gunners and to control his light machine as it was buffeted by the eddies of hot, displaced air, his attention was arrested by the clatter of machine guns coming from above and behind him. Two German machines, no doubt attracted by the black clouds of their own AA shells blossoming around the Allied aeroplanes, had swooped down to attack. They opened fire at maximum range and 'there was some long range fire on both sides'.[26] The German pilots seemed unwilling either to engage more closely or, more understandably, to relinquish the advantage their height gave them and they soon made off.

In the fighting Bickerton had become separated from Booth and now he continued alone to engage three observation balloons at the east end of the forest: 'I went over towards the nearest balloon which was about 30 feet from the ground and fired off about 20 rounds at it. I saw two machine-guns firing tracers at me and had a burst at each gun but did not observe any result. I attacked the personnel pulling down one balloon and they scattered; I then attacked the balloon about five or six times, one gun jammed which I cleared. I then fired a burst into a hut into which the men had gone, and finding all the ammunition in one gun expended, started home.'[27]

The stability of balloons made their observations more accurate than those of aeroplane crew, albeit in a more limited area, and they were considered a very real threat to ground operations. The balloonists depended for their protection on the pilots of friendly aircraft, on the gunners on the ground and on the crews who operated the lorry-mounted winches that reeled them in and out, allowing them to descend or rise into cloud cover. For all their comical appearance, therefore, the balloons were a force to be reckoned with and some pilots even specialised in their destruction. Attacking pilots usually utilised one of two weapons: barbed rockets, mounted in tubes on their wing struts and intended to tear through the skin of the balloon and explode within, or tracer bullets that contained phosphorus.

The standard .303 bullets Bickerton appears to have used were less likely to be effective, but a target of opportunity could not be neglected.

Deciding to conserve the rest of his ammunition for any targets that might present themselves during his return flight, he turned the Camel's nose west; but, with his machine struggling against the prevailing westerly wind, and having reduced his altitude, Bickerton's luck was about to run out. His report continues: 'I fired into a hut in the Forest and found my gun had jammed and could not remedy it. I was then at about 200 feet. Machine-gun and AA fire was very severe as I approached the trenches, and a bullet struck me in the left leg and left hand.'[28]

Despite the pain from his wounds, Bickerton had to reach his airfield if possible and avoid damaging the Camel with a landing on the heavily shelled terrain immediately behind the front line. With a nearly empty tank, the counterbalancing effect of the fuel would have been noticeably reduced, making the Camel nose-heavy, and he would have had to fight to keep the aeroplane flying straight and level. After crossing the lines, he had to gain height and then begin to throttle back, coming down in a fast glide. He managed to reach the ground safely, though not quite in one piece. As the ground crew pulled him from the cockpit, he asked one of the air mechanics to look for his left little finger, which had been severed by the German bullet. When the grisly article was found, he carefully transferred the gold signet ring, which was still attached to it, to the little finger, of his right hand. He had flown his last combat mission of the war but, with what Percy Gray had called 'the Luck of a Scout, and the Pity of Christ',[29] he had survived.

Nine

The Restless Heart

*In New York, I have always found, one gets off the mark quickly in
matters of the heart. This, I believe, is due to something in the air.*
P.G. Wodehouse, *Thank You, Jeeves*

Categorised as 40 per cent disabled from his multiple wounds
and in receipt of an annual RAF pension of £66, Captain F.H.
Bickerton was transferred to the 'Unemployed List' on 7 August
1919. It was almost exactly five years since Britain had declared
war on Germany and four years and eleven months since
Bickerton had signed his enlistment papers in St James's Street.
After another lengthy period of recuperation, largely spent at
Castle Malwood, a convalescent hospital owned by Daniel and
Sylvia Hanbury, he had ended his flying career as a test pilot at
the Aeroplane Experimental Station at Martlesham Heath in
Suffolk. Here he not only earned his last wound stripe of the
war but also embarked on three friendships that would prove to
be the most enduring of his life.

Having reported to Martlesham on 28 February 1918, on
17 May Bickerton was ordered to test B9953, a Vickers Vimy
bomber powered by twin Maori engines. During the flight, the

bomber suffered catastrophic engine-failure and the ensuing crash-landing reduced it to a ball of twisted and unrecognisable wreckage. Amazingly, Bickerton escaped with only shock and some broken fingers. To aid his recovery, he was invited to stay with another test pilot, Captain Cuthbert 'Turps' Orde, and his wife, Lady Eileen, youngest daughter of the fourth Duke of Wellington, at 'Brook House' in Woodbridge. A portraitist by profession, in a later decade and another war Orde would become well known as the artist commissioned to draw many of the pilots of the Battle of Britain, and his first portrait of Bickerton, dated 15 December 1918, prefigures those pencil sketches in both its intimacy and immediacy. During his convalescence, Bickerton was also introduced to Irene Lawley, the 29-year-old heiress to Escrick Park in Yorkshire. Writing to Irene in May 1918, the matchmaking Lady Eileen stated that 'we've got a Perfect Person for you here. He is the second nicest man there is. He's got every conceivable merit … he would do splendidly and I shall be deeply disappointed if you don't meet him.'[1] Although Eileen's schemes came to nothing – Irene eventually married Colin Forbes Adam of the Indian Civil Service – the two did meet and formed an extraordinarily strong and loving friendship. Over the coming decades, they exchanged letters sometimes once or twice a week, and their correspondence provides the clearest picture of Bickerton's life throughout this period. One other outcome of the meeting with the Ordes was that the explorer was renamed. Following the example set by the artist and his wife, from this point forwards, all but his family and oldest friends would know him simply as 'Bill'.

With the end of hostilities, the question facing Bickerton was the same question that faced millions of other unemployed veterans worldwide: how should he occupy himself in peacetime? In 1911, he had been called a 'first rate engineer, and a scientific one at that';[2] more importantly, having qualified as a specialist in aeronautics, he could claim quite reasonably to be one of a very small and select band, possessing expertise in a field occupied by few others. With hindsight, it is also possible to see that in 1911 he had been standing on the threshold of a world in which such talents would be called upon with an ever-increasing urgency. But four years of war had seen to it that those skills had been widely disseminated and many who had followed in his footsteps had overtaken him in terms of their practical application. Combat and his own high jinks had also come close to destroying two of the most essential tools of his trade – his hands. In the previous three years, both thumbs had been all but severed, a little finger had been blown off and other fingers had been broken. He would remain interested in mechanical matters for the rest of his life, but the inevitable reduction in his manual dexterity meant that there was no immediate likelihood of his being able to pursue a career in engineering. Nonetheless, as the long-dead Ninnis had observed, inactivity was anathema to him and there could be no question of his remaining idle for long.

In contrast to his multiple physical injuries, mentally Bickerton seems to have ended the war in something approximating rude health. A medical board that was convened some two and a half months after his wounding over Houthulst stated that he had 'not yet recovered from nervous disturbance'[3] but later army examiners could find no signs of continuing psychological problems. On 15 March 1918, six months after his wounding, his doctor reported that he 'Sleeps well, no dreams, no tremors, anxieties or headaches, enjoys flying, memory and vitality normal',[4] and confirmed that Bickerton was fit for duty: hardly a report haunted by the spectre of shell shock or repressed trauma. In the lives of many veterans, the legacy of their wartime experiences could be most readily identified in their inability to pick up the threads of their peacetime existence. Four years of mud, blood and mayhem had incapacitated them for the stability and fundamental mundaneness of civilian life. Seemingly, no changes of a comparable gravity had been wrought in Bickerton's character. Even before enlisting, he had been remarkable for his lack of predictability, for his insistence upon placing himself in situations of danger, excitement and uncertainty. In the postwar world his predilections remained unaltered. Two years in Antarctica had demanded courage, fortitude and stoicism; the war had merely honed these characteristics further. Now, as peace descended on war-ravaged Europe, he simply sought another arena in which they might be further exercised, and once again he turned towards the globe's least-frequented tracts.

For his next destination, Bickerton chose East Africa. Unfortunately, none of his diaries or letters survive from this period and snippets of information in his later writings provide the only evidence upon which to speculate regarding his activities. Travelling through the region in the early 1930s, he kept a diary of his journey from Cape Town to Cairo, and in this diary, he makes frequent reference to his previous acquaintances, primarily in the British Protectorate of Nyasaland.* Of Blantyre, the Protectorate's commercial capital, he commented that 'I didn't recognise any of it till I saw the Court House, there was one street then, now there are lots all with names.'[5] Other entries make it clear that he was familiar with many of the government officials and farmers: he reminisced with John Scott, a resident of Blantyre for thirty years, 'talked to Murray, whom I knew before' and 'met Saunders again'. In a letter to Irene Forbes Adam, he also commented that the death of his friend Count Stanislaus Steblecki had robbed him of any desire ever again to reside in the Protectorate.

Sometimes referred to as 'The Land of the Lake' – Nyasa is the Bantu word for 'broad water' – Nyasaland lies in the basin of Lake Nyasa and its outlet river, the Shire. Although as long as the British mainland, it boasts only 36,000 square miles of habitable territory, much of it dominated by spectacular mountain scenery, which Bickerton found 'inspiring'. But the Protectorate was

---

* Modern Malawi.

far from wealthy: it lacked the rich mineral deposits of neighbouring Rhodesia and achieved little more than subsistence with
its staple crops of cotton, tobacco and tea. It also suffered from
low wages and high emigration as its menfolk sought employment in the farms and mines of its wealthier neighbours. The
communications infrastructure was poor and its railway network both woefully inadequate and prone to exorbitant rates
for the movement of freight. If, therefore, Africa as a whole
was looked upon with aversion by most Britons, who thought
it dangerous and unprofitable, then Nyasaland might be seen as
exemplifying the worst of the continent's features and, by 1929,
its European population numbered less than 2,000. On the other
hand, its lack of appeal to the majority of would-be investors
and colonists might well have made it attractive to someone of
Bickerton's peculiar bent. In the absence of an established cadre
of colonial administrators, many of Britain's African colonies
became dependent for their development upon stray adventurers
and missionaries, men driven either by a lust for excitement and
exploration or by religious zeal. The authorities also revealed
a pronounced inclination towards military veterans. If, then,
Bickerton lacked any evangelical drive, in many other respects
he could be seen as an ideal candidate for the colonisation of
Africa, a tool to enable the colonial government to lay the foundations for a long-term and remunerative future.

Although at least one friend later referred to him as exploring in Africa, it is, perhaps, more likely that it was here that
Bickerton first turned his hand to farming, an occupation that
he would experiment with twice again, in very different parts of
the world. Most European farmers in Nyasaland concentrated on
capital-intensive, flue-cured tobacco, and between 1917 and 1937,
tobacco constituted the Protectorate's chief export. Given the
prevalence of tobacco in the area he knew best, it seems probable
that he would have owned or run a tobacco plantation, though
tea and cotton are also possibilities. In the postwar economic climate, however, conditions were far from ideal; many estates went

bankrupt and the likelihood of a farming novice like Bickerton being able to succeed when far more experienced agriculturalists were failing in such large numbers was small indeed.

Whether as explorer or farmer, Bickerton was the fourth AAE veteran to try settling in Africa in the postwar years: Cecil Madigan worked in the Sudan during 1920; Frank Wild turned his hand to cotton-planting in Nyasaland between 1920 and 1921; and Percy Gray emigrated to Natal in 1922. Although there is no real proof that any members of this Antarctic quartet met in Africa, Bickerton and Gray did stay in touch for a while, Bickerton even providing a brief foreword to the Antarctic letters that his erstwhile cabin-mate hoped to publish. That Wild and Bickerton, who were certainly on friendly terms, should also choose, independently, to take up residence in the same small, backward African protectorate at exactly the same time seems almost incredible. Even if their decisions were made without reference to each other, the tiny size and close-knit nature of the expat community practically guaranteed their meeting. Wild and his cotton-planting partner, Dr James McIlroy of the *Endurance*, returned to England in 1921 to join Shackleton's *Quest* expedition to Antarctica. Whether because of worsening economic conditions or his insatiable wanderlust, Bickerton also decided to abandon the blue strip of Lake Nyasa and its crown of mountain peaks. By 1922, he was staying with the Ordes among the clutter and canvases of their Paris apartment. It was here that Orde painted his first large-scale portrait of the explorer, showing him seated in a log cabin, gazing directly out at the viewer, sleeves rolled for action. The scowl on the sitter's face, however, belies the prevailing atmosphere in the studio, where amateur theatricals and high-spirited tomfoolery were the order of the day. The picture would be shown at the Alpine Club Gallery in Savile Row between 25 March and 7 April 1925, but by then, Bickerton had moved on to his next adventure, heading this time for altogether colder climes.

* * *

This INDENTURE made the 24th day of April between Joseph Keefe of Humbermouth, Bay of Islands, Newfoundland ... and Francis Howard Bickerton of Black Duck, Stephenville Crossing, Newfoundland ... WITNESSETH that in consideration of the sum of eleven hundred dollars ... the vendor as beneficial owner hereby grants to the purchaser all that piece and parcel of land abutted and abounded as follows ...*

This masterpiece of arcane legalese confirms that, by mid-1925, Bickerton had become the legal owner of a 160-acre farm near Black Duck, some 7 miles north of Stephenville Crossing on the craggy and precipitous western coast of Newfoundland.

At a glance, it might appear that he had deliberately chosen to move between extremes, just as he had once stepped from the equatorial forests of Cocos Island to the frigid wastes of Antarctica. Nyasaland was land-locked and subject to pre-rainy season conditions so oppressive that the white settlers knew them as 'the suicide season'. Newfoundland, on the other hand, boasts a 6,000-mile long coastline indented with innumerable bays and fjords, is covered with dense conifer forests and is clad in snow and ice for long months each year. For all their apparent dissimilarity, however, these two outposts of the British Empire shared a number of common features. Both were remote, poor and sparsely populated; even more important for Bickerton, they each offered an atmosphere in which the spirit of early colonialism lived on. In Newfoundland's tiny communities, strung out along a coastline longer than Ireland's, self-reliance, independence and hardihood were the character traits not only most admired but also most essential to survival.

His move also indicates that, despite his reputation for being a tardy and reluctant letter-writer – McLean thought him 'not a good correspondent'[6] and Madigan went so far as to send an ultimatum threatening to sever all links unless he

---

* Punctuation has been adjusted for clarity.

improved – Bickerton had made some effort to stay in contact with members of the small and close-knit circle of Antarctic veterans. In 1923, a handful of British settlers had established themselves at Black Duck with the intention of enjoying what they viewed as an Arcadian lifestyle, offering ample opportunities not only for farming but also for hunting and fishing. They were led by Victor Campbell, who, as a petty officer on the *Terra Nova*, had commanded the Northern Base Party on Scott's final expedition. Having visited Newfoundland with the Royal Navy in the last years of the nineteenth century, Campbell had become so enamoured of the countryside that he decided to retire there after the war. According to one resident who knew Bickerton during this period, 'It was probably through Captain Campbell that Mr Bickerton got the urge to acquire land also; which he did… . He built a comfortable home but seemed a more retiring sort of person than … the Campbells so he did not entertain visitors as they did.'[7]

On first arriving in Newfoundland, Bickerton stayed with Campbell at Black Duck, spending his time becoming acquainted with other members of the 'colony' and touring the area in search of a patch of land on which to build a homestead. The site he eventually selected was on Harry's Brook, 3 miles to the east of Black Duck.

The area as a whole might have seemed unprepossessing to any but a hardened adventurer, thick, almost primeval woods being interspersed with dank, fly-infested marshland, often hot in summer and bitterly cold in winter. Bickerton's childhood guardian, Dr Fox, had a pronounced taste for clearing woodland and heather, and for designing and constructing log cabins on and around Dartmoor. Bickerton now followed his uncle's example, clearing a space on the banks of Harry's Brook and building his own single-storied, wide-verandahed log cabin. The cabin was small, probably consisting of no more than two or three rooms, but it contained, as well as essentials, a gramophone and a ukulele for entertainment, just as Dr Fox's had been furnished with a piano. To all intents and purposes, Bickerton now became a self-reliant backwoodsman, the food that he caught, shot and grew on his own land being only occasionally supplemented by tins purchased at nearby Stephenville Crossing.

Another visitor to Black Duck during the summer of 1925 was the young Charles Ritchie, diarist, future career diplomat and celebrated lover of the novelist Elizabeth Bowen, who spent a month labouring for an English couple named du Plat Taylor. His account of his first meeting with Bickerton presages Vita Sackville-West's description of the explorer: 'In the evening Mr B. came to supper. He is an Englishman, a "remittance man": his family in England pay him a certain amount each month to stay away. He lives in a dishevelled house near here with a local girl whom he may have married. He is good company, talks a lot and drinks a lot. He has a bald head on top, curly ringlets about his ears, flashing dark eyes, and looks like a pirate. He has been all over the world and is a wanderer.'[8] Ritchie may have been letting his imagination run away with him. The 'local girl' was probably Beatrice Messervey, Bickerton's housekeeper rather than his mistress, and the suggestion that he was paid 'to stay away' from England does not stand up to scrutiny, as he was financially self-sufficient and on good terms with his family. Alternatively, the diarist may have been repeating gossip overheard at the du Plat Taylors' home.

If the piratical-looking Bickerton represented the adrenalin-fuelled and adventurous side of colonialism, then the du Plat Taylors epitomised its zealous and evangelical alter ego, and their opposing philosophies led to mutual suspicion. Ritchie found that his hosts were 'quite feudal in their outlook'[9] and that they disapproved of at least some of their neighbour's more 'modern' ideas, particularly his liberal, even admiring, attitude towards Americans. On Saturday 25 July, he noted: 'Bickerton here for lunch[.] He is a highly intelligent man and said of Americans that while he was thinking out something indefinable slowly they would suddenly express it in a word or 2. Thus as he said appearing to have great insight (v.true).'[10] This sympathy with other nationalities was characteristic of Bickerton. Although he sometimes remarked on how he felt a stranger in foreign lands and 'would so love to hear my own true language and know the restfulness that can go with it',[11] his journals and letters are devoid of any of the 'mother country' condescension exhibited by Percy Gray and attributed to Frank Wild.

On 26 July, Ritchie was allowed a holiday and he chose to join Bickerton and Campbell as they surveyed the neighbourhood, travelling 'up stream in canoes exploring. The scenery was topping green and luxuriant alders rapids of light sparkling water and vistas of … country so far away… . It is rather a lark for me to be exploring with a man who was on Scott's expedition.'[12] On this and similar excursions, Bickerton found that 'the freedom was intoxicating' and 'the canoe, so buoyant, holding our few essentials' reminded him of 'a boat I used to sail or push about on a pond at 6 years old'.[13]

On another occasion he 'was tying labels on turnips' when a neighbour approached and reported a bear in the vicinity: 'We – he and I – did a hunt the next day, through bogs and woods and up steep places till we had climbed 2,000ft or so and came to rocky places, ponds, cliffs and stunted tree growth. We saw no bear but it was the first time I had been on what they call "the barrens". I took an axe, tea and sugar, salt and a small saucepan and was prepared to stay out for a night if there was anything doing.'[14] Such adventures were, however, only a part of his life in Newfoundland. His motivation for settling there was farming, and while many of the locals looked upon the British settlers as wealthy dilettantes, their sporadic attempts at agriculture being more of a quest for novelty than a genuine means of subsistence, it is clear that, for a time at least, Bickerton took the occupation seriously.

Although the alluvial deposits that enrich the soil around Harry's River are relatively small, and opportunities for agriculture limited, his attempts at cultivation met with some success.

Furthermore, despite the remoteness of the area, he found a ready market for his produce. In 1923, the Newfoundland Power and Paper Company commenced the construction of a new, large-scale pulp and paper mill at Corner Brook. The mill opened in 1925 and rapidly became one of the island's major employers, with the small local population expanding rapidly with the growth of a raw company-town. An increase in the population necessarily meant a burgeoning demand for food and other goods and Bickerton's farm, with its crop of cabbage and root vegetables, was ideally placed to meet the needs of the factory workers. Soon, he had seventy or eighty customers and he admitted that 'Selling potatoes was amusing and profitable and so took no time.'[15]

But he found the life a lonely one and welcomed interruptions, whether for exploration or sport. Newfoundland's west coast generally, and Bay St George in particular, are noted for their fishing, and in the twenties, 10lb salmon were common. Bickerton was both a keen fisherman himself and happy to play host to others. Victor Campbell did not keep a personal diary but he did maintain game and fishing records and these contain various references to catches at 'Bickerton's'.[16] Adventurous anglers from further afield also brought some additional income, as well as welcome company, and Bickerton hoped to 'keep my small guest house doing its job, instead of having the dynamite drying on its floor as at present'.[17] One guest was Cuthbert Orde, who, during his three-week stay, completed a sketch in oils of his friend, choosing to depict him in front of a luxuriant crop of cabbages. When Turps left for home, having grown tired of an unvarying diet of salmon,[18] Bickerton accompanied him. It would prove to be the first in a series of fleeting visits to England and would mark the beginning of a curiously schizophrenic existence in which the untamed wildernesses of Newfoundland and the febrile atmosphere of London in the 'roaring twenties' each exerted a powerful influence over the explorer.

During his first visit, the BBC invited Bickerton to make a radio broadcast, and on Thursday 17 March 1927, he read a paper entitled, simply and somewhat inaccurately, 'The Australian Antarctic Expedition'. Although still in its infancy, the Corporation had already made a number of forays into the realms of Polar exploration. Appropriately enough, Frank Wild had been the first 'Heroic Age' explorer to recount his experiences over the airwaves, reading his 'Incidents and Adventures in the Antarctic' on 1 June 1923. The subject must have proved popular because, over the next four years, another six Antarctic broadcasts had been made: by Louis Bernacchi of the *Southern Cross* and *Discovery* expeditions, Herbert Ponting of the *Terra Nova* and Leonard Hussey of the *Endurance*.

When his turn came, Bickerton chose to concentrate on some of the seldom-considered aspects of Antarctic exploration: he spoke of the problems faced when washing and cooking; of the atmosphere in the hut; and of the entertainment that the explorers created for themselves. Most importantly of all, he outlined how 'the difficulties overcome brought a certain sense of achievement and venture'.[19] In conclusion, he offered one of his few attempts at analysis of the benefits of exploration: 'People sometimes say, Well, how extraordinary, but what is the good of it all? One can answer that by talking of the scientific results, but to many people that is not a wholly satisfactory reply. But if travels are reasonably made, the traveller brings back something which can help the imagination and add romance to those who cannot travel. So if this has interested anyone, then that interest has in some degree justified the expedition.'[20] Overall, he seems to have taken the broadcast seriously: humorous, self-mocking, fast-paced and full of incident, it bears the hallmarks of having been carefully crafted to suit the likely tastes of its intended audience.

It was not uncommon for the colonists of Black Duck to vacate their log cabins for portions of the year and by February 1928 Bickerton was in England again, dividing his time between his uncle's house in Plymouth and rooms at the Royal Air Force Club on Piccadilly. Taking the opportunity to enjoy pastimes unavailable in western Newfoundland, he played squash and golf during the day and spent his evenings with the Ordes who, with Irene Forbes Adam, were now firmly established as his most intimate friends. By virtue of their position as artists and of Eileen's aristocratic lineage, the Ordes played an active part in fashionable society, wining, dining and dancing in all the best venues and mixing with London's literary and artistic elite. Exchanging his plaid shirt for white tie and tailcoat, Bickerton joined them, and on 19 February, they introduced him to the novelist and former suffragette, Stella Benson.

Described by Vera Brittain as 'delicate, witch-like, remote' with 'penetrating blue eyes and the chill whisper of a voice that her deafness gave her',[21] Benson appears to have been almost bowled over by this apparition from a different world. Over the coming weeks, she and Bickerton met regularly in company with the Ordes, often playing poker until the early hours and listening to 'heartrending blues songs' from across the Atlantic. Soon, Benson felt that she had identified the inner man lurking beneath the hardened, scarred veteran of so many adventures: 'He is intelligently – even subtly – interested in people – an unusual thing for such a man of action – besides going about hunting risks, he hunts understanding of people and new aspects of people. People, in fact, are more to him than a kind of by-product of a life of exploration and battle.'[22]

Despondent over her childlessness and trapped in an unhappy marriage – she feared that her literary friends found her diplomat husband, 'Shaemas', dull – Benson quickly began to weave for herself a romantic idyll in which Bickerton was to play, more or less, her Prince Charming. He was, she opined, 'so exactly what the human intelligent Man was supposed in the beginning to be – a rare success, in fact, on the part of God'.[23] There appears to have been some flirtatiousness, possibly encouraged by the Ordes, who revelled in the freer atmosphere of the postwar

period, and Bickerton certainly opened up sufficiently to share
with her some of his Antarctic anecdotes. But if he found her
company pleasant and easy, Benson was beginning to conjure
fantasies of which he knew nothing or believed to be mere fal-
lalery designed to pass the time. In fact, for most of the twenties,
Bickerton seems to have had eyes for no one but Irene Forbes
Adam. Irene had married in 1920 but this had done little to
curb her increasingly passionate friendship with the explorer.
Although they appear not to have had a physical affair, at times
the emotional intensity of their correspondence was sufficient
for Irene to ask him to burn some of her letters, while he stated
his belief that 'no decent person ought ever to marry anyone
if he couldn't marry you.'[24] The waif-like Benson was not the
woman to threaten such an attachment.

The pleasures of London society may have added to
Bickerton's growing weariness with the primitive life of Black
Duck. While still in Newfoundland, he had admitted that 'My
interests dislike me and always preceed [sic] me, one might as
well try and catch a kangaroo. I'm slightly alarmed, as I think
I recognise something in common here with the majority of
emmigrants [sic], who imagine a change of character or habit
may be made easier, if not automatic, by a change of place.'[25]

These feelings came to a head in April 1928 when he
announced his intention of selling his farm. The immediate
temptation was an offer to join, as second in command, a surveying expedition to Rio de Janeiro, possibly that being funded
by the Chicle Development Company to search for chicle and
gutta-percha. Bickerton wavered. On the one hand, his dwin-
dling cash reserves made the annual salary of £975 seem very
attractive; on the other, he found the idea of three years in Brazil
'a grim prospect'. Eventually he decided against the expedition
but admitted to being 'hanged if I know whether to be glad or
sorry'.[26] Ironically, while he mocked his own indecision, his
sister Dorothea, a woman who, in widowhood, had successfully struggled to bring up three small children, complained

of her 'sense of inferiority to Frank' and bemoaned the 'vague and muddy'[27] nature of her mind when compared with the clarity of his. Clearly, whatever doubts he may have harboured regarding his future course, he did not share them with his most uncritical admirer.

Benson, meanwhile, acknowledged that the prospect of Bickerton's departure for South America 'made me think I minded very much that he should go'.[28] Her relief at the abandonment of the Rio plan, however, was short-lived because on 2 May he left for Newfoundland to 'immediately collect my debts there and clean up and return with moveable property worth moving'.[29] A day earlier, the besotted writer had admitted that 'thoughts of dear Bill towards me are sending my emotional temperature rather high' and, on his departure, she was left 'roaring with tears'. This emotional suscept-ibility had led many of her friends to comment on her fragility; Winifred Holtby had described her as looking 'as though a wind could puff her away'[30] and the repercussions of her infatuation with Bickerton would soon prove the accuracy of this prediction.

But Benson was not the only celebrated novelist to meet the explorer during this visit to England. Bickerton had indulged himself with the purchase of a powerful Bentley motor car, and on the day that Benson described his 'subtle' interest in people, he had driven her and the Ordes down to 'Long Barn', the rambling, low-ceilinged medieval house in which, reputedly, William Caxton had been born. Now, the house belonged to Vita Sackville-West and her husband, Harold Nicolson. Although Bickerton's acquaintance with Vita was short-lived, he made a lasting impression both on her and on her son, Nigel: 'He entered my mother's life very briefly in 1930 [*sic*] ... and I (aged 13) just remember him as a burly, romantic figure who came to Long Barn, our home near Sevenoaks, once or twice, but then vanished from our lives.'[31]

Vita left no mention of Bickerton in her sketchy diary entries for this period, but Nigel later remembered that she 'was much impressed by him, and hoped that one of her two sons might emulate him, but neither of us did'. Two years later, she also decided to use Bickerton as the model for the character of the explorer Leonard Anquetil in her most commercially successful novel, *The Edwardians*. In her 'Author's Note', the novelist mischievously admitted that 'No character in this book is wholly fictitious' and Anquetil's physical appearance matches Bickerton's precisely, even down to the statement that, in certain moods, his features could assume an 'almost diabolic' appearance (even Dorothea had referred to his looks being 'Mephistophelian'[32]): 'He was very dark, even sallow, with two puffs of frizzy black hair standing out from either temple, bright black eyes, and a sword-cut running from chin to ear. A startling face; pocked, moreover, by little blue freckles, where a charge of gunpowder had exploded'.[33] As for his adventures: Anquetil 'had been marooned for a whole winter somewhere near the South Pole in a snow-hut with four companions, one of whom had gone mad'.[34] There are also references to his being connected with both Devon and Oxford, of his love of adventure, of his being seldom in England and of his 'piercing up tropical rivers',[35] just as Bickerton and Mackintosh had done on Cocos Island.

More interesting, however, are the subtler shades of Anquetil's characterisation. He is described as being a loner and as a man whose companions 'knew nothing of him beyond his qualities as a cheerful, resourceful, and reliable companion'.[36] He is also referred to as enjoying the company of children, a trait which Bickerton particularly demonstrated at this period with the children of Irene Forbes Adam, and of 'deep, wise women, with whom he could talk'[37] – a reference, perhaps, to Benson, or to Vita herself. Like Bickerton, 'it was difficult to make him talk of his experiences'[38] and yet, with only a handful of meetings to play with, Vita succeeded where many failed. Although only a small proportion of the novel's 350-odd pages deal explicitly with Anquetil, those pages contain a remarkably astute analysis of Bickerton's character; details contained within the novel's last pages also reveal an extraordinary degree of prescience in forecasting his choices in marriage.

While settling his affairs in Newfoundland, Bickerton expressed a desire to 'see USA or at least one of them', thinking it 'absurd not to'. By September 1928 he was in New York and voicing his intention of 'going to look at some land which has been bought by the people I know well and admire considerably'.[39] The admired purchasers were Cecil Baker, an English financier, and Marion Hollins, US Women's Amateur Golf Champion, three times winner of the Metropolitan Golf Championship and captain of the first US Curtis Cup team. The land was some 600 acres of real estate at Pasatiempo, overlooking the town of Santa Cruz on the Californian coast south of San Francisco.

As well as being a sportswoman par excellence, Hollins, whom Bickerton thought 'Not sylph like but a charming character', was a shrewd businesswoman and self-made millionaire. Now she believed that, with its salubrious climate and extensive views over the Pacific Ocean and of the rolling foothills of the Santa Cruz Mountains, the site that she had found was ideal for a new and exclusive sports complex, to incorporate facilities for golf, tennis, bathing and horse-riding. There would also be a residential development which, with her large experience of real estate, she expected to sell to golfers and non-golfers alike. But to turn her vision into profitable reality, she needed like-minded investors such as Bickerton and Baker. Hollins engaged the eminent British golf-course designer Alister MacKenzie[40] to lay out the course, and the landscape architects the Olmsted brothers to create a plan for the scheme.

In a letter of 9 October 1928, the Olmsteds' representative, George Gibbs, makes reference to meeting 'Mr Bickerton, whom I understood to be a friend of Miss Hollins, and interested in the financial possibilities of the proposed development'.[41] Initially, Bickerton was doubtful about his involvement – he wrote to Stella Benson that he resented a long journey to California with, perhaps, only 'a busted flush at the end of it'[42] – but clearly the landscape and its dramatic views impressed him. Gibbs stated that Bickerton 'wanted to know a little about the possible cost of development and the possible magnitude of the entire undertaking... . He jotted down some figures just as the train was leaving.'[43] Whether it was Gibbs' positive answers to his questions, his enthusiasm for golf or Hollins' salesmanship that most influenced him, Bickerton decided to invest some of his capital in the venture. The Santa Cruz Development Company was formed under Hollins' presidency and, for the first and last time in his life, he became a company director.

It comes as no surprise to find that he soon became dissatisfied with the role of office-bound and silent partner. By the end of October, he was personally representing Hollins on site and had even taken up residence in the main building purchased with the plot. Ground was first broken at Pasatiempo on 12 November 1928 and, as the weeks passed, Bickerton took on an increasingly active role in the development. His remit included at least some responsibility for the routing and staking out of roads, the provision of an adequate water supply for irrigation and the usage of existing buildings. According to legend, a retired English privateer named William Buckle had buried treasure at Pasatiempo but, whether or not a chest of doubloons came to light during the earth-moving operations, Bickerton was confident that the club would yield gold. The estimated value of the real estate lots alone convinced him that 'I shall make a good deal when we begin to sell here.'[44]

Filled with these happy expectations, he made another flying visit to England in December, and again he spent much of his time in the company of the Ordes and their circle, including the lovelorn Stella Benson. While Bickerton had been supervising work in California, she had continued to construct castles in the air. By the time of his return, she had even 'made a great resolve ... to ask Bill to be my lover – on condition that I didn't claw at his freedom at all – and give me a baby'.[45] Perhaps hoping to engineer an opportunity to make this suggestion, on 28 December Benson invited him to a party at the fashionable Gargoyle Club in Soho. With its interiors designed by Matisse, its select membership and its free-and-easy atmosphere, the Gargoyle seemed a perfect, if highly populous, venue for a romantic tryst. But the party was a disaster. Bickerton arrived 'a little tight and got tighter' and quickly succeeded in shattering her illusions. In a 'hard and obstructive mood' he wounded her artistic vanity by calling her books 'damn modern' and she retorted waspishly. A few days later, at another party, he built upon the foundations already laid: 'They turned out the lights – and Bill and Retta came and sat on my feet, (on the sofa) – and Bill deliberately forced me to know he was making love to Retta – he had his hand down inside her clothes, and whenever I shifted a little up the sofa so as not to be obliged to be a 'tangible witness' of this, they pushed up too, on to me – so it must have been sadistic.'[46] Masochistic also, perhaps, on the part of Benson as she elected not to change seats.

At best, Bickerton's behaviour lacked subtlety and sensitivity, but there are a number of possible explanations for it. The first is that it was an exhibition of pique. Earlier in the year, Benson had noted that he had murmured 'plaintively in a veiled way about my lack of expressed feeling'. She, meanwhile, had been savouring the inherent dangerousness of her position: married, but physically and emotionally attracted to another man; more than willing to flirt but refusing to commit. It may be that the nuances of her feeling were simply too subtle for Bickerton and that he resented being toyed with. And yet, his behaviour does not seem to indicate any real indignation at a perceived slight. Benson herself acknowledged that, even when 'tight', he had remained 'gentle and thoughtful'[47] when commenting on her latest story, *The Man Who Missed the Bus*, and that, in the days following the Gargoyle debacle, he had been 'kindly and easy'. Alternatively, although it is unlikely that he had any prescience of her plans for a baby, he may have been all too aware of the complicated emotional web that Benson was beginning to weave and resolved to disillusion her. The third possible, and perhaps most likely, explanation for Bickerton's behaviour is that he was completely ignorant of the intensity of Benson's feelings towards him. In his letters to Irene, he is disarmingly frank about his affairs, revealing all the subtleties of his own emotions. In none of them is there even a passing reference to Benson, implying that he was entirely unaware of the seriousness of her interest in him. Unfortunately, and perhaps unwittingly, in resolving the situation, he delivered a fatal blow to the novelist's fragile self-esteem, leaving her with the conviction that no one could ever again 'want a scratchy thin poor mistress of 37'.[48] Within a few days of the fiasco, Bickerton sailed for America while Benson soon afterwards accompanied her husband on a posting to China, where she devoted herself to campaigning on behalf of the enslaved prostitutes working in the country's legalised brothels. She and Bickerton would never meet again, but she would continue to watch his progress with a melancholy interest.

On his return to California, Bickerton found that his remit was expanding still further. Now it included publicising the work at Pasatiempo, a task which involved him in writing for local newspapers. On 20 February 1929, for example, the *Santa Cruz Evening News* carried an article in which he allowed full play to both his imagination and his enthusiasm for golf:

> Some of the subtleties of Dr. Alexander Mackenzie [*sic*], the architect who designed the course make one smile. The tempting way he offers an open route to the hole for the hero who hopes to drive far and straight, but at the same time provides a safe road for the more modest who are enticed to the hole by a longer but easier route. One hole in particular which presents three possible methods of attack will make it necessary for the player to decide whether he will be a tiger, a

short but accurate lynx or just a rabbit. It is this kind of thing which gives character to a golf course. If one walks to the tee feeling aggressively efficient and looking for difficulties to laugh at, well, there they are and may the player finish with a broad smile and a chest extended with achievement.[49]

As a keen golfer, Bickerton's complimentary remarks on the club's design were almost certainly sincere but, in making them, he of course had an ulterior motive. As well as being an investor in Pasatiempo, soon after publication of the article, he became one of Alister MacKenzie's 'associates'. While the term might ordinarily indicate a loose business connection – in the past, MacKenzie had called Hollins, his employer, an associate – Bickerton's role was sufficiently formalised for his name to be added to the headed notepaper of 'MacKenzie and Egan, Golf Course Architects'. By successfully advertising MacKenzie's talents, therefore, he would maximise dividends from both of his speculations. But, to balance the happy prospect of sharing profits with one of the world's foremost golf architects, association brought with it the burden of coping, on a day-to-day basis, with a particularly difficult business colleague. Many thought MacKenzie cantankerous but Bickerton also found him dilatory and, after only two weeks of association, he admitted that 'the result to date is the loss of a good job for Stanford University ... lost through apathy on Mackenzie's part'.[50] A few days later, he ended another letter with the world-weary statement that 'by the time we next meet I may be full of sorrow and worn out with the minor aggravations incident upon such work as ours',[51] a prediction hardly indicative of a match made in heaven.

In addition to his irascibility, MacKenzie's approach to the job of design and construction was markedly idiosyncratic: 'He makes a little sketch for each green with its hazards and bunkers and traps and instructs his foreman quite fully as to his wishes regarding each one. Then he starts for a trip around the world and later returns to see what the course looks like.'[52] Despite

such difficulties and aggravations, the Olmsteds' correspondence makes it clear that Bickerton possessed a well-developed
understanding of his partner's design principles and golfing
philosophy, and J.F. Dawson, another member of the Olmsteds'
staff, acknowledged that 'between Dr MacKenzie's periodic
trips to California', it was Bickerton who 'handled the work'.
Bickerton, himself, had also noted that 'when Mackenzie is
away I am – in his opinion – quite capable of seeing his plans
are being carried out correctly.'[53] This being the case, it might
reasonably be claimed that he shared a large part of the credit
for making the design and realisation of Pasatiempo such an
overwhelming success.

The club opened to the public on 8 September 1929, amidst
much fanfare. To mark the occasion, Marion Hollins opened
play with Bobby Jones, considered by many to be the father of
modern golf, against Glenna Collett, the US Women's Amateur
Champion, and Cyril Tolley, Britain's Amateur Champion.
Their game was watched by a crowd of some 2,000 spectators,
which included many more golfing greats and celebrities from
other fields. Over the coming years, Pasatiempo would become
a favoured resort for many of Hollins' friends from the sporting
and show business worlds, including the likes of Will Rogers,
Mary Pickford, Walt Disney and Spencer Tracy. Hollins entertained these and other stars at lavish parties held at her house in
the club's grounds, the champagne cocktails and jazz lasting far
into the night. Bickerton had been willing to participate in the
somewhat louche parties hosted by the Ordes in London and,
as director, part-owner and on-site manager of the Santa Cruz
Development Company, there can be little doubt that he also
took part in Hollins' glitzy gatherings.

How comfortable he might have felt mixing with the
Hollywood glitterati is, however, open to doubt. Despite his
liking for Americans, he admitted to often feeling 'so much a
stranger here' and he could display a distinctly satirical turn of
mind when confronted by anyone courting or championing

celebrity. In 1932, while flying in stages down the Nile, he would mock those who championed the idea of a memorial to Gordon of Khartoum, 'Murdered by Dervishes, he died as he lived, Sir, fighting for a great ideal'. He would go on to laugh at the 'expensive red leather embossed loose-leaf ledger' recording the names of 'the impressed and generous. Americans, bless their memorial-loving hearts, give handsomely: £10, 50 dollars, £20. Some day, if someone will bet me, in case I fail, I will travel the States, black clad and white fingered, collecting for a memorial to Earl P. Cinch, the first man to print the printed word in America, and his brother Royal, who made the first piece of paper (since used).'[54] It may be that this sardonic brand of humour accorded ill with the prevailing atmosphere at Pasatiempo. At least one resident[55] remembers his being referred to as 'Lord Bickerton': an affectionate nickname, perhaps, deriving from his accent and manner; or maybe a sarcastic response to what was considered his aloofness and pretended superiority.

Despite these latent discords, by 1931 there were clear indications that Bickerton was giving very serious thought to settling permanently in the United States. As early as September 1928, he had mentioned to Eileen Orde that he was considering the possibility of marriage, and on 6 April 1931, the *San Francisco Examiner* carried an announcement that 'Miss Hope Hollins, daughter of Mr and Mrs Harry B. Hollins Jr of East Islip, L.I. and New York, and Mr Francis Howard Bickerton' were to be married on 30 May. The newspaper went on to state that, after the wedding, 'the couple will reside at Pasatiempo'. Although he had once stated his belief that 25 was the most suitable age for matrimony – being, in his view, 'the best time of a man's life'[56] – war, isolation and, perhaps, Irene's marriage to another man had all conspired to see to it that Bickerton was 42 before his first recorded proposal. Hope, who was Marion's niece, was in her twenties. Their relationship was certainly a sexual one and, according to Cuthbert Orde, it was with Hope that the explorer at last lost his virginity.

Years earlier, when describing his ideal woman to Eileen Orde, Bickerton had stipulated that '1. She must be a good linguist; 2. She must love travelling; 3. She must have blue eyes.'[57] One further characteristic, which he did not enumerate but which was common to all the women with whom he formed strong attachments, was a highly developed independence of spirit. Despite her sexual freedom, Hope seems to have lacked this independence and Bickerton was certainly frustrated by her reliance upon her parents and by her apparent inability to resist what he saw as their bullying. These views undoubtedly caused friction in his relations with Hope's parents, and at first, Harry Hollins refused his consent to the match. He relented, but arguments over the date ensued and Bickerton, while he looked 'forward immensely to living with Hope', vowed 'not to be eaten up by this family and to marry only one member of it'.[58] For a while, it seemed that all the problems and disagreements had been resolved, but then, almost exactly one month later, the *San Francisco Examiner* carried another headline: 'Troth Cancelled by Hope Hollins and British Flyer'.[59] Although Bickerton declined to explain the causes of the split to the newspaper reporters, in the days following, he did write to Irene Forbes Adam to outline the circumstances. After proposing, he had remained in California while Hope stayed in New York; to bridge the gap, he had written 'letters and letters in every vein and let my imagination run free with passion. I overdid it. I was a fool, she was young and got frightened, then with fear and help she saw all manner of meaning in other words and actions of mine, which was never really there. It was broken off and I have had no chance to clear it up. I know I couldn't now, because we are both so hurt.'[60]

On a brief visit to England from China, Stella Benson, who continued forlornly to follow Bickerton's progress, shared with her diary her version of the story as it was being disseminated by Cuthbert Orde. She reported that the offending letters were 'extremely sadistic', 'talking about love-tortures and "beating her insensible"' and that, in addition to these billets-doux,

Bickerton had written other 'dreadful letters against the girl – fulminating with insults'.[61] In fact, although he was clearly angered by what he saw as Hope's impetuosity, Bickerton's surviving letters are far more self-accusatory than critical of her. Writing in May, he stated that 'My glimpse of a happiness such as I have long imagined and hoped for has gone out' and admitted that 'The fault is mine I suppose if there is fault.'[62] The people he considered most responsible, however, were Hope's parents, whom he thought both 'stupid' and 'puritanical', and he bemoaned the fact that Hope and he 'could have been so happy for many years if only left alone and encouraged'.[63]

In relating the story, Benson accused Bickerton of sadism, treachery, insanity, ingratitude, stupidity, sexual naivety and even homosexuality. And all of these crimes she attributed to a man whom, only a short time previously, she had described as the epitome of 'intelligent Man', one whose company left her feeling 'like one of those hot chocolate dishes encased in cream'.[64] Having herself been reduced to near-hysteria by his rejection of her advances, she also accused him of being an adventurer in the Don Juan mould, obsessed with sexual conquest. In fact, far from being the depraved and arrogant Mr Hyde-like figure conjured by Benson, it is clear that Bickerton was left depressed and demoralised by the affair. He feared becoming 'distrustful, cynical and dull' and began to doubt his own character: 'I got so worried over all this I doubted my decency and went to a doctor and showed him my returned letters and told him the entire story to the minutest amorous details. He said I was perfectly normal and had only done as any sane passionate man would and he was prepared to back his opinions by getting in consultation various medical heads of depart[ments] in universities and other prominent people.'[65]

These feelings of self-doubt and anxiety would continue to plague him for months to come. The impact on Hope is more difficult to gauge but, in spite of the fact that she had herself invited her parents' involvement, she expressed dissatisfaction both at their high-handed actions and at the termination of her engagement. Rumours of a tragic love affair clung to her for the rest of her life and she would eventually die a spinster. In the short term, others, too, frowned on the actions of the Hollins family. Cecil Baker, the English banker who had done so much to support the Pasatiempo development, sided with Bickerton and even offered to foreclose on the club's mortgage – an offer Bickerton declined.

The events of May 1931 undoubtedly constituted a watershed in Bickerton's life. Initially, he hoped to win over Marion Hollins, but his attempts came to nothing and, siding with her family, she persisted in thinking him 'no person to be associated with in business'.[66] Eventually, he resigned, or was sacked, from the board of the Santa Cruz Development Company and left California under a cloud. The affair also had a negative impact on his increasingly troubled finances. By the time of his departure, the company was sinking deeper and deeper into the prevailing financial quagmire; Hollins herself acknowledged that the project had been started 'at a time when business conditions of the country were good, but as soon as our plans were completed the entire picture had changed'.[67] The success of the club as a business venture was almost wholly dependent upon the ability to sell its land for residential development; profits from the golf course itself were almost incidental. But, after the Wall Street Crash, those who had been expected to buy land were either too concerned with the collapse of the stock market to listen to such proposals or else no longer able to afford them. Investors found that their much-needed cash had become irre-trievable, while creditors were left to pursue the increasingly impecunious Hollins as best they might. As for Bickerton, for the foreseeable future, his money remained locked in the rolling landscape of Pasatiempo, as unobtainable as the fabled treasure of William Buckle.

By the end of 1931, he was back in London and again resident at the Royal Air Force Club. There are signs, however, that even before the catastrophe of May 1931, his thoughts had been turning towards the wild places of the Earth and to his earlier adventures. First, he accepted an invitation to join the prestigious Antarctic Club, its membership being 'restricted to members of British Expeditions which have been engaged primarily in exploration work within the Antarctic Circle'.[68] Then, in April 1931, he had written to the RGS in London, 'under the impression that the members of the Land Party of the Australian Antarctic Expedition of 1911 to 14 were presented with some commemorating medal by the Society.... the point of this letter is to let you know that I have never received any medal and was a member of the Main Base Party for two years. Needless to say, it would give me great pleasure to have any medal given by the Society, and I am rather ashamed of myself for not having brought this matter up before.'[69] The medal referred to was the RGS's Special Antarctic Medal but, as the Society's Secretary explained, while the medal had been awarded to the men of Scott's and Shackleton's expeditions, it had never been presented to the veterans of the AAE.

Soon after his return to Britain, Bickerton also wrote to Douglas Mawson who, on his British, Australian and New Zealand Antarctic Research Expedition of 1929–31, had visited the AAE huts at Cape Denison and photographed the remnants of the air-tractor, still anchored to the ice: 'I saw in the *London Daily Telegraph* a picture of the old aeroplane or remains of it – taken outside the hut at Commonwealth Bay. Have you written any description of your visit because if so I would awfully like to read it, as I can't talk to you about it. I wonder how long before the mast fell that we tended so dutifully[?]'[70] In his reply, Mawson confirmed that 'the remains of your old bus were still protruding from the ice', but admitted that 'There was less of it remaining when we departed, for various members ... of the party took away small pieces as curiosities.'[71]

Bickerton's years in civilisation had brought him nothing but financial loss and emotional turmoil. It was time to return to

the wildernesses in which he thrived. Two years later, returning
from his next adventure, he would bump into Mawson on board
the SS *Strathnaver* as it sailed from Port Said for London. Writing
to his wife, Paquita, the Australian summarised Bickerton's
recent experiences: 'after giving up his farm in Newfoundland,
Bickerton put money into a new golf links and club in California
– they just about got it ready for big business when the financial
slump hung them up – he may or may not get his money out of
it when times improve.'[72] Although any disagreements between
the two men had long since been resolved, it is perhaps not surprising that Bickerton told only a part of his story and that he
concealed the true cause of his departure from California. Had
he been relating it to Madigan or to Ninnis, with whom he had
once 'got very confidential and swapped ... affaires de coeur',[73]
he might have told an altogether different tale.

Ten

From Cape to Cairo

*The would-be shikari has a great longing for the three great attractions
of Big Game; firstly, travel and exploration, secondly, hunting, and
thirdly, collecting*

Major H.C. Maydon, *Big Game Shooting in Africa*

Bickerton's depression continued throughout the remainder of
1931 and the beginning of 1932. Irene Forbes Adam remained
his loyal confidante and he told her that 'if God gave me a choice
of what I would have happen to me, I should ask that he made it
possible for me to fall in love again.'[1] However he also expressed
his determination 'not to be damaged by this mess but somehow
get the better for it'.[2] In the short term, he needed employment,
but in England the economic climate of 1932 was no more promising than in the States and it was unlikely that an ex-explorer,
ex-flyer, ex-cabbage-farmer, ex-business-manager would be
able to find any work commensurate with his age and peculiar
experience. In telling the story of a man who 'got into his car
in Hampstead and started driving to the bank to cash a cheque'
and who, a week later, '"came to" sitting in a café in Tangiers'
Bickerton wondered, 'Why can't great things like this happen

to us?'[3] Shortly after asking the question, he was approached by a man named Cecil Hanbury, whose family he had first met at Castle Malwood during the war. Hanbury came with a proposal which, if not quite the 'great thing' that Bickerton dreamed of, did at least offer foreign travel, a salary and, most importantly, distraction.

Hanbury's 17-year-old son, Tom, just up from Eton, had fallen in love. Only his father's last-minute dash to Gretna Green and a frantic trawl through the town's guesthouses had foiled Tom's plans for a runaway marriage. In the hope that separation would cure him of his precocious attachment, Hanbury proposed to send his son on a nine-month expedition intended to incorporate as many new experiences and foreign scenes as possible: a veritable whirligig of adventure to distract a lovelorn boy. He now required a guide, mentor and chaperone. Somewhat ironically, given his recent experiences, the role was offered to Bickerton. All his expenses would be paid and, in addition, he would receive a handsome allowance of £700 a year. Bickerton agreed.

The expedition would begin in April, sailing for New York on the *Berengaria*, before heading towards the Canadian Rockies. After some grizzly-bear hunting in the mountains, it would then cross to Cape Town, with the intention of proceeding by rail, road and air the 4,500 miles to Cairo, stopping periodically to hunt whatever game presented itself. The party would consist of three: Bickerton, Tom and one of Tom's Eton friends, William 'Hen' Rhodes-Moorhouse. Hen was the son of Will Rhodes-Moorhouse, the first RFC flyer to win the Victoria Cross, and already the boy had demonstrated a desire to follow in his father's footsteps. Even before leaving school, he had won his pilot's 'ticket', thereby earning the sobriquet of the 'Flying Etonian'. Over the coming months, Bickerton would become increasingly grateful for Hen's company, as it provided a pleasing counterbalance to the resentment and ill humour displayed by Tom. In the meantime, there were tickets to purchase, routes to determine and kit to source.

At Southampton Bickerton was introduced to Hen's mother, Linda. Her vitality and enthusiasm impressed him immediately and, in truth, her intrepidity equalled her late husband's. In 1912, Will, Linda and a reporter named Ledeboer had flown a Breguet biplane from Douai in northern France to England. They became the first trio to achieve this feat, and astonishingly, all survived their spectacular crash-landing near Romney Marsh. Will had been mortally wounded in April 1915, while undertaking a lone bombing raid on the German-held railway junction at Courtrai, and Linda had then devoted herself to bringing up their infant son. If Bickerton warmed to Hen's spirited and independent mother, she thought him 'an extremely nice person, and full of resource' and believed that a trip in his company must be considered 'a chance not to be missed'.[4] But there was little enough time now to develop the friendship.

Having reached New York, the party crossed to California and then into British Columbia, shooting a few bear and canoeing down the mighty Fraser River, before heading eastwards again to look at Niagara Falls. No passenger steamers plied the route between New York and Cape Town so, instead, Bickerton chartered cabins on a cargo vessel named the SS *West Cawthorn*. Their month-long voyage passed without incident and, after a brief stay in the exclusive Mount Nelson Hotel, they caught the train from Cape Town to Bulawayo. Most of the African rail network had been developed to link the previously inaccessible interior to the coastal ports, facilitating the export of Africa's bulk commodities while, at the same time, opening up the African markets for European manufactured goods. But the railway also made passenger travel far easier than it had ever been, and Bickerton and the boys were able to continue their journey in relative comfort in the company of farmers, soldiers and government officials. Arrival in Bulawayo was to mark the real beginning of their adventure.

This was the 'golden age' of the African safari, a time when many considered big-game hunting to be the finest test not only of a man's skill as stalker and marksman but also of his hardihood, determination and self-control. If the decision was taken to hunt dangerous game on foot – elephant, rhinoceros, buffalo and the big cats – then courage might be added to the list of determinants. Land grants to veterans and a massive increase in population since the war had resulted in a significant reduction in game, but there were still plenty of herds to be found, although in some cases the habitats had changed, often from the open veldt to scrub and forest.

Rather than undertake a traditional safari, when a white hunter would be accompanied by a veritable army of native trackers, guides and servants, all travelling on foot, Bickerton decided they would attempt one of the newfangled 'motorised safaris'. The increased availability of tough and reliable motor transport in the postwar period had led to a massive increase in the number of roads in Africa, making the continent as a whole far more accessible. Outside the cities, however, few of the roads were tarred and many would become completely impassable during the rainy season. This meant that, while the use of a motor vehicle might result in the loss of some of the exoticism of the earlier safaris, it still entailed some degree of risk, as well as demanding an independent spirit and a willingness to attempt the local languages, Swahili and Chinyanja in particular. Proceeding gradually northwards towards Cairo, where they planned to rendezvous with the Hanburys and Hen's mother, Bickerton and the boys would camp some nights and, on others, use the various hotels and primitive rest houses that had sprung up all along the routes most commonly used by the colonial couriers and officials.

In compliance with this plan, Bickerton decided to buy a Ford lorry to carry his party from Bulawayo to Nairobi. Fords were by far the most popular choice of vehicle for such work, with a reputation second to none for rugged reliability. Only a few years before, four had been salvaged from a three-month-old wreck at the bottom of Mombasa's Kilindini Harbour and, after cleaning, they had gone on to give splendid service on the veldt. Since the vehicles were held in such high regard, with anecdotal evidence of this kind to bolster their reputation, discounts proved difficult to obtain and it was only after 'hours of delay, negotiation and irritation' that a new half-ton pick-up was purchased. For all its newly acquired mobility, however, Bickerton's party was not travelling light: besides the nineteen main packages, trunks and cases, a bewildering assortment of smaller parcels and bags must be stowed, unpacked and restowed before they could finally get under way. The journey was uneventful and the road fair. Nevertheless, with regular stops to change drivers and the care they needed to exercise to prevent damage to the overloaded springs, it took the best part of 15 hours to reach Salisbury.* They arrived at 3 a.m. and the day ended amid complex negotiations with a deaf lodging-house keeper who seemed 'mixed between the meaning of yes and no'.

The next morning, 17 August 1932, they began to explore the town. Bickerton found it 'very American to look at with square angles to all streets and concrete buildings with showy fronts.... But as usual no trees in the main streets, though on the water part of the town the designing is more pleasant and the streets are vastly broad with grass and trees.... There are no buildings of modern design and anything handy in the way of a house seems to satisfy both the business man and the householder. Many people pass through here and in prosperous times there must have been much gaiety.'[5] The peaceful atmosphere was deceptive. Only a few years earlier, the immigration of unskilled labourers had given rise to savage faction-fights among workers fearful of a labour surplus, and now the economic impacts of the Depression were being felt all over East Africa, threatening further civil unrest.

---

* Modern Harare.

They prolonged their stay for a week, meeting the Governor and five or six 'agreeable and helpful people', including a man whose cartographic leanings seemed likely to prove highly beneficial to their expedition: 'By extraordinary fortune I find a man who has been over our road in the last 3 months and moreover is so statistically minded he made a note of every corner, culvert and hill – a most astonishing thing that anyone should do this, and I expect [it] to be quite accurate too. I made a pile of notes, maps and information of all that may concern us between here and Nairobi and it seems quite a formidable book.'[6]

On leaving Salisbury, it took them a day and a half to cover the 250 miles to Tete in Portuguese East Africa,* over roads which were, for a large part of the way, 'bloody' and often little more than a series of potholes and dried-up wheel ruts. The countryside was impressive, consisting of 'large hills of granite smoothed and rounded by some ice age',[7] but Tete failed to live up to expectations. Once a centre for the ivory and slave trades, now, except for the hotel's German beer, there was nothing to recommend it to anyone.

On the morning of 25 August, they crossed the Zambezi on a flat-bottomed, steel-sided ferry and entered a landscape that was fly-infested and wretched, its woebegone aspect being further heightened by a collection of 'awful looking baobabs'. With its enormous girth – the tree is nearly as wide as it is tall – its irregular, barbed-wire-like crown and smooth, grey bark, the baobab is always something of a spectacle. But these examples seemed particularly contorted and diseased-looking, and made Bickerton think that 'they would make a good avenue for a hospital for small-pox.'[8] The road improved, however, and they made rapid progress. The only delay occurred when some tsetse flies got into the cab, sending Tom into fits. Comical though the boy's reaction might be, the threat was real enough. With a sting similar to that of the African honeybee, the tsetse introduces

---

*   Modern Mozambique.

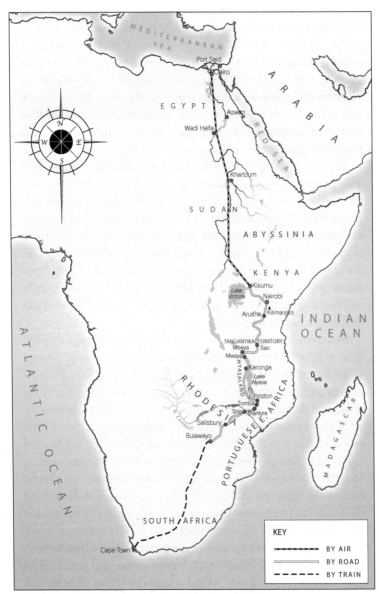

From Cape Town to Cairo, 1932–33.

the trypanosomiasis parasite into the bloodstream. Slowly but surely, it works its way through the arteries and veins of its victim, attacking heart, kidneys and nervous system – quite literally driving the sufferer insane, before coma and death. Humans and domestic animals were equally prone to the disease and whole tracts of land were left uninhabited. Since wildlife remained immune, these areas then attracted intrepid or foolhardy hunters, unable to resist the lure of virgin game country.

They entered British-controlled Nyasaland at lunchtime and, passing through an increasingly lush landscape of large and impressive hills, reached Blantyre that evening. Ten years had passed since Bickerton had last seen the town and it had changed beyond recognition. Serving as the commercial heart of the Nyasaland highlands, the town had thriven in his absence: then, there had been only one street, now there were many, crisscrossing in all directions. Their hotel even boasted electric light and baths with plugs, though the evidences of civilisation did not stretch to running water.

Bickerton intended to start their safari in the Kasungu district, west of Lake Nyasa, but wanted to find a man who knew the area and who, as well as acting as a guide, might be able to provide a lorry and camping gear for a few weeks' hunting. Many on safari paid professional white hunters to guide them and provide all the equipment, beaters, skinners, gun-bearers and domestic servants, but this expedition was to be altogether less formal – and significantly cheaper. The individual recommended to Bickerton was called Alexandre, the owner of a tobacco plantation on the outskirts of Blantyre. The Crash that was destroying the economies of North America and Europe had also devastated East Africa's: coffee alone had lost nearly half its value and many crops were now proving more expensive to produce than to buy. Despite reduced incomes, most Africans were still expected to pay taxes (which had not fallen) and many white farmers had large debts to service. This being the case, Alexandre proved willing to sell his services, leaving his plantation in the hands of his workers. He agreed that Kasungu was the place to go, but believed that while there should be plenty of elephant, their tusks were unlikely to be very large. Negotiations were quickly completed and it was decided that Alexandre would meet the rest of the party at Dedza in a week's time. Once they arrived there, their safari would begin in earnest.

On 30 August, Tom, Hen and Bickerton set out for Zomba, the administrative capital of Nyasaland. The Governor resided there, and it was to him that they must apply for their hunting licences. A personal interview was essential, as Bickerton wanted to request an exception to the usual licensing rules. Various licences were available, at different prices and valid for different periods. Having considered the options and the time available to them for their hunting, he wished to obtain fourteen-day licences of the kind often purchased for wives and children. Moreover, he required two for each member of the party, instead of the usual one, and he wanted them to run back-to-back. To his surprise, he found that he not only managed to persuade the Governor to look upon their request sympathetically, but also to undertake a full review of the licence laws. The only disadvantage was that the revised laws would not come into force until 28 September, entailing a delay of a fortnight before the safari could properly begin. Despite this hitch, overall, Bickerton felt pleased with his achievements. Not only had month-long licences been granted, but a respected and knowledgeable guide had been engaged and all other arrangements had been made.

They drove to Dedza on the afternoon of the 3rd, passing, on the way, elephant droppings and footprints as well as baboons and small buck, turkey buzzards and guinea fowl, and a single kudu with its corkscrew horns and welt-like markings across its flank. A number of factors had contributed to a massive reduction of game since the war. The increases in population, the clearing of land and the resulting loss of habitats, the slaughter of 40,000 head to supply the army, and the soldiers' indiscriminate use of military weapons for recreational hunting had all taken their toll.

But here, the abundance of game seemed to bode well for their shoot. Alexandre arrived soon afterwards, the back of his lorry crowded with native guides, gun-bearers and skinners.

To occupy the time before their licences would become available, the next day they decided to drive to the free shooting area between Dedza and Fort Manning, 120 miles west of Lake Nyasa. The road was broad and quite level for much of the way, lined with scrubby trees, and with the mountains in the distance quivering in the heat haze. They spent the night at a house belonging to a friend of Alexandre's and, leaving the trucks there, hiked to the spot chosen for their first camp, a few miles distant. By the standards of the champagne safaris that were becoming so popular with wealthy westerners, with their portable shower-baths and refrigerators, the camp they built was primitive but fit for its purpose. They had folding tables and chairs and, at mealtimes, white tablecloths; their camp beds were protected by jointed frames draped with mosquito nets, but the lavatory was no more sophisticated than a latrine-trench dug a hundred yards or so downwind and made private by a grass screen.

Their routine was quickly established and varied very little. The party rose at about 5 a.m. and had some tea, then they split into pairs. Over the previous week, Bickerton's relations with Tom had become increasingly difficult. He admitted to feeling 'somewhat cramped with T. about, he contributes nothing of course, but doesn't even give the impression of wanting to',[9] and it came as a relief when Alexandre volunteered to partner Tom, while Bickerton accompanied Hen. Usually, they congregated again around 9.30 to 10 a.m. and breakfasted on porridge and eggs bought from the nearest village. During the heat of the day they lounged around, sleeping or reading or writing letters or diaries. At 4 p.m. they had more tea and then hunted again until just after dark. 'The fruit of these expeditions', Bickerton noted, 'has been various.... The lads do most of the shooting of course but we blokes get most of the game. Hen has got a reed buck with horns, and 3 oribi; Tom got a reed buck and has fired about

40 rounds some under the best possible conditions. My best was a reed buck in full flight across me at 100yd, and this evening a good shot at about the same range in a bad light. We have also got some guinea fowl and seen some wart hog, one or two roan, 1 water-buck and a small herd of eland.'[10]

They left the area on 13 September and headed for Fort Manning. Bickerton and Tom sought an interview with the relevant officials to collect the first of their fourteen-day licences, while Hen set off with Alexandre to establish their next camp. The spot they chose was an excellent one, allowing an awning to be slung between some large, shady trees with, here and there, a stringy, laurel-like bush to break the monotony of the grassland. Early next morning, they took their rifles out by moonlight, Hen with Bickerton, Tom with Alexandre. Hen showed that he was learning to stalk and they soon managed to pick up a well-defined elephant trail: 'we came to some broken trees which seemed quite fresh, then while we were going through long grass, we came to a spot where one had been standing quite recently, and at the same moment saw what I thought was smoke but was dust raised by the herd hurrying off. We came out of the long grass to see the last 2 elephants about 90yd from us . . .'[11] Hen was 'absolutely thrilled' but they didn't follow, as the elephants were moving at about four miles an hour and, as they had clearly heard or smelled their pursuers, they would probably keep up that pace for some hours.

Bickerton's main concern at this time was that the boys were firing too many shots, either at the wrong animals or without taking a careful enough aim. In order to reduce the risk of unnecessarily injuring their prey, he devised a point-scoring system that would focus their minds a little better. For an animal brought down and killed with one shot, ten points would be awarded; five points if further stalking and a second shot were required; and ten points would be deducted if an animal was fired at and then lost, whether hit or not. This competition would serve to discourage 'vague firing and possible wounding'.

The local elephants, however, seemed reluctant to help prove the efficacy of the new regime. Here and there, the hunters found fresh spoor, sometimes only five or six hours old, and trees recently pushed over, but the boys had to satisfy themselves with hunting deer of various types. Perhaps they were fortunate. Elephant had killed more hunters and tribespeople than any other animal, buffalo and lion included. Hunting them required skill and nerve, and stopping their steamroller charge could be nigh on impossible. Once enraged, the elephant could show incredible ferocity, using its front knees to crush unwary hunters, and its trunk to bind them and force them on to its tusks. Despite the disappointment, Bickerton found that he was enjoying himself in Hen's company and the weather continued to be marvellous. He thought it 'a delightful climate, cool nights and today just warm enough under our shelter not to wear a coat, and no mosquitoes at all'.[12]

Over the next month, they moved camp three times and, on each occasion, found themselves in different countryside. On 19 September, Bickerton selected 'the most attractive place, a decent distance from the village, water close, and on the edge of the forest with green grass in front'.[13] But, despite early sightings of wart hog, hartebeest, sable and eland, they discovered that, for most of the time, the area was all but devoid of game; day after day passed and they saw nothing but 'dull horse-faced hartebeest'. This scarcity was particularly frustrating because the landscape seemed to offer 'Perfect stalking country' and was 'a delight to look on'. After a disappointing week, they moved to the village of Longwe. Although the new camp proved uncomfortable and unsatisfactory in a number of ways, being extremely dusty and too close to the village and its noises, they hoped for better sport: 'The country for hunting is different again. The River Rusa is nearby and floods during the rains for miles. All this some time flooded land is now dry and flat except for a lot of large anthills mostly with trees on them. On this great plain herds of zebra, hartebeest and roan and reedbuck wander about.'[14] But, for all this plenitude, the shooting proved difficult. The anthills provided cover, but getting to them without being seen was practically impossible and, once alerted to their presence, the herds proved alert and nervous. Everyone felt dissatisfied and, to make matters worse, Alexandre knelt on a thorn, poisoning his knee. If the infection spread, there would be no alternative but to break camp and seek out the nearest hospital. It seemed that the expedition was turning into a disaster.

Fortunately, Alexandre's knee improved and they decided to move towards Chikonsas. On the whole, the hunting here was significantly better and the guides proved to be intelligent and skilled at their jobs. Always willing to acknowledge the talents of the Africans, Bickerton confessed that he thought their system of firing the bush 'most skilfully arranged'. They set fire to the dry grass and scrub and succeeded in trapping a large number of animals in a confined area of unburned country. Everyone did well in the shoot, but Hen outshone them all: 'in the evening he was coming home late and saw a leopard drinking at a waterhole, at about 50yd with its back to him. Fortunately he was carrying his rifle, and immediately shot it in the behind, when it roared across his front and he had a running shot with his second barrel. The beast dropped into long grass, and the boys were all against following it and, though he had hit it, made him leave it and they all arrived in camp rather hot.'[15] The leopards' astonishing speed and secretive, nocturnal habits made shooting them a matter of the merest chance.

The next morning, Hen and Bickerton returned to the spot and, with their rifles at the ready, moved slowly into the scrub. Even severely injured, in the undergrowth the animal would have the advantage, and wounded leopards were notorious for taking cover and then attacking their pursuers. Its attack could be swift and terrible. Leaping at its victim's shoulders, it would seek his throat with its sharp white incisors, while attempting to scoop out his entrails with the powerful motion of its rear claws. The only defence was to kneel on the ground and roll into as tight a ball as possible, protecting face, throat and intestines with arms, elbows and hands. But the cat was dead and they found it lying where it had fallen in the thicket.

The sport ended on 15 October and they parted company with Alexandre, who intended to pass through Dedza on his way home. Bickerton, Tom and Hen continued northwards, passing through the tobacco-producing areas of Lilongwe and Dowa on the way to Mzimba, a journey of about 250 miles. At Mzimba, Bickerton asked about a huge, rocky hill that lay on the horizon and learned that it was Hora Mountain, site of an inter-tribal massacre in 1878. According to an account written by the British Resident, the mission set up by David Livingstone had rather naively attempted to inculcate an understanding of the principles of human freedom among the local tribespeople. The lesson had been taken to heart by the enslaved Ngoni tribe, who had risen in bloody revolt against their oppressors, the Tongas and Tumbukas. The Tongas had escaped but the Tumbukas had been cornered and forced up on to Hora Mountain. During the night, their chief, Baza, had planned his escape while the Ngoni watchfires twinkled on the plain below. Unable to carry his hoard of ivory to safety and, refusing to let it fall into the hands of the Ngoni, Baza had ordered that it be thrown into a deep gorge on the northern side of the mountain. Under cover of darkness, he then slipped through the enemy's cordons and fled, leaving his people to their fate.

At dawn, the Ngoni offered a truce and allowed the Tumbukas to descend the mountain to drink from the springs that bubble at its foot. Once the Tumbukas were away from their rocky fastness, the Ngoni fell on them with rocks, knives and spears, and slaughtered them all. Over the succeeding years, a number of attempts had been made to retrieve Baza's hoard but each had ended in disaster. The bark ropes made by the tribesmen frayed as they came into contact with the jagged rocks around the mouth of the gorge, and while the treasure-hunters were being hauled to safety astride their prizes – some of the tusks were reputed to exceed 9ft in length – the ropes parted and they hurtled to their deaths. Having listened to this story of treachery, bloodshed and hidden treasure, Hen and Tom expressed a wish to see the site and Bickerton agreed.

The next day, by the time the sun grew hot, they were camped in the shade of a large tree at the foot of the mountain, where the Tumbukas had been slaughtered a little over fifty years earlier. About 2 p.m. they began their climb to the summit, accompanied by guides hired in one of the local villages: 'We spent four hours on the hill, and I have reasons to believe we were shown the wrong treasure hole. The natives watched us like cats and were full of the danger of going here and there, and the snakes which waited for us at this place and the other. But it was afterwards that I thought this. The hole we were shown was most unimpressive, but I believed it to be the true one then.'[16] Given his experiences on Cocos Island twenty years earlier, it seems surprising that there is no trace of irony in Bickerton's assertion that 'I can see exactly where the real one should be looked for.' Hen had already stated his rather macabre desire for a skull, which he hoped to locate at the site of the massacre, and perhaps it was this sacrilegious aim that made the guides so watchful; after all, they might be the grandchildren of the skulls' original owners. Perhaps, also, they wanted to preserve the secret of Baza's treasure so that they might themselves benefit at a later date. Continuing his climb through 'an enormous number of broken pots and many human bones', Bickerton noted that 'The view from the top was grand and would have been grander if the bush fires hadn't made so much smoke.' All around, the level plain stretched for miles, undisturbed by any sign of human habitation. The boys rooted about in the undergrowth, hoping for some interesting or ghoulish memento, while Bickerton admired the mountain with its 'wild and sudden shapes which I delight in'.

After an uncomfortably cold and windy night spent in the truck at the foot of Hora, they continued their journey towards

Karonga on the north-west edge of Lake Nyasa. Once again, the
roads were appalling, one stretch of 70 miles taking 9 hours, and
they didn't reach their destination until 22 October. The next
afternoon a favourable wind brushed the surface of the lake
and they loaded the van on to a lake barge, with the intention
of sailing to Mwaya, where they could again pick up the road.
The manoeuvre turned out to be a delicate one. The vessel was
steel-hulled and about 50ft long, with a single, stumpy mast
positioned near the bow. It was also hardly any wider than the
Ford itself, so the margin for error in getting the vehicle up the
ramps and safely aboard seemed slim indeed.

Once the van had been manhandled on to the barge, the
crew adopted a novel method of securing the vehicle, swarming
around it like Lilliputians around the captive Gulliver:

> The natives tying it on in great loose loops of rope round the
> weak parts if allowed. I think it will be all right if there is only
> a little roll, but the whole affair looks most odd and unlike
> a voyage of 30 miles in an open lake subject to winds down
> 400 miles of its length.
>
> Lord, how she rolled. The native idea of tying on the car
> to the barge was to get a very long and very large rope; then
> ten of them shouted and sang as they made a perfectly use-
> less cobweb around everything, regardless of its use for fixing
> purposes, lamps, number plates, handles and brake rods, etc.
> I was terrified when I found how the barge rolled, and was
> thankful when I got some spare rope to deal with by myself.[17]

The instability didn't worry the crew as they used their 15ft poles
to push the boat along at a rate of three miles an hour. They numbered twelve, working in shifts of six 'with song and darkness
and plenty of roll'. In the gloaming, clinging to the shoreline,
it seemed to Bickerton that an upset constantly threatened but
he 'decided to let the crew do whatever they thought fit, as they
knew their job and I would make no comment'. They continued

their slow progress throughout the night; the darkness was complete and the silence unbroken, except for the cry of an animal somewhere inland, the buzz of the insects attracted by the light and the incessant whoosh of the waves on the beach. Lulled by the gentle motion, Bickerton drifted off to sleep and woke to find dawn breaking over the lake. The shore stretched for miles, flat and uninteresting, the monotony of its sands broken only by clumps of reed that rose to chest height and sometimes formed small, dank islets a few feet from the banks. As the sun rose, the rocky prominences of the Livingstone Mountains came into view across the lake, some 25 miles away to the east, 'very steep and sudden'. At about 8 a.m. the wind picked up for the first time and, at last, they could hoist the sail. The unwieldy barge began to move more swiftly through the water and, soon, a roof appeared on the horizon: Mwaya.

'Mwaya is nothing,' Bickerton thought, 'just a name on the map.' But as they approached, a number of villagers put out towards them in dugout canoes, handling them with a skill that won his admiration. The captain ran the barge up on to the gently shelving coast and, as soon as the van had made its jerky way down the ramps, they continued their journey towards Tukuyu, on the very edge of the British-mandated Tanganyika Territory.* The territory had been created in 1919 when, by the terms of the Treaty of Versailles, most of German East Africa passed into British hands. They paused at Tukuyu only long enough to laugh at the 'large fort built by Arabs or by Germans in Arab style for fun' before moving on towards Mbeya, 40 miles to the north and the midway point between Lake Nyasa and Lake Rukwa. After a tedious ride over more bad road, they were lucky to find beds at the hotel, which was crowded with men employed at the nearby gold workings. With the onset of the Depression and Britain's abandonment of the gold standard in 1931, the value of gold had risen dramatically. The exploitation

---

*   Modern Tanzania.

of East Africa's scattered deposits had become big business and soon gold would become Tanganyika's largest export. Everywhere shovels, picks and crowbars lay strewn about, as though the miners simply threw them down before launching themselves into their beds or the bar, which, with the lavatory, formed 'the most evident parts of the hotel'.

They set off towards the Southern Highlands on 27 October. At first the road was abysmal, potholed and tortuous, but gradually it improved and they passed through some fine game country, once the preserve of the German Crown Prince. Around 180 miles from Mbeya and at an altitude of 6,500ft above sea level, Sao was cold and windy. At their hotel they met a gregarious and cheerful man named Bentley, who was travelling with his wife and their friend, Miss van Rynveldt. Since the plans of the two parties tallied, they agreed to continue together. Over the next few days, in company with the 'comic, rather slapdash but victorious Bentley outfit', they motored the 400 or so miles from Sao to Arusha. Descending into the low plain of the River Rhuha, which drew in the sun's rays and formed a strong contrast with bleak Sao, they followed the course of the brown river.

Gradually, the flat, featureless landscape became more populated and they caught glimpses of giraffe, reedbuck, wild pig and a hyena. Bickerton marvelled at the ungainliness of the giraffes' gait, imagining 'the first was lame until I saw they all had an odd clumsy motion'. Travelling in the hours of darkness, every now and then he stopped the van and tried to catch the nocturnal wildlife in the beam of the windscreen-mounted spotlight. Mostly, the startled animals moved too quickly to be followed with the beam but, at least once, they caught a glimpse of a ghost-like cheetah, and once they came across a mob of eight lions lying in the road. Two young animals ambled about in front of the car and none showed any inclination to hurry away; it made, Bickerton thought, 'A fine sight'. He also found himself admiring the beauty of the local tribespeople – members of the Mbulu tribe whose chief, Michaeli, had provided 500 warriors to act as beaters for the Prince of Wales in 1928: 'The natives here are magnificent, tall, most graceful, straight necks, wide eyes, clear and smiling always, I never knew any pure coloured people could be so attractive. When young they wear nothing or a single string of beads. They live in what are practically holes in the ground, generally made on the side of the hill; this I am told was developed because the Masai used to raid them. They are great runners and the District Officer told me two men once ran with a message from Mbulu to Arusha, 87 miles, in 12 hours.'[18]

The Arusha hotel, which they reached on 2 November, proudly advertised on a large hoarding the fact that it stood exactly halfway between Cape Town and Cairo. Situated in the beautiful, lush foothills at the base of the volcanic Mount Muru, for many years the town had enjoyed a 'Wild West' kind of reputation. For all its cosmopolitan atmosphere, however, it had been under British rule since 1918 and, after a late breakfast, they underwent the tedious rigmarole of customs checks prior to entry into Kenya.

The resident Europeans all told Bickerton that the road to Nairobi was too bad to be attempted in a single day. Since his trip was one of pleasure, interspersed with hunting, they suggested a stopover in Namanga just over the Kenyan border. There they would find a decent rest house inside the Masai Reserve, and all manner of animals, including elephant. Before moving on, however, they decided to try a buffalo hunt. In Nyasaland, buffalo were too rare to be shot, but around Arusha the locals looked upon them as vermin. In compliance with this plan, they drove for about 12 miles and found themselves 'on a huge plain with herds of zebra and wildebeeste and small game and secretary birds'. The ground proved flat enough and hard enough for them to drive anywhere and soon the Ford was careering 'alongside the galloping herds... . On one front mudguard sat Hen with a rifle, on the other a man with unpleasant suggestions about him, hair lengthened with sheep's wool and hanging in rolls made up with red ochre and mud, ears hanging down to his shoulders with

metal ornaments in them, a slight beard, long eyelashes and big
eyes, sleepy and dopey looking, something lecherous about the
whole animal ...'[19] Great clouds of dust rose and the air was filled
with the sound of thousands of hooves drumming the earth, the
masses of zebra overtaking each other and confusing the eye with
the dazzling effect of their stripes as they charged. This kind of
activity made the true white hunters despise the amateurishness
of most motorised safaris. But the adventure was drawing to a
close and here they 'saw more game at one time than ever before'.

That night they pitched camp amid scrub and thorn trees,
and Bickerton lay awake, listening to the chorus that began as
darkness closed in: 'crickets continual, frogs not quite so much,
monkeys and birds often, hyenas occasionally, and from time
to time something big moving through the undergrowth'.[20]
Early next morning they split up to hunt in pairs. Bickerton
had impressed on the boys that they must not underestimate
the buffalo. Up to 5ft high at the shoulder, single-minded and
astonishingly belligerent, the 'buff' was an adversary to be reckoned with. Most people chose to hunt it in open country, where
its charge could be seen from a distance. Here, they were in terrain where the animal could ambush the unwary and, having
run down its opponent, bring its meat-hook-like horns to bear
with devastating effect. Moreover, unlike the more stupid rhino,
the buffalo charged with its head raised so that it could watch
its victim until the very last moment before impact. Its charge
could prove nearly unstoppable, with some continuing in full
career despite four or five mortal wounds.

Tom and Bickerton soon found fresh buffalo spoor near the
river and decided to follow it: 'The undergrowth was thick,
visibility about 10yd and audibility 50. Nothing but elephant
could be hunted in such stuff, buffalo are not high enough to
be seen. Twice we got close and heard something big rush off
unseen. We did this – very tiringly – for four hours, saw several animals but no buffalo, and got close to one rhino without
seeing it... . The bush near the river is most tropical, large

trees, huge creepers, some crushing the smaller trees, black monkeys and large-leafed undergrowth; buffalo spoor everywhere.'[21] Back at camp, no one had enjoyed any better success and they decided to return to Arusha and then, after lunch, on to Namanga.

The various pessimistic predictions they had heard regarding the quality of the road soon proved to be well founded. It was appalling: 'The road passed all understanding. It had got so bad in many places people had driven beside the road, then these tracks had got bad and others had been made further afield still. The result being awful, and wherever we were it seemed worse than anywhere else. The dust was immense and we had a following wind just our wretched speed, so travelled in a thick cloud of our own dust, at one time this was so bad we had to stop as we could see nothing. To make it worse, as no draught went through the radiator the water boiled continually and not expecting this, we had no spare water. This went on for two hours.'[22] Eventually, like many others before them, they decided to leave the track altogether and drove instead over steep, rolling downs which, for all their unmade surface, turned out to be less tortuous than the alternative. The cool of the evening came as a relief and the sight of Kilimanjaro's snowy summit made them feel a little less jaded. Tired and filthy, they drove into the Namanga rest house at 8.30 p.m., Bickerton feeling 'too sleepy to undress rapidly, or to keep awake if I undressed slowly'.

The following morning, the strain and discomfort of the previous day's journey had been forgotten after a decent night's sleep. Nothing had been shot in the Masai Reserve for twenty years and game was abundant. As they breakfasted, they heard reports that elephant had been seen in the near vicinity, so they decided to investigate. The temperature remained as hot as it had been the day before and even a relatively brief walk made them sweat but, unusually, the hitherto elusive elephant were exactly where they were supposed to be. Bickerton had expected to see nothing more than 'the line of a back and perhaps flapping ears' but, instead, in an open clearing, four elephant obligingly ambled about in clear view, presenting the spectators with ample opportunities to photograph them. They enjoyed another close encounter the following day when Bickerton was woken by their native guide:

Sumaili woke me at 6 – 'There is an elephant eating close by.' I gave [Bentley] a shake and we went out. The elephant was 100yd from our hut feeding slowly up a small river. We watched him from within 10yd. Mrs B. and Miss van R. and Tom turned up too. The light was bad for photography so we just watched for quarter of an hour, then a native got to windward of him and Sumaili pointed this out to me and said, 'He will become fierce,' so we moved off. Almost immediately he made a noise like a boy learning the bugle and gave a short rush our way and we scattered, two men in blue pyjamas, one in pink, one woman in a quilted blue dressing gown and the other in pyjamas and a dressing jacket. The elephant came through the thick stuff to where we had been standing and stood looking very large with outspread ears; he then walked across our front.[23]

It had been, Bickerton thought, 'A good show'.

After another eight and a half hours of motoring, they reached Nairobi at 5.30 p.m. on 6 November and, that evening, Bickerton toasted their safe arrival in the hotel bar. It had been nearly four months since they had first stepped from the gangplank of the *West Cawthorn* on to the quayside at Cape Town and, in that time, they had covered over 2,500 miles by train, truck and lake barge. Now, the last leg of their journey lay before them.

After a stay of six weeks in Nairobi, a highly anglicised city popular with hunters because of the accessibility of the Serengeti and with others because of its louche reputation, Bickerton, Hen and Tom sold their truck and boarded a seaplane at Kisumu on the north-eastern edge of Lake Victoria. From here they would fly to their final destination: Cairo. Stretched below them, the lake presented a marvellous spectacle. With a surface area of some 27,000 square miles, it is really more of an inland, fresh-water sea and Bickerton enjoyed looking down on the numerous islands dotting its surface, varying from tiny barren rocks to some of a few square miles, covered with trees, and with their own villages and harbours. For three hours the seaplane clung to the water's edge and then turned inland: 'All trees here and get-ting flatter. At first there were high mountains to the west and later to the east, which must be Abyssinia. There seem to be no villages in Northern Uganda, just everlasting forest for hours, and we could see no game. Towards evening, we found the Nile which ran fast over rocky bottom, and the forest opened out fre-quently, about the spot where Uganda, Soudan [*sic*], and Congo meet.'[24] As the hours passed, however, the scenery began to fail in distracting him from the discomfort of his immediate sur-roundings: 'The noise is terrific,' he commented in his diary. 'I didn't use cottonwool at first but it is absolutely necessary, and conversation is impossible.'

After a night spent at Juba, which he thought 'A hell of a place' remarkable only for its 'Mosquitoes and heat', they continued to follow the Nile northwards. The river grew ever wider and more distorted, 'a thing of endless curves and very little progres-sion', and the discomfort of the flight was partly compensated for by the sight of a herd of elephant, which the noise and low altitude of the aeroplane caused to stampede: 'I saw lots of other game after this, mostly hippos and a few more elephants. The Nile here is wide and getting wider still, the ground flat, trees up to a mile or two of the river, then long grass, then swamp, then papyrus, then water.'[25] Here and there, little islands might be seen and on some of them stood a few huts. It seemed a dreary spot for human habitation, surrounded by acres of morass and large clumps of papyrus, through which watery lanes ran from island to island. Bickerton wondered what could have induced

people to live in such a wilderness and guessed that it might be
fear of the Abyssinian slave-traders who used to raid the district.
As the aeroplane skimmed the surface, sometimes only 100ft
above the water, the startled wildlife fled: 'Crocodiles splashed
into the Nile as we passed,' he observed, and 'immense flocks of
birds went into confusion.'[26]

At Khartoum they exchanged their seaplane for a wheeled
model of advanced antiquity, with 'the engines tied on anywhere
and a tail which looks ready to go off on its own'. Temporarily
leaving the river as it diverged westwards, they flew over a monstrous expanse of desert, 'Like flying over a calm sea of weak tea'
and marked only by the web of tracks leading to and from desert
wells. The vast stretches of sandy, barren wilderness revolted
Bickerton, and his fertile imagination began to turn over plans
for their reclamation, including a scheme along the lines of that
first mooted by the Frenchman François Roudaire, in the 1870s:
'some thought of water, and then it is green anywhere apparently in the desert. Why shouldn't the Sahara be made a sea, and
then have the granaries of Europe round its shores?'[27]

Two more nights were spent near Khartoum and at Wadi
Halfa and then they began the approach to Cairo. Notes were
occasionally passed down the cabin, drawing attention to sites
of particular interest: the Island of Philos, the Temple of Huron
and Luxor, with its 'temples and grey ruins round a swimming
pool, and two large monuments in a field, green irrigated square
and precise'. At last, the pyramids came into view: '"Forty centuries," Napoleon said to his soldiers, when they fought near the
Pyramids, "look down upon you." I wonder if he thought we
should look down on the forty centuries in a hundred years from
then.'[28] Bickerton resolved to visit the Pharaohs' tombs over the
next few days but first he must brace himself for 'Passports, bag-
gage, Customs'.

Eleven

Movies and Marriage

I am a part of all that I have met;
Yet all experience is an arch wherethrough
Gleams that untravelled world, whose margin fades
For ever and for ever when I move.

Alfred, Lord Tennyson, *Ulysses*[1]

Although the African safari had succeeded in diverting Bickerton's mind from the Hollins debacle, his mood remained gloomy. Of course, most recently, his despondency and dissatisfaction had been due, in part at least, to Tom's presence. Bickerton usually sympathised with young people and he admitted to feeling 'awfully sorry'[2] for the lovelorn swain, but there could be no denying that the boy's presence had effectively spoiled the pleasure of his companions.

There were, however, other, more deeply rooted, causes for his depression. With the conclusion of another adventure, he was becoming painfully aware of the passage of time, of his failure to find a permanent or comfortable niche for himself. Since his early twenties, he had never spent more than two or three years in pursuit of the same goal, or even in the same occupation: treasure hunting had given place to Antarctic exploration; exploration to soldiering and flying; flying to farming and business. His own inclinations or pressure of circumstances had caused him to abandon each activity and now, as he entered his forty-fifth year, his future path remained as uncertain as at any time in his life. In the early days, his comparative wealth had made occupation a choice rather than a necessity but his cash reserves were not inexhaustible and his speculations had tended rather to deplete than to increase them. Constantly on the lookout for investments, during the late twenties he had considered putting money into a variety of projects, often of a mechanical nature, and ranging from fire extinguishers to Philo Farnsworth's electrical television. Bickerton thought the latter speculation 'looks like being a great payer'[3] but so far he had seen no return on his investments and employment was no longer merely a means of vanquishing his habitual boredom and impatience with inactivity.

In recent years, he had also begun to question whether his lust for new challenges was beginning to wane. As early as 1928, having refused the Brazilian Survey Expedition, he had wondered 'whether I am not getting soft in body and will and letting beds, books, food and philandering have too much attention'.[4] More recently, during his overnight stay at Wadi Halfa, he had noted in his diary: 'I don't want to be in a desert alone in an air mail, eating cold lunches. I want a warmed, curtained, quietly lit room, with a big fire, all wood; and a big bed, all warm; after a bath, soft, slewshy and scented; to warm a naked back by the fire, and plunge between sheets, creep between the arms of gentle sleep, into a heart-resting oblivion.'[5] It was a mood far removed from that which he had experienced at the end of the AAE, nearly twenty years earlier, and which had given rise to Percy Gray's comment on his friend's love of the explorer's life. Despite these doubts, however, Bickerton admitted that, when his companions were sympathetic, he continued to enjoy fresh adventures. If Hen had been his sole companion on the safari, the two of them might have continued their journey from Nairobi by driving through the desert and, on reaching Cairo, the presence of Linda Rhodes-Moorhouse soon had him waxing enthusiastic at the prospect of accompanying the adventurous widow to Petra. This last plan was defeated only by his obligations to the Hanburys, who intended to sail from Port Said to Europe on the SS *Strathnaver*.

He also continued to turn over in his mind the possibility of other enterprises, even ones which would lead him back to the African deserts that he found so unappealing. One such was the prospect of sailing on the massive lake at Aswan to study opportunities for the exploitation of the desert's latent fruitfulness: 'I shall study irrigation on a large scale, and hire a sail boat. We shall have to take a Primus stove, as there is no wood; have to take water too. Water in Africa may be bad, if natives live upstream. Seven million people have been polluting 2,000 miles of this river for 4,000 years at least, so we will take water.'[6] For the time being, however, he must once again answer the question that faced him at the conclusion of each of his adventures: what next?

In the period immediately following his return from Africa in February 1933, Bickerton devoted his time to seeking employment and to an activity which his hitherto peripatetic existence had rendered all but impossible: the consolidation of friendships. Unable to justify the expense of maintaining rooms at the RAF Club, he took a flat in Whitelands House on the King's Road, but much of his time was spent with Irene's family at Escrick Park and with the Ordes. The artists' bohemian lifestyle had been curtailed by Eileen's having fallen a victim to multiple sclerosis; now wheelchair-bound and a prey to uncontrollable twitches and shakes, she remained as outspoken and amusing as ever, but Bickerton found that his visits to their house made him 'feel like crying'.[7] Perhaps through his membership of the Antarctic Club, he also established contact with other Antarctic veterans – most notably Joe Stenhouse, who had taken over command of the *Aurora* from Aeneas Mackintosh during the *Endurance* expedition and who had subsequently married Mackintosh's widow, Gladys. Most importantly of all, he cemented his friendship with Linda and Hen Rhodes-Moorhouse. Linda owned a house overlooking Constantine Bay in Cornwall, a home designed to help its visitors 'shed the worries and perplexities of civilisation',[8] and Bickerton became a regular guest, fishing, swimming and sailing along the rugged coastline. If he entertained any hopes of becoming more than a friend to Linda, he was to be disappointed. While she enjoyed the company of strong-minded and adventurous men in the mould of her late husband, she kept aspiring lovers at arm's length. She did, however, encourage romance among her friends and, as a matchmaker, she was to succeed where others had failed.

During the summer of 1935, Lady Joan Chetwynd-Talbot, the granddaughter of the twentieth Earl of Shrewsbury and sister of the twenty-first, was a guest at Constantine Bay. Slim, with a sensitive and slightly aquiline face, Lady Joan was humorous, down-to-earth and constitutionally drawn towards people with unconventional backgrounds, individuals who, like Bickerton, stood apart from the commonalty. Impatient of the constraints normally imposed on girls of her class, she had also demonstrated her independence by taking a job in London, as an assistant to the celebrated interior designer Syrie Maugham, and by renting a flat with Didi Ryle, Linda's niece. Despite the disparity in their ages – Bickerton was twenty-two years her senior – Joan was strongly attracted to the explorer, perhaps finding in him an antidote to her more conventional and less experienced suitors. He was rather more reticent. In the aftermath of his affair with Hope Hollins he had repeatedly stated his hope that he might again fall in love, but his Californian experiences made him feel that the age difference might prove an insurmountable barrier. A lesser obstacle was his dislike of the name Joan, but this was overcome by their agreement that he should be allowed to call her Jane instead, much to the confusion of their mutual friends. The two continued to frequent Linda's house and, at last, persuaded by a combination of Joan's obvious indifference to the age gap and by his hostess's determined advocacy, Bickerton proposed and was accepted.

While Bickerton enjoyed the company of intelligent and experienced women near his own age – including Vita Sackville-West, Marion Hollins and Linda Rhodes-Moorhouse – with the exception of Irene Forbes Adam, physically and emotionally he appears most often to have been attracted to younger women. Both Hope Hollins and Lady Joan were more than twenty years his junior but the attraction was clearly mutual. That his romances were with representatives of society's upper echelons on both sides of the Atlantic is less surprising. With some degree of financial self-sufficiency, Marlborough-educated, made eligible for lionisation by his Antarctic experience, the associate of knighted explorers such as Mawson and Shackleton and, perhaps, also possessed of his father's social facility, it is unremarkable that Bickerton was welcomed into society drawing rooms. His friendship with the Ordes, doyens of the cocktail-fuelled and self-consciously decadent arts scene of postwar London, had also given him entrée into both fashionable and artistic circles.

A few years earlier, Vita Sackville-West had concluded her novel *The Edwardians* by marrying off Leonard Anquetil to her youthful and patrician heroine, Viola. In thus consummating the fictional union, the novelist was prescient in more ways than one. Not only does Anquetil's fiancée bear a striking resemblance to Lady Joan in terms of age, independence and aristocratic background, but the explorer himself is 48 when he marries, exactly the same age as Bickerton at the time of his nuptials. The marriage was solemnised on 27 May 1937 at St Nicolas's Church in Cranleigh, with Cuthbert Orde acting as Bickerton's best man. Despite the groom's unconventional background, the Shrewsbury family approved the match – the Earl gave his sister away and later admitted to getting on 'pretty famously'[9] with his new brother-in-law. Another guest, whose presence raised eyebrows in some quarters, was Irene Forbes Adam, whose long and passionate friendship with the explorer had made her an object of some suspicion – at least to Linda, who saw the bride as one of her particular protégées. But, whatever suspicions Joan's friends may have entertained, Irene would remain firmly within Bickerton's inner circle.

On the subject of financial security, Joan's well-wishers had fewer reasons for doubt. As Britain staggered from beneath the shadow of the Great Depression, fresh opportunities had begun to open up, particularly to those who demonstrated a willingness to turn their hands to new things. It seems to have been shortly before his first meeting with Joan that Bickerton had taken advantage of just such an opportunity, in the world of professional cinematography.

The move was not, perhaps, quite as surprising as it might appear at first glance. Bickerton had taken photographs on his Cocos Island expedition, in the Antarctic and in Africa[10] and, while he had never shown any great inclination to crank the handle of Frank Hurley's Prestwich movie camera on the AAE, his enthusiasm for photography and film-making was an enduring one. As a regular film-goer, he frequently expressed his opinion on the merits of the films he watched, and early in 1932, shortly after his return from California and immediately before his safari, he had even asked Douglas Mawson whether it would be possible to obtain a copy of the AAE films: 'I was wondering if you would let me have a copy of the films of the AAE for my private cinema ... of course it would never be used except for purely private [viewing] nor be copied in part or whole. Would you let me know?'[11]

At around the same time, in 'a very small and cheap movie theatre in some back street' he had watched two masterpieces of European cinema: Josef von Sternberg's *Der Blaue Engel* and René Clair's *Sous les Toits de Paris*. Still smarting from the wounds inflicted by the Hollins family, he had responded enthusiastically to these tales of love, betrayal and sexual jealousy. He thought them both 'most excellent … and both un-Hollywood-like', with photography that was 'soft and gentle instead of hard and glaring' and admitted that 'I haven't enjoyed any movie … so much ever before'.[12] This sensitivity, particularly to lighting and photography, would serve him well over the coming years.

Quite how Bickerton achieved his entrée into the world of British film-making is uncertain but, in the preceding years, he had made a number of contacts in the industry. In particular, during the latter stages of his connection with Pasatiempo, Marion Hollins' guests had included members of the Hollywood elite including Walt Disney, Douglas Fairbanks and Mary Pickford, any of whose names might have opened doors across the Atlantic. These celebrities were, however, the friends of a woman with whose family Bickerton had quarrelled and their loyalties would have been expected to lie with the Hollinses, who lived on their doorstep, rather than with an English adventurer now thousands of miles distant. Another and perhaps more likely advocate was Hurley, who had added to his reputation as an Antarctic cameraman with his work as an official photographer during the First World War and, in the early twenties, with his ground-breaking documentary films about the natives of Papua New Guinea. Not only had Hurley spent time in the English studios, building up contacts and learning about the new technology of the 'talkies', he had also entered into a contract with an English cinema proprietor and film producer named Sir Oswald Stoll. Stoll, in turn, was a business partner of John Argyle, the producer who was to become Bickerton's employer. Argyle's productions, by and large, were distributed by the Associated British Picture Company (ABPC), which often used the lesser studios in and around London, and it was at the studios in Welwyn Garden City that all but one of the five films for which Bickerton received a major credit were made.

By the mid-thirties, the industry generally had shed much of the risqué reputation of its earliest years, but the films on which Bickerton worked were far removed from the glossy and highly polished features made by the Hollywood producers. Even in their highest echelons, British film-makers were little more than poor relations, and any actor or technician who distinguished himself was more likely to seek his fortune in America than to stay at home. In most British studios, employees worked on a jobbing, film-by-film basis without the security of a long-term contract. In such an environment, actors, writers, cameramen and even directors often moved from one role to another to ensure their income. Argyle himself had worked as actor, screenwriter and director before becoming a producer. Only the more senior and recognised roles received a formal credit and it is possible that, prior to 1935, Bickerton fulfilled other, unbilled functions before he received his first credit – for the screenplay of *Happy Days Are Here Again*. Many of Argyle's films revealed the cinema's vaudeville lineage, being hackneyed variations on a melodramatic, musical or romantic theme and often starring music hall performers keen to make the transfer to film. *Happy Days Are Here Again* was a typical example of the genre and its screenplay was no more remarkable than any of its other attributes.

Although Bickerton enjoyed writing, having attempted poems, short stories and newspaper articles, his next job was perhaps altogether better-suited to his peculiar talents and required many of the skills that he had amply demonstrated in the Antarctic and elsewhere, including methodical working and the ability to innovate and improvise. The role was that of film editor. In fact, this was perhaps the closest he had come to utilising his engineering skills since the end of the war and he enjoyed the challenge. His primary responsibility was to prepare the separate film and sound reels for screening. This involved logging the contents of each reel according to the slate numbers on the clapperboards and then synchronising the image of the pre-shot clapperboard with the sound of it snapping shut. This process guaranteed that sounds and images matched throughout the film. The reels would be viewed at lunchtime and then, later on each day, by Bickerton, the director and the producer. Only when shooting had been completed would final editing take place. Soon he was able to tell Irene Forbes Adam that 'I am more than considerably thrilled because I had been imagining that I was rather slow at "cutting" but find that with good organising I am as quick as any.'[13] His confidence seems to have been well placed, because the veteran cinematographer Bryan Langley, who worked with Bickerton at Welwyn, has commented: 'It is obvious to me that he was highly skilled by the way he intercut the many shots of actuality ... with studio scenes.'[14] Despite these skills and his position as one of the senior technicians, however, Bickerton's work required long hours, and his earnings were unlikely to have exceeded £20 per week. But the hours were not too long to prevent him from entering – and winning – the stroke competition for the Deane Mann Challenge Cup at the meeting of the 12th Division Golfing Society at Royal Wimbledon on 12 October 1936. Nor was his pay too small to stop him from wining and dining Joan at such fashionable nightspots as the Florida Club, in company with other representatives of stage and screen.

Although ABPC tended to consider quality an expensive and unnecessary luxury, the films produced under their banner occasionally rose above the mediocre and, while costs were closely controlled – not least by the astute Argyle – they sometimes invested in performances from recognisable actors. One such was the Irish-American Sally O'Neil, who starred in the first film that Bickerton edited, *Kathleen Mavourneen*, released in February 1937. *Kine Weekly* described how 'The Welwyn Studios have been resounding to the strains of Irish folk songs and dances'[15] and called the result 'unpretentious musical romantic melodrama' and 'good fare for simple folk'.[16] Bickerton, however, was altogether less enthusiastic, dismissing it as 'an unimaginative and simple soppy story for sentimental mothers'[17] and the film did little to revive O'Neil's waning star.

Altogether more successful was *The Mutiny of the Elsinore*, starring the future Oscar-winning Hungarian–American actor Paul Lukas.[18] Ostensibly at least, this is also the only film that bears any relation to Bickerton's life and propensities. Released in September 1937, and based on a novel by Jack London, the story is one of nautical derring-do aboard a mutinous ship in the age of sail. It was the only film on which he worked that was given an 'A' certificate, indicating that children under 16 years of age must be accompanied by a parent or guardian, and many of the contemporary reviews focused on the adult nature of its material. *To-Day's Cinema* reported: 'Jack London's story is certainly rip-roaring melodrama, and the patron who requires his film entertainment to be full-blooded will acclaim this one with delight … the stirring maritime backgrounds, the stark characterisations, and the melodramatic punch of the incident leading up to, and involving, the mutiny – these are the things on which John Argyle is entitled to praise, for they comprise the red meat of the entertainment.'[19]

Unusually for a low-budget British film, after its New York premiere, *The Mutiny of the Elsinore* attracted large audiences in America with many film-goers enjoying both its 'red meat' and the maritime atmosphere, which *Kine Weekly* found 'always realistic and convincing'.[20] Bickerton could take some small credit for the achievement of this realism, as it was almost certainly through his good offices that the role of adviser on nautical matters was offered to his friend Joe Stenhouse. As well as lending the film authenticity in details ranging from rigging to sea shanties, Stenhouse's involvement also helped to make the film unique in its genre, boasting not one but two 'Heroic Age' Antarctic explorers among its crew.

Bickerton's next two films could hardly have offered a stronger contrast with *The Mutiny of the Elsinore*, exchanging decks awash with blood for rustic charm and sentimental songs.

Little Dolly Daydream and *My Irish Molly* both starred the diminutive Binkie Stuart, considered by some to be Britain's answer to Shirley Temple. But, while Bickerton thought the second film offered 'some interesting farmyard scenes with all the propper [*sic*] animals' he found Binkie and her entourage rather more trying:

> Binkie Stewart [*sic*] is the star in our picture she is aged 5½. Yesterday I saw the family leaving, Father Stewart with Binkie preceeded [*sic*] by their chauffeur to their car, then Mother Stewart who does Binkie's make up followed by a nurse with a six weeks old baby which Mrs B is still feeding (while at the studio) then a man carrying a bassinette followed by Binkie's 'stand in' & the 'stand in's' mother. Binkie has a dressing room especially built on the set, but there is no lavatory in it & she seems to need one more than I do for instance, and yesterday all was ready but when she was called 'Gone to the telephone' was the answer which was code. So the Director and assistants, 4 camera men, 2 sound men, 4 artists, and 12 electricians, and 1 editor had to stand and wait.[21]

Despite such frustrations and the film's failure to rise above melodramatic mediocrity, *My Irish Molly* did earn a place in cinema history because of its casting of the 17-year-old Irish actress Maureen O'Hara in a supporting role. The following year, O'Hara would achieve fame and fortune in Hollywood playing opposite Charles Laughton in *The Hunchback of Notre Dame* and it was during the shooting of *My Irish Molly* that Laughton visited the studio to offer her the role of Esmeralda.

My Irish Molly proved to be Bickerton's last film. During its making, he had responded to Hitler's annexation of the Sudetenland with the opinion that 'it has been so clearly and cleverly shown to the whole world that Germany is now in the wrong that they will funk starting a really big war and cry off.'[22]

His optimism quickly waned, however, and by the middle of the following year he had joined the Royal Air Force Auxiliary Reserve (later the Volunteer Reserve, or RAFVR). Although this decision must have been taken in response to the growing threat of National Socialism in central Europe, he knew that the chances of his serving in an operational capacity in the event of conflict were remote. Not only had it been two decades since he had last piloted an aeroplane but, in 1939, he was 50 years old. Nevertheless, within a few short months he was not only back in uniform but serving close to the front line.

On 26 September 1939, just over three weeks after Britain's declaration of war on Germany, Bickerton was granted a commission as a pilot officer in the RAFVR's Administrative and Special Duties Branch. Five months later, as the so-called 'phoney war' drew to a close, he was posted to France to join the administrative contingent of the Air Component of the British Expeditionary Force (BEF). When he joined 14 Group in the area around Arras, France was gripped in one of the severest winters experienced in years. But the cold was among the least of his worries. Group Captain Victor Goddard commanded the Air Component's administration wing and he later described the arrangements that he and his staff officers, like Bickerton, inherited:

> This was a nightmare situation. The Army was responsible for supplying all the common needs of the whole of the BEF including some of our more uncommon needs. Pay, rations, petrol, oil, fuel of all kinds ... works services, tentage, quartering, canteens, postal services, billeting, furniture, kitchen equipment, stationery and all kinds of consumable stores – for all those things the squadrons and units of the Air Component attached to an army in the field were to be entirely dependent upon the Army.[23]

Bickerton's role, as a mere pilot officer, was to throw himself into the ensuing chaos and to help to achieve something approximating order and efficiency. With 10,000 men to feed, clothe, accommodate, bathe and pay, and hundreds of aircraft to fuel, arm and repair, the task facing the administrators was colossal. But, just as order was achieved, *blitzkrieg* began. By late May 1940, within three months of Bickerton's arrival in France, the BEF was in full retreat, outnumbered and outwitted by vastly superior German forces. Unfortunately, there are practically no records relating to the work and manoeuvres of the Air Component: all official documents were thrown into Calais harbour during the pell-mell retreat and, while some officers ignored the embargo on personal diaries, Bickerton was not among them. On 17 May, the headquarters staff began its movement towards the Channel ports, many being evacuated from Cherbourg and Boulogne. Most of the staff made their own way, commandeering whatever motor transport they could find, and the one surviving photograph taken of Bickerton at this time shows him apparently supervising the loading of a French civilian lorry.

Victor Goddard later commented that his more-capable staff officers had soon recognised that 'regulations mainly existed to regulate fools' and, with his scant regard for bureaucracy, Bickerton appears to have been numbered among the more capable. Certainly the ability that he demonstrated both in France and in the disbanding of 14 Group on its return to England was recognised by the RAF's higher authorities and, within less than twelve months, he was promoted from pilot officer to flight lieutenant, to squadron leader, and finally to wing commander. For much of the rest of the war, he moved from station to station, sometimes setting up new units, including 9 Group Headquarters near Preston and 82 Group in Belfast, before handing them over to a senior air staff officer when they became fully operational. None of his postings lasted for more than fourteen months but, despite the strain of constant upheavals, his marriage thrived. Since their union, Joan had always sought to stay close to her husband, even choosing to share uncomfortable and dirty lodgings in Welwyn during filming, rather than remain alone in their flat on the King's Road. Now they gave up the flat altogether and she accompanied him in all of his home postings, sometimes hosting tea parties at their digs in order to make the young members of the Women's Auxiliary Air Force feel less homesick. She would later state that this period of constant activity and movement was perhaps the happiest time of their married life, not least because her husband was filled with a sense of purpose and usefulness.

Inevitably, the administrative nature of Bickerton's duties meant that he endured mundane tasks such as chairing 9 Group's Waste Committee and solving the logistical problems involved in ensuring that every man on a 1,000-strong base received an egg for breakfast. But there was also plenty of variety in terms of people and places and these factors helped to counterbalance the depressing news of friends being killed – like Hen Rhodes-Moorhouse, shot down during the Battle of Britain, and Joe Stenhouse, lost while serving with the Royal Navy in the Red Sea. There were also opportunities to display flashes of his old adventurous spirit, particularly when the tide turned in favour of the Allies. By July 1944, he was back in France helping to construct airfields for Allied squadrons raiding German military installations and cities, and taking the opportunity to arrange 'joy rides' for his friends and acquaintances. One such was Cuthbert Orde's son-in-law, Major David MacIndoe. Having served with the Royal Artillery through D-Day and beyond, MacIndoe met Bickerton in Brussels and, as he wrote to his wife, Jane, he was soon being treated to 'Bill's' particular brand of hospitality:

> Darling, your godfather is a *magnificent* man. I can't tell you how much I like him. I turned up at 1230, had lunch, met the CO and Wing Comd (flying) … in the afternoon I went in a Mitchell to Courtrai, and actually steered the aircraft … in the evening I had much whisky (on the Group Captain at

Bill's invitation!), dinner, fine frantic game of shove-ha'penny at which Bill beat me by sound tactics rather than exquisite stroke-production, then beer and further chat and so home to bed. I talked a most awful lot, bummed my load a bit in fact, and Bill listened as if he was really enjoying it. A most excellent man, and himself a most interesting talker...[24]

MacIndoe was somewhat less thrilled when, on a later leave, the 'magnificent' Bickerton offered him a seat on an offensive sortie. Unable to convince his benefactor that he would simply prefer to enjoy his leave among the cafés of the Belgian capital, the battle-weary young officer was saved from a flight over Nazi Germany only by bad weather.[25]

But the adventure was, to all intents and purposes, over. When he left the RAF on 26 August 1945, Bickerton was 56; the limited number of more-senior administrative posts had restricted his promotion beyond the rank of wing commander, but his services were acknowledged by a 'Mention in Despatches' for meritorious conduct and devotion to duty.[26] The postwar years would prove a lean time, offering few opportunities for a veteran of his particular stamp. Inevitably, sudden unemployment came as a shock, and uncertainty and frustration placed a strain upon his marriage, though unhappiness and disagreement were more likely to produce a sullen silence than open discord. An attempt at farming at Cliddesden, near Basingstoke, came to nothing and, in 1947, he eventually accepted a post as assistant manager to a friend's engineering works in London. At the same time, he and his wife purchased the last fourteen years of a 99-year lease on 10 Carlyle Square in Chelsea. In these genteel and bohemian surroundings their neighbours included the novelist Osbert Sitwell, the artist Anthony Devas, and, next door at number eleven, the Colditz escapee Airey Neave. Enjoying some degree of security, Bickerton filled his study with poetry and with books of travel and exploration, and sought to contribute to local life by becoming chairman of the committee for the maintenance of Carlyle Square's communal garden. He and Joan were also frequent guests at 'Ingestre', her brother's home in Shropshire, and, in recognition of Joan's aristocratic lineage and his own military service, they became regular attendees at the royal tea parties at the Palace.

This rather sedate lifestyle was perhaps driven as much by necessity as by desire, because Bickerton had at last become a family man. In May 1943, after two miscarriages, Joan had given birth to their only child, a daughter, whom they named Rosanna. Bickerton had always evinced a deep affection for children and demonstrated an affinity with them. He had been named as god-father on nine occasions but his rootless existence had meant that he attended the christening of only one of his godchildren. His nephews and niece had grown up in his absence, but he had paid regular visits to the sons and daughter of Irene Forbes Adam and, in his many letters to her, he had almost invariably asked to be remembered 'with a kiss'. During the thirties he had also used his editorial skills to help them produce two of their own films: *The Lost Ball* and *Miss Otis Regrets*. He enjoyed thrilling Linda Rhodes-Moorhouse's great-nephews with ghost stories told round a campfire in a Cornish sandpit and shared with his own great-niece tales of his treasure hunt on Cocos Island. Although he had hoped for a son, believing, perhaps, that a boy would be more likely to share his interests, he willingly attempted to imbue his young daughter with his enthusi-asm for challenges and for the odd and unusual. He lectured to her classmates on the mysteries of Antarctica, tormented her with tests in mental arithmetic and, when her own drawing skills proved inadequate to the challenge, even completed her art homework. On another occasion, he dashed home to share with her his excitement at finding an ugli on the stall of a King's Road greengrocer – a rare discovery in ration-weary London.

Bickerton remained active, yachting with his brother-in-law and fishing with friends in Cornwall and County Durham. Rather belatedly, he even taught himself to ride a bicycle and terrified Joan with his precarious circuits around the square. But the years and a lifetime of pipe-smoking were beginning to exact a physical toll. Weight gradually fell away from his previously stocky frame and, early in 1954, he was struck down with pleurisy and pneumonia. Ordered by his physician to convalesce in the country, he took up residence with his family in a small, terraced house in the Welsh seaside village of Borth, on Cardigan Bay. The house, 'Ocean Wave', practically sits on the long, curving, shingle beach and it was here, in mid-August, that he suffered a stroke, which was further complicated by coronary thrombosis and renal failure. He rallied briefly, and in his last conversation with the 11-year-old Rosanna, thanked her for her attentions when he was taken ill. But the combination of ailments quickly proved fatal to the 65-year-old explorer and, on the 21st, his struggles and adventures finally came to a close. Perhaps appropriately for such a wanderer, instead of being buried and his body anchored in the earth, Bickerton was cremated and his ashes scattered in the vicinity of the bay – to be picked up by the coastal breezes and carried out on their last expedition, over the equally restless, rolling ocean.

Although the obvious seriousness of his illness prior to the trip to Wales may have prepared some of Bickerton's friends for the worst, the suddenness of his death came close to overwhelming his wife. In the postwar years their marriage had passed through a difficult period as, approaching old age, Bickerton struggled to find a congenial and remunerative occupation, but uncertainty had at last given way to something approximating security and contentment. Dorothea, who, despite her love for her brother, had remained to some degree on the periphery of his existence, sought to support and assist her widowed sister-in-law, but she could do little to mitigate the devastating impact of the blow.

In the weeks and months following the explorer's death, friends rallied round and one summed up their feelings of loss in an anonymous obituary for *The Times*: 'His loyalty to his friends, his gallantry … and the unembittered courage with which he continued to meet the difficulties of a world which gave little recognition in peace to men of his mould – leave to us who shared in one way or another his various life the memory of a rich, rewarding and abiding spirit.'[27] The same writer also stated that Bickerton 'preserved to the very end the zest and enthusiasm which formerly took him on expeditions of exploration to the then odd and unfamiliar places of the world and gained for him the Polar Medal before the 1914–18 War'. Another obituarist naturally focused upon his involvement with the AAE and upon his leadership of 'the western sledging party which traversed the inland ice sheet of Terre Adelie',[28] and it is natural to look to the Antarctic when considering the influences that shaped his life.

In reviewing the annals of Polar exploration, it is impossible not to believe that Antarctica somehow infects the blood of its explorers; that the continent acts as a magnet, forever drawing them back and making it impossible for them to settle down successfully. This certainly appears to have been the case with men like Shackleton and Wild, but the pull was exerted even upon the dour, rigidly scientific Mawson who, in his account of the AAE, *The Home of the Blizzard*, describes the power of the lure: 'once more a man in the world of men, lulled in the easy repose of routine, and performing the ordinary duties of a workaday world, old emotions awakened, the grand sweet days returned in irresistible glamour, far away "voices" called:

"… from the wilderness, the vast and Godlike spaces,
The stark and sullen solitudes that sentinel the Pole".'[29]

Was Bickerton's insatiable restlessness a product of this same disease? It is easy to believe that, in originally volunteering for the AAE, he might simply have been exorcising the common youthful urge to 'sow his wild oats', to purge himself of the romantic leanings of adolescence before settling down to a more mundane existence. The Antarctic was merely the fashionable arena for such an exercise in the Edwardian world. But, perhaps, once he had been subjected to its influence, the infection took root and a return – or, at least, an attempt at a return – became inevitable and a more humdrum existence impossible. Add to this the impact of the Great War on his psychology. For millions of young men, four years of unmitigated horror permanently disturbed the natural warp and weft of their existence, making a 'normal' life quite impossible.

In addition to these factors, vanity and self-delusion might play a part in a man's choice of career. In the aftermath of Bickerton's rejection of her love, Stella Benson stated her belief that his character as an adventurer was his own creation: 'he has been so noticed for his "[indecipherable] he-man's life" exploring in Africa and the South Pole – getting those interesting scars in the war etc – and also so written up by V. Sackville-West (in the *Edwardians*) – that he now almost worships himself as a romantic adventurer and deliberately lives a romantic he-man's life … he is doing his best, I imagine, to make an artificial life for himself.'[30] Considered in this light, it seems credible that, in conjunction, these influences might have forced Bickerton into a mould which was not his by nature. And yet all the evidence suggests that these factors merely reinforced traits already embedded in his character. Most importantly of all, the date of his trip to Cocos Island – March 1911 – proves that even before the war and his expedition to Antarctica, he was demonstrating a strong desire to reject the trammels of a routine existence. He went to Cocos Island for the fun of it, not for riches. He returned to England in May 1911, and by the end of the following month, he had signed up for Mawson's expedition; two and a half years later, while still awaiting rescue from Cape Denison – and long before his ego could have been inflated by lionisation – he offered his services to Shackleton.

There is ample proof that Bickerton's experience of exploration was not one of unalloyed pleasure and that he sometimes doubted the impulses that drove men into such a life. But the inclination towards adventure was too deeply rooted to be easily overthrown by doubt, danger or discomfort. When trapped in the Antarctic and experiencing some of the worst climatic extremes ever suffered by man, he confided to his diary that 'These present conditions are nearly enough to cure a man of a desire to poke his nose into the odd corners of the earth.'[31] But while such conditions were 'nearly enough' they were never sufficiently strong to overcome his curiosity. Bickerton was not much inclined towards analysis of his own motivations; but there are indications that he was himself puzzled by the origins of his compulsion, that he was 'continually mystified by my desire never to settle down and do not understand it at all'.[32] However, in looking back over his own life, he might, perhaps, have been content to accept the simple explanation offered by the friend who wrote his obituary for *The Times*: that 'Adventure was in his blood and expressed itself in everything he said and did.'[33]

Notes

Introduction

1. Philip Ayres, *Mawson: A Life* (Melbourne, Miegunyah Press, 1999), pp. 95–7.
2. Thor Heyerdahl, *The* Kon-Tiki *Expedition: by raft across the South Seas*, tr. F.H. Lyon (London, HarperCollins, 1950).
3. *The Times*, 30 August 1954.
4. F.H. Bickerton, African Diary, 1932, p. 51.

Chapter One: Of Ice and Treasure

1. Michael L. Turner and David Vaisey, *Oxford Shops and Shopping* (Oxford, Oxford Illustrated Press, 1972), p. 12.
2. Eliza Frances Fox to Agnes Russell, *c.* 1883.
3. F.H. Bickerton, *African Diary*, 1932, p. 58.
4. Dorothea Bussell, *The New Wood Nymph* (London, Stanley Paul & Co., undated), pp. 37–8.
5. Mrs Sally McNally, in conversation with the author.
6. A.L.A. Mackintosh, 'Diary of Events on Treasure Seeking Expedition to Cocos Island', by permission of Mrs Elisabeth Dowler and Mrs Anne Phillips, 6 May 1911.

7. *Ibid.*, 18 April 1911.
8. *Ibid.*, 22 April 1911.
9. *Ibid.*, 28 April 1911.
10. *Ibid.*, 7 May 1911.
11. *Ibid.*
12. *Ibid.*, 9 May 1911.
13. *The Times*, 15 June 1911.
14. *Sphere*, 33 (1908), p. 122.
15. SPRI, MS1618, B.E.S. Ninnis, AAE Diaries, by permission of Mr Allan Mornement, 13 July 1911.
16. MAC, AAE 12/81, Douglas Mawson to F.H. Bickerton, 22 June 1911.
17. E.A Reeves, *Recollections of a Geographer* (London, Seeley, Service & Co., undated), p. 88.
18. SPRI, MS1618, Ninnis, AAE Diaries, 13 July 1911.
19. City & Guilds College, Student Programme, quoted in Adrian Whitworth (ed.), *City & Guilds College: a Centenary History* (London, City & Guilds College, undated), p. 115.
20. *Flight* magazine, 5 August 1911, quoted in Philip Ayres, *Mawson: a Life* (Melbourne, Miegunyah Press, 1999), p. 50.
21. SPRI, MS944/8, Frank Wild to Fred Pinfold, 30 October 1911.
22. SPRI, MS1509, F.H. Bickerton, 'Western Sledging Journey', p. 1.
23. Watkins continued to fly and was again injured in a crash in a Spencer biplane at Brooklands. He attended a Central Flying School (CFS) course on 17 January 1913 but served with the infantry throughout the First World War, and not with the Royal Flying Corps. If he failed the CFS course this might lend some credibility to Mawson's rather belated doubts about his abilities as a pilot.
24. SPRI, MS1509, Bickerton, 'Western Sledging Journey', p. 1.
25. *The Times*, 10 May 1911.

Chapter Two: Tempest-Tossed

1. ML, MSS2893, Percival Gray, 'Antarctic Voyages', 3 December 1911.
2. *Ibid.*
3. SPRI, MS1509, F.H. Bickerton, 'Western Sledging Journey', p. 1.
4. ML, MSS2893, Gray, 'Antarctic Voyages', 9 December 1911.
5. ML, MSS382/2, A.L. McLean, AAE Diaries, undated.
6. SPRI, MS1509, F.H. Bickerton, 'A Log of the Western Journey', 13 January 1913.

7. J.K. Davis, *With the* Aurora *in the Antarctic* (London, Andrew Melrose, 1919), p. 23.
8. Cecil Madigan, AAE Diaries, by permission of Mr D.C. Madigan, 20 December 1911.
9. D.C. Madigan, Vixere Fortes: *a Family Archive* (Kingston, privately printed, 2000), p. 243.
10. MAC, 80AAE, Alec Kennedy, AAE Diaries, 29 January 1911.
11. ML, MSS2893, Gray, 'Antarctic Voyages', 24 January 1912.
12. Douglas Mawson, *The Home of the Blizzard* (abridged 1930, Edinburgh, Birlinn, 2000), p. 41.
13. ML, MSS2893, Gray, 'Antarctic Voyages', 9 January 1912.
14. ML, MSS382/2, McLean, AAE Diaries, 8 January 1912.
15. SPRI, MS1618, B.E.S. Ninnis, AAE Diaries, by permission of Mr Allan Mornement, 13 January 1912.
16. ML, MSS382/2, McLean, AAE Diaries, 14 January 1912.
17. SPRI, MS1509, Bickerton, 'Western Sledging Journey', p. 1.
18. BBC, 2LO-5XX-S.B., F.H. Bickerton, 'Australian Antarctic Expedition', 17 March 1927, p. 1.
19. *Ibid.*

Chapter Three: Terre Adélie

1. BBC, 2LO-5XX-S.B., F.H. Bickerton, 'Australian Antarctic Expedition', p. 1.
2. *Ibid.*
3. Windchill comparisons are taken from: Francis Ashcroft, *Life at the Extremes: the Science of Survival* (London, Flamingo, 2001), p. 152.
4. BBC, 2LO-5XX-S.B., Bickerton, 'Australian Antarctic Expedition', p. 1.
5. Charles F. Laseron, *South With Mawson* (Sydney, Australian Publishing Co., 1947), p. 59.
6. SPRI, MS1509, Bickerton, 'A Log of the Western Journey', 25 December 1912.
7. SPRI, MS1509, Bickerton, 'Western Sledging Journey', p. 1.
8. *Ibid.*, pp. 1–2.
9. *Ibid.*, p. 2.
10. *Ibid.*, p. 3.
11. BBC, 2LO-5XX-S.B., Bickerton, 'Australian Antarctic Expedition', pp. 3–4.

12. F.H. Bickerton to Dorothea Bussell, 31 January 1913.

13. BBC, 2LO-5XX-S.B., Bickerton, 'Australian Antarctic Expedition', p. 2.

14. SPRI, MS1509, Bickerton, 'A Log of the Western Journey', 13 January 1912.

15. SPRI, MS1618, B.E.S. Ninnis, AAE Diaries, by permission of Mr Allan Mornement, 19 March 1912.

16. SPRI, MS1509, Bickerton, 'A Log of the Western Journey', 13 January 1913.

17. *Ibid.*, 9 January 1913.

18. BBC, 2LO-5XX-S.B., Bickerton, 'Australian Antarctic Expedition', p. 3.

19. *Ibid.*

20. SPRI, MS1509, Bickerton, 'Western Sledging Journey', p. 2.

21. SPRI, MS1618, Ninnis, AAE Diaries, 18 April 1912.

22. Bickerton to Dorothea Bussell, 31 January 1913.

23. BBC, 2LO-5XX-S.B., Bickerton, 'Australian Antarctic Expedition', p. 2.

24. SPRI, MS1509, Bickerton, 'Western Sledging Journey', p. 2.

25. *Ibid.*

26. *Ibid.*

27. *Ibid.*, pp. 3–4.

28. *Ibid.*, p. 4.

Chapter Four: This Breezy Hole

1. BBC, 2LO-5XX-S.B., F.H. Bickerton, 'Australian Antarctic Expedition', p. 4.

2. Douglas Mawson, *Antarctic Diaries*, ed. Fred and Eleanor Jacka (Sydney, Unwin Hyman, 1988), p. 81, 13 May 1912.

3. BBC 2LO-5XX-S.B., Bickerton, 'Australian Antarctic Expedition', p. 3.

4. SPRI, MS1618, B.E.S. Ninnis, AAE Diaries, by permission of Mr Allan Mornement, 31 August 1912.

5. ML, MSS382/2, A.L. McLean, AAE Diaries.

6. SPRI, MS1509, F.H. Bickerton, 'A Log of the Western Journey', 11 January 1913.

7. SPRI, MS1618, Ninnis, AAE Diaries, 19 May 1912.

8. ML, MSS382/2, McLean, AAE Diaries, 15 June 1912.

9. Quoted in Charles F. Laseron, *South With Mawson* (Sydney, Australian Publishing Co., 1947), p. 98.

10. BBC, 2LO-5XX-S.B., Bickerton, 'Australian Antarctic Expedition', pp. 2–3.

11. Cecil Madigan, AAE Diaries, by permission of Mr D.C. Madigan, 21 May 1912.

12. SPRI, MS1509, Bickerton, 'A Log of the Western Journey', 23 December 1912.

13. Laseron, *South With Mawson*, p. 13.

14. SPRI, MS1509, Bickerton, 'A Log of the Western Journey', 23 December 1912.

15. *Ibid.*, 11 January 1913.

16. BBC, 2LO-5XX-S.B., Bickerton, 'Australian Antarctic Expedition', p. 2.

17. *Ibid.*

18. Madigan, AAE Diaries, 20 December 1911.

19. ML, MSS382/2, McLean, AAE Diaries, 29 August 1912.

20. SPRI, MS1618, Ninnis, AAE Diaries, 13 October 1912.

21. Laseron, *South With Mawson*, p. 128.

22. ML, MSS 382/2, McLean, AAE Diaries, 21 July 1912.

23. *Ibid.*, 12 August 1912.

24. F.H. Bickerton to Dorothea Bussell, 31 January 1913.

25. SPRI, MS1509, Bickerton, 'A Log of the Western Journey', 11 January 1913.

26. SPRI, MS1509, F.H. Bickerton, 'Western Sledging Journey, p. 4.

27. *Ibid.*, p. 5.

28. BBC, 2LO-5XX-S.B., Bickerton, 'Australian Antarctic Expedition', p. 4.

29. SPRI, MS1509, Bickerton, 'A Log of the Western Journey', 7 December 1912.

30. SPRI, MS1509, Douglas Mawson, 'Instructions to F.H. Bickerton', 9 November 1912.

31. D.C. Madigan, Vixere Fortes: *a Family Archive* (Kingston, privately printed, 2000), p. 301.

32. BBC, 2LO-5XX-S.B., Bickerton, 'Australian Antarctic Expedition', p. 5.

33. Madigan, AAE Diaries, 9 November 1912.

Chapter Five: Westward Ho!

1. SPRI, MS1509, F.H. Bickerton, 'Western Sledging Journey', p. 1.
2. *Ibid.*, p. 3.
3. *Ibid.*, p. 5.
4. *Ibid.*
5. *Ibid.*, pp. 4–5.
6. *Ibid.*, p. 6.
7. *Ibid.*
8. *Ibid.*, p. 7.
9. *Ibid.*
10. ML, MSS2893, Percival Gray, 'Antarctic Voyages', 16 January 1913.
11. SPRI, MS1509, Bickerton, 'Western Sledging Journey', p. 8.
12. SPRI, MS1509, Bickerton, 'A Log of the Western Journey', 4 December 1912.
13. SPRI, MS1509, Bickerton, 'Western Sledging Journey', p. 9.
14. SPRI, MS1509, F.H. Bickerton, 'A Log of the Western Journey', 4 December 1912.
15. *Ibid.*, 5 December 1912.
16. *Ibid.*
17. I am indebted to Dr W.A. Cassidy of the Department of Geological & Planetary Science, University of Pittsburgh, and to Dr Balthasar Indermuehle and Michael Burton of the School of Physics, University of New South Wales, for their analyses of the Adelie Land meteorite.
18. SPRI, MS1509, Bickerton, 'Western Sledging Journey', p. 11.
19. SPRI, MS1509, Bickerton, 'A Log of the Western Journey', 5 December 1912.
20. *Ibid.*, 5 December 1912.
21. *Ibid.*, 6 December 1912.
22. *Ibid.*
23. *Ibid.*, 7 December 1912.
24. *Ibid.*, 8 December 1912.
25. SPRI, MS1509, Bickerton, 'Western Sledging Journey', p. 14.
26. SPRI, MS1509, Bickerton, 'A Log of the Western Journey', 9 December 1912.
27. SPRI, MS1509, Bickerton, 'Western Sledging Journey', p. 15.
28. SPRI, MS1509, Bickerton, 'A Log of the Western Journey', 11 December 1912.
29. SPRI, MS1509, Bickerton, 'Western Sledging Journey', p. 18.

30. ML, MSS2893, Gray, 'Antarctic Voyages', 14 January 1913.
31. SPRI, MS1509, Bickerton, 'A Log of the Western Journey', 20 December 1912.
32. *Ibid*., 23 December 1912.
33. *Ibid*., 25 December 1912.
34. *Ibid*., 26 December 1912.
35. *Ibid*., 28 December 1912.
36. *Ibid*., 29 December 1912.
37. *Ibid*.
38. *Ibid*., 30 December 1912 [*sic*].
39. BBC, 2LO-5XX-S.B., F.H. Bickerton, 'Australian Antarctic Expedition', p. 4.
40. SPRI, MS1509, Bickerton, 'A Log of the Western Journey', 31 December 1912.
41. *Ibid*., 4 January 1913.
42. *Ibid*., 5 January 1913.
43. *Ibid*., 9 January 1913.
44. *Ibid*., 11 January 1913.
45. *Ibid*., 15 January 1913.
46. *Ibid*., 16 January 1913.
47. *Ibid*., 17 January 1913.
48. *Ibid*., undated.

Chapter Six: Hope Deferred

1. ML, MSS2893, Percival Gray, 'Antarctic Voyages', 16 January 1913.
2. *Ibid*., 17 January 1913.
3. Canterbury Museum, Christchurch, MS203, Leslie Whetter to Robert Edgar Waite, 3 March 1913.
4. ML, MSS2893, Gray, 'Antarctic Voyages', 21 January 1913.
5. BBC, 2LO-5XX-S.B., F.H. Bickerton, 'Australian Antarctic Expedition',p. 5.
6. Cecil Madigan to Sir Samuel Way, 31 January 1913, quoted in D.C. Madigan, *Vixere Fortes: a Family Archive* (Kingston, privately printed, 2000), p. 206.
7. F.H. Bickerton to Dorothea Bussell, 31 January 1913.
8. *Ibid*.
9. Dorothea Bussell, *The New Wood Nymph* (London, Stanley Paul & Co., undated), p. 70.

10. F.H. Bickerton to Dorothea Bussell, 31 January 1913.
11. ML, MSS382/2, A.L. McLean, AAE Diaries, 20 January 1913.
12. BBC, 2LO-5XX-S.B., Bickerton, 'Australian Antarctic Expedition', p. 5.
13. ML, MSS382/2, McLean, AAE Diaries, 8 February 1913.
14. BBC, 2LO-5XX-S.B., Bickerton, 'Australian Antarctic Expedition', p. 5.
15. Douglas Mawson, *The Home of the Blizzard* (abridged 1930, Edinburgh, Birlinn, 2000), p. 201.
16. SPRI, MS1509, F.H. Bickerton, 'A Log of the Western Journey', n.d.
17. BBC, 2LO-5XX-S.B., Bickerton, 'Australian Antarctic Expedition', p. 5.
18. *Ibid.*, pp. 5–6.
19. Canterbury Museum, Christchurch, MS203, Leslie Whetter to Robert Edgar Waite, 3 March 1913.
20. ML, MSS384, Walter Hannam, AAE Diaries, 23 January 1913.
21. Cecil Madigan, AAE Diaries, by permission of Mr D.C. Madigan, 13 February 1913.
22. SPRI, MS1618, B.E.S. Ninnis, AAE Diaries, by permission of Mr Allan Mornement, 9 July 1912.
23. *Ibid.*, 27 October 1912.
24. Mawson, *Home of the Blizzard* (1930), p. 315.
25. BBC, 2LO-5XX-S.B., Bickerton, 'Australian Antarctic Expedition', p. 6.
26. F.H. Bickerton to Dorothea Bussell, 31 January 1913.
27. ML, MSS382/2, McLean, AAE Diaries, 28 February 1913.
28. *Ibid.*, 23 February 1913.
29. *Ibid.*, 12 September 1913.
30. Transcribed by Robyn Mundy and reproduced by courtesy of MAC.
31. I am most grateful to Dr Elle Leane of the University of Tasmania for sharing with me her extensive research into the *Adelie Blizzard*.
32. MAC, *Adelie Blizzard*, June 1913.
33. MAC, 28AAE/1, Leslie Whetter to F.H. Bickerton, 17 August 1913.
34. ML, MSS382/2, McLean, AAE Diaries, 17 August 1913.
35. *Ibid.*, 8 June 1913.
36. *Ibid.*
37. CUL, MSS6762-6803, Stella Benson, diary, 23 April 1928.
38. ML, MSS382/2, McLean, AAE Diaries, 11 July 1913.
39. Madigan, AAE Diaries, 8 July 1913.
40. CUL, MSS6762-6803, Stella Benson, diary, 23 April 1928.

41. ML, MSS382/2, McLean, AAE Diaries, 5 August 1913.

42. MAC, MS 28AAE/1 and 29AAE/2, Macquarie Island wireless log.

43. SPRI, MS996/1-2, Douglas Mawson to Professor Bragg, 1 January 1913.

44. BBC, 2LO-5XX-S.B., Bickerton, 'Australian Antarctic Expedition', p. 6.

45. Douglas Mawson, *Antarctic Diaries*, ed. Fred and Eleanor Jacka (Sydney, Unwin Hyman, 1988), pp. 191–2, 26 May 1913.

46. *Ibid.*, p. 192, 6 June 1913.

47. *Ibid.*, p. 200, 5 August 1913.

48. Madigan, AAE Diaries, 30 October 1913.

49. SPRI, MS1509, Bickerton, 'A Log of the Western Journey', 25 December 1912.

50. ML, MSS382/2, McLean, AAE Diaries, 20 August 1913.

51. *Ibid.*, 20 November 1913.

52. *Ibid.*, 9 September 1913.

53. Mawson, *Home of the Blizzard* (1930), p. 330.

54. BBC, 2LO-5XX-S.B., Bickerton, 'Australian Antarctic Expedition', p. 6.

55. ML, MSS2893, Gray, 'Antarctic Voyages', 18 December 1913.

56. *Ibid.*, 21 December 1913.

57. BBC, 2LO-5XX-S.B., Bickerton, 'Australian Antarctic Expedition', p. 6.

Chapter Seven: Endurance

1. SPRI, MS1456/38, Report of a conference of the Royal Geographical Society with Sir Ernest Shackleton, 4 March 1914.

2. Royal Geographical Society of South Australia, Frank Wild to Ellen Augusta James, 28 January 1912.

3. ML, MSS2893, Percival Gray, 'Antarctic Voyages', 24 February 1913.

4. MAC, 29AAE/2AAE, Log of Wireless Transmissions, 8 April 1913.

5. *Morning Post*, 6 February 1914.

6. ML, MSS2893, Gray, 'Antarctic Voyages', 16 January 1914.

7. SPRI, MS1509, F.H. Bickerton, 'A Log of the Western Journey', 11 December 1912.

8. *Ibid.*, 26 December 1912.

9. Douglas Mawson, *The Home of the Blizzard*, 2 vols (London, Heinemann, 1915), vol. 2, p. 6.

10. SPRI, MS1509, F.H. Bickerton, 'Western Sledging Journey', p. 9.

11. SPRI, 1456/64, conversation between Sir Harry Brittain and James Fisher, 20 August 1955.

12. *Ibid*.

13. Hampshire Record Office, George Marston to Hazel Marston, May 1914.

14. ML, MSS 2198/2, Frank Wild, Memoirs, by permission of Mrs Anne Fright, p. 120.

15. SPRI, MS1456/38, Report of a conference of a committee of the RGS with Sir Ernest Shackleton, 4 March 1914.

16. *Ibid*.

17. *Ibid*.

18. SPRI, MS1456/64, conversation between Sir Harry Brittain and James Fisher, 20 August 1955.

19. Edvard Welle-Strand in the *Bergens Aftenblad*, 20 May 1914, translated by Finn R. Jørstad.

20. *The Times*, 28 May 1914.

21. Edvard Welle-Strand in the *Bergens Aftenblad*, 20 May 1914, translated by Finn R. Jørstad.

22. ML, MSS 2198/2, Wild, Memoirs, p. 120.

23. Hampshire Record Office, George Marston to Hazel Marston, May 1914.

24. Members of the ITAE to Joseph Klem, 26 May 1914, reproduced by kind permission of Mr Trygve Norman, Finse 1222 Hotel.

25. SPRI, MS1456/44, Sir Ernest Shackleton to Lady Shackleton, May 1914.

26. Recruitment figures quoted in this chapter are taken from Peter Simkins's excellent study, *Kitchener's Army* (Manchester, Manchester University Press, 1988).

27. Alexander Turnbull Library, Wellington, New Zealand, Thomas Orde-Lees, *Endurance* Diaries, 1914–16.

28. Sir Ernest Shackleton, *South* (London, Robinson, 1999), p. 93.

29. MAC, 175AAE, F.H. Bickerton to Sir Douglas Mawson, undated.

30. NA, ADM1/8407/491, Douglas Mawson to the Secretary of the Admiralty, 21 December 1914.

31. ML, MSS2893, Gray, 'Antarctic Voyages', 9 January 1913.

32. Captain Hugh Bowlby's letter was published in the magazine of Marlborough College, *The Marlburian*, July (?) 1914, p. 121.

33. *Ibid*.

34. F.H. Bickerton to Dorothea Bussell, 31 January 1913.

35. *The Marlburian*, July 1915.

36. Owen Rutter (ed.), *The History of the Seventh (Service) Battalion, The Royal Sussex Regiment* (London, Times Publishing, 1934), p. 43.
37. West Sussex Record Office, MS25001, Ralph Ellis, 'A March with the Infantry'.

Chapter Eight: Air War

1. F.H. Bickerton, African Diary, 1932, p. 56.
2. *Ibid*.
3. IWM, MS P359, Captain Ewart Garland, DFC, diary, 21 July 1916.
4. Patrick Garland, son of Ewart Garland, in a letter to the author, 4 September 2004.
5. IWM, MS P359, Ewart Garland, diary, 15 August 1916 [*sic*].
6. NA, WO339/39605, proceedings of a medical board, 30 August 1916.
7. University of Sydney Archives, Edgeworth David Papers, Series 7, Douglas Mawson to Edgeworth David, 9 September 1916.
8. MAC, 184AAE/6/30.2 (178AAE), A.L. McLean to Douglas Mawson, 6 September 1916.
9. ML, MSS389/2, Item 6, Diary No. 3, Frank Hurley, diaries, by permission of Ms Toni Hurley, 20 November 1916.
10. NA, WO339/39605, medical report, 15 March 1918.
11. NA, AIR1/404/15/231/45, quoted in C.G. Jefford, *Observers and Navigators* (Shrewsbury, Airlife, 2001), p. 28.
12. NA, AIR1/176/15/184/1, 'History of 70 Squadron'.
13. NA, WO339/39605, medical report, 15 March 1918.
14. Bickerton, African Diary, 1932, p. 54.
15. NA, AIR1/1226/204/5/2634, F.H. Bickerton, 'Combats in the Air', 5 August 1917.
16. *Ibid*., 15 August 1917.
17. *Ibid*., 20 August 1917.
18. *Ibid*., 22 August 1917.
19. *Ibid*.
20. Bickerton, African Diary, 1932, p. 52.
21. Bickerton was one of only six men qualified to wear the Polar Medal ribbon on their RFC tunics. The others were Tryggve Gran and Cecil Meares of the *Terra Nova* and Thomas Orde-Lees, Irvine Gaze and L.A. Hooke of the ITAE.
22. Recollections of Captain Cedric N. Jones, *Cross and Cockade Journal*, vol. 1 (1970), no. 3, 53.

23. Captain Clive Franklyn Collett was killed on 23 December 1917, while demonstrating a captured Albatros D-V over the Firth of Forth.

24. NA, AIR1/1226/204/5/2634, Bickerton, 'Combats in the Air', 10 September 1917.

25. *Ibid.*

26. *Ibid.*, 20 September 1917.

27. *Ibid.*

28. *Ibid.*

29. ML, MSS2893, Gray, 'Antarctic Voyages', 14 January 1913.

Chapter Nine: The Restless Heart

1. HUA, DDFA3/6/49, Lady Eileen Orde to Irene Lawley, [May 1918].

2. SPRI, MS1618, B.E.S. Ninnis, AAE Diaries, by permission of Mr Allan Mornement, 13 July 1911.

3. NA, WO339/39605, proceedings of a medical board, 8 December 1917.

4. NA, WO339/39605, medical report, 15 March 1918.

5. F.H. Bickerton, African Diary, 25 August 1932.

6. MAC, 178AAE, A.L. McLean to Douglas Mawson, 11 January 1916.

7. Mrs Jean Messervey (1905–2003), in a letter to the author, March 2003.

8. Charles Ritchie, *An Appetite for Life*, p. 84.

9. *Ibid.*, p. 85.

10. Charles Ritchie, unpublished diary, reproduced by courtesy of Ms Judith Robertson, 25 July 1925.

11. HUA, DDFA3/6/74, F.H. Bickerton to Irene Forbes Adam, 1 April 1931.

12. Charles Ritchie, unpublished diary, 26 July 1925.

13. HUA, DDFA3/6/74, F.H. Bickerton to Irene Forbes Adam, 17 October 1927.

14. *Ibid.*

15. *Ibid.*, 27 May 1928.

16. Centre for Newfoundland Studies, Campbell Papers – 4.01, Victor Campbell, Game Book 1925–28.

17. HUA, DDFA3/6/74, F.H. Bickerton to Irene Forbes Adam, 17 October 1927.

18. Angus MacIndoe, grandson of Cuthbert Orde, in conversation with the author.

19. BBC, 2LO-5XX-S.B., F.H. Bickerton, 'Australian Antarctic Expedition', 17 March 1927, p. 3.
20. *Ibid.*, p. 6.
21. Vera Brittain, *Testament of Friendship* (London, Virago, 1980), p. 172.
22. Cambridge University Library, MSS6762-6803, Stella Benson, diary, 22 April 1928.
23. *Ibid.*, 25 April 1928.
24. HUA, DDFA3/6/74, F.H. Bickerton to Irene Forbes Adam, 1 April 1931.
25. *Ibid.*, 17 October 1927.
26. *Ibid.*, 18 April 1928.
27. Dorothea Bussell, 'Dream Diary', 11 December 1926.
28. Cambridge University Library, MSS6762-6, Stella Benson, diary, 30 April 1928.
29. HUA, DDFA3/6/74, F.H. Bickerton to Irene Forbes Adam, 18 April 1928.
30. Winifred Holtby, *Letters to a Friend*, ed. A. Holtby and J. McWilliam (London, Collins, 1937), p. 454.
31. Nigel Nicholson, in a letter to the author, 14 February 2003.
32. Dorothea Bussell, '*Remarquez que Frank est très mephisto*', note on the back of a photograph, *c.* 1935.
33. Vita Sackville-West, *The Edwardians* (London, Virago, 2000), p. 61.
34. *Ibid.*, pp. 27–8.
35. *Ibid.*, p. 78.
36. *Ibid.*, p. 73.
37. *Ibid.*, p. 79.
38. *Ibid.*, p. 28.
39. HUA, DDFA3/6/74, F.H. Bickerton to Irene Forbes Adam, 22 September 1928.
40. MacKenzie's other important commissions include Cyprus Point, on California's Monterey Peninsula, the Augusta National in Georgia and the Royal Melbourne, Australia.
41. George Gibbs to Olmsted Brothers, 9 October 1928, courtesy of the National Park Service, Frederick Law Olmsted National Historic Site.
42. CUL, MSS6762-6803, F.H. Bickerton to Stella Benson, quoted in Benson's diary, 18 September 1928.
43. George Gibbs to Olmsted Brothers, 9 October 1928, courtesy of the National Park Service, Frederick Law Olmsted National Historic Site.
44. HUA, DDFA3/6/74, F.H. Bickerton to Irene Forbes Adam, 7 May 1929.

45. CUL, MSS6762-6803, Stella Benson, diary, 28 December 1928.
46. *Ibid*., 31 December 1928.
47. *Ibid*.
48. *Ibid*., 28 December 1928.
49. F.H. Bickerton, 'Work Going Forward on New Marion Hollins' Golf Links', *Santa Cruz Evening News*, 20 February 1929. I am most grateful to Bob Beck, resident historian at Pasatiempo for his transcription of this article.
50. HUA, DDFA3/6/74, F.H. Bickerton to Irene Forbes Adam, 7 May 1929.
51. F.H. Bickerton to J.F. Dawson, 10 May 1929, courtesy of the National Park Service, Frederick Law Olmsted National Historic Site.
52. George Gibbs [?] to Frederick Law Olmsted, 20 May 1931, courtesy of the National Park Service, Frederick Law Olmsted National Historic Site.
53. HUA, DDFA3/6/74, F.H. Bickerton to Irene Forbes Adam, 7 May 1929.
54. F.H. Bickerton, African Diary, 1932, p. 58.
55. The daughter of Hollins' attorney, William Boekel, in conversation with Bob Beck.
56. Cecil Madigan, AAE Diaries, by permission of Mr D.C. Madigan, 3 July 1912.
57. HUA, DDFA3/6/49, Lady Eileen Orde to Irene Lawley, [May 1918].
58. HUA, DDFA3/6/74, F.H. Bickerton to Irene Forbes Adam, 1 April 1931.
59. *San Francisco Examiner*, 5 May 1931.
60. HUA, DDFA3/6/74, F.H. Bickerton to Irene Forbes Adam, May 1931.
61. CUL, MSS6762-6803, Stella Benson, diary, 24 April 1932.
62. HUA, DDFA3/6/74, F.H. Bickerton to Irene Forbes Adam, May 1931.
63. *Ibid*., 25 June 1931.
64. CUL, MSS6762-6803, Stella Benson, diary, 1 May 1928.
65. *Ibid*., 25 June 1931.
66. *Ibid*.
67. Marion Hollins to Olmsted Brothers, 24 December 1933, courtesy of the National Park Service, Frederick Law Olmsted National Historic Site.
68. Antarctic Club Rules, 1929.
69. Royal Geographical Society, F.H. Bickerton to the Secretary of the RGS, 29 April 1931.

70. MAC, 175AAE, F.H. Bickerton to Douglas Mawson, 9 February 1932.

71. MAC, 158AAE, Douglas Mawson to F.H. Bickerton, 12 April 1932.

72. Douglas Mawson to Paquita Mawson, 4 January 1933, courtesy of the State Library of South Australia, Adelaide.

73. Madigan, AAE Diaries, 23 July 1912.

Chapter Ten: From Cape to Cairo

1. HUA, DDFA3/6/74, F.H. Bickerton to Irene Forbes Adam, 31 July 1931.

2. *Ibid*., undated.

3. *Ibid*.

4. Linda Rhodes-Moorhouse, *Kaleidoscope* (London, Arthur Barker, 1960), p. 104.

5. F.H. Bickerton, African Diary, 17–22 August 1932.

6. *Ibid*.

7. *Ibid*., 23 August 1932.

8. *Ibid*., 25 August 1932.

9. *Ibid*., 1 September 1932.

10. *Ibid*., 5–8 September 1932.

11. *Ibid*., 14 September 1932.

12. *Ibid*., 16 September 1932.

13. *Ibid*., 29 September 1932 [*sic*].

14. *Ibid*.

15. *Ibid*., 6 October 1932.

16. *Ibid*., 20 October 1932.

17. *Ibid*., 24 October 1932.

18. *Ibid*., 29 October 1932.

19. *Ibid*.

20. *Ibid*.

21. *Ibid*.

22. *Ibid*.

23. *Ibid*., 6 November 1932.

24. F.H. Bickerton, African Diary, 1932, p. 50.

25. *Ibid*., p. 52.

26. *Ibid*., pp. 54–5.

27. *Ibid*., p. 59.

28. *Ibid*., p. 61.

Chapter Eleven: Movies and Marriage

1. These lines from Tennyson's *Ulysses* were quoted by Bickerton on the endpaper of Dufferin's *Letters from High Latitudes*, given by him to Eileen and Cuthbert Orde in September 1918.

2. HUA, DDFA3/6/74, F.H. Bickerton to Irene Forbes Adam, 27 July 1932.

3. *Ibid.*, 4 February [1931?].

4. *Ibid.*, 18 April 1928.

5. F.H. Bickerton, African Diary, 1932, p. 57.

6. *Ibid.*, pp. 59–60.

7. HUA, DDFA3/6/74, F.H. Bickerton to Irene Forbes Adam, undated.

8. Linda Rhodes-Moorhouse, *Kaleidoscope* (London, Arthur Barker, 1960), p. 142.

9. The Earl of Shrewsbury, in a letter to the author.

10. Of these photographs, only one survives from Cocos Island and none from the Antarctic. Many survive from the African safari.

11. MAC, 175AAE, F.H. Bickerton to Douglas Mawson, 9 February 1932.

12. HUA, DDFA3/6/74, F.H. Bickerton to Irene Forbes Adam, undated.

13. *Ibid*.

14. Bryan Langley, in a letter to the author, 25 September 2004.

15. *Kine Weekly*, 5 November 1936.

16. *Ibid.*, 11 February 1937.

17. HUA, DDFA3/6/74, F.H. Bickerton to Irene Forbes Adam, undated.

18. Paul Lukas (1887–1971) was awarded the Academy Award for Best Actor for his performance in *Watch on the Rhine* (1943).

19. *To-Day's Cinema*, 6 September 1937.

20. *Kine Weekly*, 9 November 1937.

21. HUA, DDFA3/6/74, F.H. Bickerton to Irene Forbes Adam, undated.

22. HUA, DDFA3/6/74, F.H. Bickerton to Irene Forbes Adam, undated.

23. Victor Goddard, *Skies to Dunkirk* (London, William Kimber, 1982), pp. 57–8.

24. Major David MacIndoe to Jane MacIndoe (née Orde), 21 March 1945, courtesy of Angus MacIndoe.

25. Angus MacIndoe, son of David MacIndoe, in conversation with the author.

26. *London Gazette*, 1 January 1946.

27. *The Times*, 30 August 1954.

28. *Polar Record*, 7, no. 50 (May 1955).

29. Douglas Mawson, *The Home of the Blizzard* (abridged 1930, Edinburgh, Birlinn, 2000), p. xvii.
30. CUL, MSS6762-6803, Stella Benson, diary, 24 April 1932.
31. SPRI, MS1509, F.H. Bickerton, 'A Log of the Western Journey', 23 December 1912.
32. HUA, DDFA3/6/74, F.H. Bickerton to Irene Forbes Adam, 7 May 1929.
33. *The Times*, 30 August 1954.

Sources and Bibliography

Abbreviations used in this section

HUA   Hull University Archives
MAC   Mawson Antarctic Collection, South Australian Museum, Adelaide
ML   Mitchell Library, Sydney
NA   National Archives, Kew
NPS   National Park Service, Frederick Law Olmsted National Historic Site
RGS   Royal Geographical Society, London
SPRI   Scott Polar Research Institute, Cambridge

This book has been based very largely upon eyewitness accounts, including the journals and letters of Frank Bickerton and those who knew him personally.

Bickerton Papers by permission of Miss Rosanna Bickerton

'A Log of the Western Journey' – a typescript of the handwritten journal kept by Bickerton between 3 December 1912 and 17 January 1913. Copies at SPRI and MAC.

'Western Sledging Journey' – Bickerton's 'written-up' version of his journal, prepared for Mawson's official account of the AAE, *The Home of the Blizzard* (1915). Portions of this version were published in the first edition of 1915 but revised and edited by Dr Archibald Lang McLean. In the popular, one-volume edition of 1930, Bickerton's contribution was again edited and reduced. The version used in this book is Bickerton's original, without McLean's editorial amendments. Copies at SPRI and MAC.

'Australian Antarctic Expedition' – Bickerton's account of the AAE, broadcast by the BBC at 10 p.m. on 17 March 1927. Copy at the BBC Written Archives Department, Reading.

Correspondence at HUA, NPS, MAC, RGS and in possession of the Bickerton / Bussell family.

'African Diary' – a three-volume journal kept by Bickerton between 15 August 1932 and 6 November 1932. The journal also contains an undated account of Bickerton's continuing journey from Nairobi to Cairo by seaplane.

Papers relating to Bickerton's military service during the First World War at NA.

Papers relating to Bickerton's military service during the Second World War – confidential personnel records of the MoD (restricted access).

Personal Interviews

These were conducted face-to-face, by telephone and by letter, between the author and: Miss Rosanna Bickerton, Mrs Karen Bussell, Mrs Henry Cavendish, Mr William Cavendish, Mrs Sophia Crawford, Mrs Elisabeth Dowler, Mrs Anne Fright, Mr Patrick Garland, Mr Angus MacIndoe, Mrs Sally McNally, Mrs Jean Messervey, Mr Andrew Morritt, Lady Angela Nall, Mr Nigel Nicolson, Mrs Elizabeth Pearce, Mrs Anne Phillips and the Earl of Shrewsbury.

Other Primary Sources

Full details of diary entries and letters cited can be found in the relevant chapter notes.

Australasian Antarctic Expedition, 1911–14. Log of AAE Wireless
     Transmissions at MAC

Benson, Stella. Diaries, 1928–1932. Cambridge University Library

British Imperial Trans-Antarctic Expedition, 1914–16. Correspondence
     by permission of Mr Trygve Norman, Finse 1222 Hotel

Brittain, Harry. Notes of an interview with Sir Harry Brittain at SPRI

Dymond, John. 'Facts and Recollections about Alec Coryton's
     Connection with Flying Training, as Known and Remembered by
     John Dymond', January 1984, by permission of Lady Angela Nall and
     Mrs S. Harrisson

Ellis, Ralph. 'A March with the Infantry', West Sussex Record Office

Garland, Ewart. Diary, April 1916–December 1918, Imperial War
     Museum, by permission of Mr Patrick Garland

Gray, Percival. 'Antarctic Voyages, 1911–1914' at ML

Hannam, Walter. AAE Diaries at SPRI and ML

Hurley, Frank. Diaries at ML, by permission of Ms Toni Hurley

MacIndoe, David. Correspondence, by permission of Mr Angus
     MacIndoe and Mrs Sophia Crawford

Mackintosh, Aeneas. 'Diary of Events on Treasure Seeking Expedition
     to Cocos Island', March–May 1911, by permission of Mrs Elisabeth
     Dowler and Mrs Anne Phillips

Madigan, Cecil. AAE Diaries, by permission of Mr D.C. Madigan

Marston, George. Correspondence at Hampshire Record Office

Mawson, Douglas. Correspondence at SPRI, MAC, NA, State Library
     of South Australia, University of Sydney and the Vickers Archive,
     University of Cambridge, by permission of the Mawson family

McLean, Archibald Lang. AAE Diaries at ML

Ninnis, B.E.S. AAE Diaries at SPRI, by permission of Mr Allan
     Mornement

Orde Lees, Thomas. *Endurance* Diaries, 1914–16. The Alexander Turnbull
     Library, Wellington, New Zealand

Royal Geographical Society. Report of a Conference of the Royal
     Geographical Society with Sir Ernest Shackleton, 4 March 1914 at
     SPRI

Shackleton, Ernest. Correspondence at SPRI

Whetter, Leslie. Correspondence at Canterbury Museum, Christchurch,
     New Zealand

Wild, Frank. Correspondence at SPRI and Royal Geographical Society of
     Australia

—— Memoirs at ML, by permission of Mrs Anne Fright

Printed Books

Ashcroft, Frances. *Life at the Extremes: The Science of Survival*, Flamingo, 2001

Ayres, Philip. *Mawson: a Life*, Miegunyah Press, 1999

Barker, Ralph. *The Royal Flying Corps in World War I*, Robinson, 2002

Blake, Robert. *A History of Rhodesia*, Eyre Methuen, 1977

Bowyer, Chaz. *Sopwith Camel – King of Combat*, Asron Publications, 1978

Brittain, Vera. *Testament of Friendship*, Virago, 1980

Burke, David. *Moments of Terror – The Story of Antarctic Aviation*, Robert Hale, 1994

Bussell, Dorothea. *The New Wood Nymph*, Stanley Paul & Co., undated (*c.* 1912)

Cameron, Kenneth M. *Into Africa: the Story of the East African Safari*, Constable, 1990

Chadwick, St John. *Newfoundland: Island into Province*, Cambridge University Press, 1967

Davis, John King. *Trial by Ice: the Antarctic Diaries of John King Davis*, ed. Louise Crossley, Bluntisham Books, 1997

—— *With the* Aurora *in the Antarctic, 1911–1914*, Andrew Melrose, 1919

Debenham, Frank. *Nyasaland: Land of the Lake*, HMSO, 1955

Fage, J.D. *A History of Africa*, Routledge, 1995

Fisher, Margaret and James. *Shackleton*, Barrie Books, 1957

Fleming, Fergus. *Barrow's Boys*, Granta, 1999

Garland, Patrick. *The Wings of the Morning*, Bantam Books, 1990

Gibbs, Philip. *Realities of War*, William Heinemann, 1920

—— *The War Dispatches*, Anthony Gibbs & Phillips, 1964

Goddard, Victor. *Skies to Dunkirk*, William Kimber, 1982

Grant, Joy. *Stella Benson: a Biography*, Macmillan, 1987

Herne, Brian. *White Hunters: the Golden Age of African Safaris*, Henry Holt, 1999

Holtby, Winifred. *Letters to a Friend*, ed. A. Holtby and J. McWilliam, Collins, 1937

Huxley, Elspeth. *Nine Faces of Kenya*, Collins Harvill, 1990

Jefford, C.G. *Observers and Navigators*, Airlife Publishing, 2001

Jørstad, Finn R. *Historien om Finse*, 1998

Kinsey, Gordon. *Martlesham Heath*, Terence Dalton, 1975

Laseron, Charles F. *South with Mawson*, The Australian Publishing Co., 1947

Lewis, Cecil. *Sagittarius Rising*, Warner Books, 1998

Livesey, Anthony. *Atlas of World War I*, Viking, 1994

Lorch, Walter. *Snow Travel and Transport*, Gawsworth Series, 1977

Low, Rachael. *Film Making in 1930s Britain*, George Allen and
     Unwin, 1985

MacDonald, Lyn. *1915: the Death of Innocence*, Penguin, 1993

Madigan, D.C. Vixere Fortes: *a Family Archive*, privately printed, 2000

Marshall, Edison. *Heart of the Hunter*, Frederick Muller, 1957

Mawson, Sir Douglas. *Antarctic Diaries*, ed. Fred and Eleanor Jacka,
     Unwin Hyman, 1988

——— *The Home of the Blizzard*, 2 vols, Heinemann, 1915

——— *The Home of the Blizzard* (abridged, 1930), Birlinn, 2000 (with a
     foreword by Sir Ranulph Fiennes)

Maydon, H.C. (ed.). *Big Game Shooting in Africa*, Seeley, Service & Co.,
     1932

Mill, Hugh Robert. *The Life of Sir Ernest Shackleton*, Heinemann, 1933

Mills, Leif. *Frank Wild*, Caedmon, 1999

Outerbridge, David. *Champion in a Man's World: the Biography of Marion
     Hollins*, Sleeping Bear Press, 1998

Price, A. Grenfell. *The Winning of Australian Antarctica: Mawson's
     B.A.N.Z.A.R.E. Voyages 1929–1931*, Angus and Robertson, 1963

Rawson, Andrew. *Loos – 1915: Hohenzollern Redoubt*, Lee Cooper, 2003

Reeves, E.A. *Recollections of a Geographer*, Seeley, Service & Co., undated

Rhodes-Moorhouse, Linda. *Kaleidoscope*, Arthur Barker, 1960

Ritchie, Charles. *An Appetite for Life, The Education of a Young Diarist,
     1924–1927*, Macmillan, 1977

Roberts, A.D. (ed.). *The Cambridge History of Africa*, Cambridge University
     Press, 1986, vol. 7: *From 1905 to 1940*

Roberts, R. Ellis. *Portrait of Stella Benson*, Macmillan, 1939

Rossiter, Heather. *Lady Spy, Gentleman Explorer: the Life of Herbert Dyce
     Murphy*, Random House, 2001

Rutter, Owen (ed.). *The History of the Seventh (Service) Battalion The Royal
     Sussex Regiment*, Times Publishing, 1934

Sackville-West, Vita. *The Edwardians*, Virago, 2000

Shackleton, Sir Ernest. *South*, Robinson, 1999

Simkins, Peter. *Kitchener's New Army*, Manchester University Press, 1988

Smallwood, Joseph R. (ed.). *Encyclopaedia of Newfoundland & Labrador*,
     Newfoundland Publishers, 1981–8

Thomson, John. *Shackleton's Captain: a Biography of Frank Worsley*, Mosaic
     Press, undated

Turner, Michael L. and Vaisey, David. *Oxford Shops and Shopping*, Oxford Illustrated Press, 1972

Walmisley, Claude. *Spacious Days*, privately printed, 1979

Whitworth, Adrian (ed.). *City & Guilds College: a Centenary History, 1885–1985*, City & Guilds College, undated

Wilkins, Harold T. *Treasure Hunting*, Ivor Nicholson and Watson, 1932

Newspapers, Magazines & Periodicals

Adelaide Mercury
Bergens Aftenblad
Coventry Herald
Cross & Cockade Journal
The Marlburian
Morning Post
Polar Record
San Francisco Examiner
Santa Cruz Evening News
Santa Cruz Sentinel
The Sphere
The Times

Index